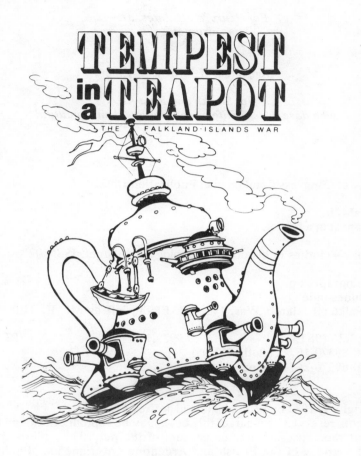

TEMPEST in a TEAPOT
THE FALKLAND ISLANDS WAR

Stokvis Studies in Historical Chronology and Thought, No. 3
ISSN 0270-5338

R. Reginald & Dr. Jeffrey M. Elliot
Research Assistants: Renata Parrino & Mary A. Burgess

R. Reginald

the Borgo Press

San Bernardino, California
MCMLXXXIII

LIBRARY
COLBY-SAWYER COLLEGE
NEW LONDON, N.H. 03257

Dedication of R. Reginald:

For Henry W. Holmes, Jr.—
"Arma virumque cano..."

Dedication of Jeffrey M. Elliot:

For Sheikh and Rina Ali,
who dare to ask of life everything good and beautiful

Library of Congress Cataloging in Publication Data:

Reginald, R.
  Tempest in a teapot.

  (Stokvis studies in historical chronology & thought, ISSN 0270-5338 ;
no. 3)
  Bibliography: p.
  Includes index.
  1. Falkland Islands War, 1982. I. Elliot, Jeffrey M. II. Title. III.
Series.
F3031.R36 1983   997'.11   83-8807
ISBN 0-89370-167-X (cloth, $12.95)
ISBN 0-89370-267-6 (paper, $6.95)

Copyright © 1983 by R. Reginald and Jeffrey M. Elliot.
All rights reserved. No part of this book may be reproduced in any form
without the expressed written consent of the publisher. Maps reproduced courtesy of the British and Argentine governments. Published
by arrangement with the authors. Printed in the United States of America by Whitehall Co., Wheeling, Illinois. Binding by California Zip
Bindery, San Bernardino, CA.

Produced, designed, and published by R. Reginald and Mary A. Burgess, The Borgo Press, P.O. Box 2845, San Bernardino, CA 92406, USA.
Cover and title page illustration by Tim Kirk. Cover and title page
design by Michael Pastucha.

First Edition————August, 1983

Contents

ACKNOWLEDGMENTS

We particularly wish to thank the governments of Argentina and the United Kingdom for their cooperation in providing documentary sources, maps, photographs, and, of course, official statements on and about the Falklands/Malvinas and the 1982 war. Thanks also to Renata Parrino for digging out articles and clippings about the conflict, and to Mary Burgess for checking the manuscript for errors of fact. Such errors as do exist are solely the responsibility of the authors.

Introduction
Tempest in a Teapot

Of all the battles, skirmishes, and wars waged among and between nations in the twentieth century, surely the Falklands Conflict must rank as the strangest. In a struggle outwardly reminiscent of the halcyon days of gunboat diplomacy and European imperialism, Argentina invaded the Falklands/Malvinas, which it had claimed since the beginning of its Republic, quickly occupying those desolate isles in an almost bloodless, one-day campaign. Within two and one-half months, Great Britain had mounted an expeditionary force, reinvaded the Falklands and South Georgia Island, and swiftly reconquered its former colony. Approximately 1,000 persons died during the campaign. Such are the facts. This brief outline scarcely conveys, however, the puzzlement which most of the world expressed at the outbreak of hostilities, or the varied complexities of the immediate and distant causes of the war itself.

Compounding this confusion is an almost complete lack of source materials other than those derived directly from the participants themselves or from their accredited war correspondents. Unlike most modern wars, which have been brought to the American public in living color directly to its television screens, the Falklands Conflict was reported primarily through radio and newspaper stories censored before release by the respective combatants, and often used by both sides as an instrument of war itself. The Argentine press was discredited early in the struggle by the rather blatant efforts of the military government to manipulate its news releases, often for home consumption. This is unfortunate, because many of the European and English-speaking countries thereafter relied almost solely upon the British reports as completely true accounts of the fighting. They were not, however, as subsequently admitted by the United Kingdom Government after hostilities had ceased. Moreover, almost all of the published book-length accounts of the Falklands War have been written by British authors, using British sources, with British points of view predominating.

Our purpose in writing this history is to provide as completely objective an account of this bizarre little war as is possible from a perspective of one year. We have not consciously sympathized with either side, but have tried to understand and present the views of *both* sides, with a straightforward account of the conflict itself. In this light, we have been fortunate to receive the cooperation of the Argentine and British Missions to the United Nations, members of which have provided two lengthy interviews detailing the official positions of each country. Our own opinions concerning the causes of the war, with possible solutions and prognostications, are provided in the final chapter of this work, "Reading the Tea Leaves."

As with most such conflicts, this is a war that never should have happened, that could, in fact, have easily been kept from reaching the shooting stage. That it did happen, that 1,000 men and women died in attacking and defending these barren little islands deep in the South Atlantic, should give all of us pause. Britain's tenuous victory has solved nothing: the basic grievances on both sides still exist, and will continue to exist until the two combatants are willing to make real compromises in their positions. Alas, we see no such signs; on the contrary, the Falklands War gives every evidence of being a continuing Greek tragedy in which the actors, doomed to their fates by the uncaring gods, must play out their hopeless drama in an endless series of bombasts, battles, and belligerencies. Whom the gods would destroy they first make mad.

Robert Reginald
Jeffrey M. Elliot
June, 1983

Chronology

1493 Pope Alexander VI divides the South American continent between Spain and Portugal.

1502 Vespucci sights "new land" while sailing near the South American coast.

1520 Magellan discovers "some islands" while exploring the east coast of South America.

1535 Simon de Alcazaba sights several islands south of the 45th parallel.

1540 Francisco Camargo describes islands in the South Atlantic—many believe his to be the strongest claim for the first sighting of the Falkland Islands.

1592 John Davis makes the first English sighting of islands near the Straits of Magellan.

1594 Richard Hawkins makes a similar sighting, but is discredited for inaccuracies.

1600 Dutch master Sebald de Weert discovers "three little islands" (named the Sebalds).

1675 Anthony de Laroche, a Briton, claims to sight what is now South Georgia Island.

1684 The British buccaneers Cowley and Dampier visit the Sebalds, and discover another island which they name "Pepys."

1690 Pirate Capt. John Strong names Falkland Sound, but does not take formal possession.

1701-1708 French explorers begin to call the islands "Iles Malouines," later corrupted to "Malvinas" by the Spanish.

1708 Privateer Woode Rogers names the islands "Falkland's Land."

1764 Antoine de Bougainville establishes the first colony on East Falkland Island (Fort Louis), with his uncle as Gov., and claims the "Malouines" in the name of King Louis XV.

1765 John Byron claims West Falkland Island (Port Egmont) for the British Crown.

1766 John McBride is dispatched by the British to remove the French settlement (which he fails to do).

1767 Bougainville, under pressure from the French, sells his interest in the colony to Spain—Port Louis is renamed "Puerto Soledad."

1770   British naval vessel *Favourite* surrenders peacefully and is evicted from the British settlement by Spanish Gen. Madariaga.

1771   War is averted by Spanish envoy Prince Masserano, who negotiates a settlement. By a supposed "secret agreement," the British promise to evacuate the islands at a later date. Resettlement of Port Egmont.

1774   The British abandon Port Egmont, but leave a plaque reiterating British claims to sovereignty over the islands.

1775   Capt. James Cook discovers and names South Georgia Island, claiming it for King George III.

1776   The Viceroyalty of Buenos Aires is established—the Malvinas are included in its jurisdiction.

1790   The Nootka Sound Convention is signed by Britain and Spain.

1806   Buenos Aires is captured by a British expeditionary force.

1810   A revolution results in the establishment of an Argentine provisional government.

1811   The provisional government abandons the Malvinas.

1816   The independent United Provinces of the Rio de la Plata are proclaimed.

1819   South Shetlands discovered by British Capt. William Smith, who claims them for King George III.

1820   The United Provinces occupies the Malvinas and warns off whalers and sealers.

1821   South Orkneys discovered by British Capt. George Powell, who claims them for King George IV.

1823   Entrepreneur Louis Vernet receives his first grants from the Provinces.

1829   Vernet is named Malvinas Gov. British Consul-General Parrish reaffirms British claims and makes overtures to Vernet.

1831   A confrontation between U.S. naval vessels and the administration of Gov. Vernet results in an international incident and diplomatic crisis between the U.S. and Argentina. Suits and counter-suits continue for decades.

1832   The Argentine Gov. Mestivier is assassinated by his own men, leaving the islands government in chaos.

1833   Acting Gov. Pinedo is ousted by the British (Jan. 3rd), the Argentine flag taken down, and British resident William Dickson left in charge. He and other British residents are subsequently murdered by gauchos who are never brought to trial.

1834   Lt. Henry Smith is installed as first British military administrator. Protests from the Argentine government continue through 1849 and are summarily rejected by the British. G. W. Whitington forms the Falkland Island Commercial Fishery and Agricultural Association.

1842   Lt. Richard C. Moody is appointed Lt. Gov.—the first beginnings of colonial administration are established.

1843   Letters Patent officially recognize the islands and their Dependencies; Lt. Gov. Moody is made Gov.

1844 Samuel Lafone makes first attempt at large-scale British colonization.

1845 Port Stanley becomes the seat of government.

1851 Lafone's enterprise fails; he is bought out by the Falkland Islands Company, Ltd. formed for that purpose.

1852 The Company introduces the first successful strain of Cheviot sheep to the islands.

1853 The United Provinces become the Argentine Republic.

1854 British insistence upon sovereignty results in a confrontation with U.S. vessels.

1881 The islands become financially independent of Britain.

1884 Argentina issues a new map designating the Malvinas as being in Argentine territory—Britain protests. Claims and counterclaims continue.

1892 The Falkland Islands are raised to the status of a Crown Colony.

1903 Argentina acquires administration of a meteorological station in the South Orkneys, and attempts to use it as evidence of a transfer of sovereignty in the Dependencies.

1914 A major naval battle takes place off the islands between British and German vessels. The Germans are defeated (a similar battle takes place during World War II).

1927 Argentina asks the International Postal Union to accept Argentine jurisdiction over the entire area of the Dependencies.

1939 Income taxes are imposed by the Falkland Islands government.

1944 Col. Juan Peron takes over Argentine government in military coup.

1947 Britain protests issuance of stamps by Argentina for use in the Malvinas and Dependencies.

1949 Universal suffrage is promulgated among British subjects on the islands.

1955 Britain attempts to place adjudication of the Dependencies issue before the International Court of Justice—Argentina refuses to recognize the court's authority.

1964 Argentine pilot flies plane to Port Stanley.

1965 U.N. General Assembly urges Britain and Argentina in Res. 2065 to negotiate on Falklands question.

1966 Operacion Condor, in which twenty Argentine nationals hijack plane to Port Stanley. Talks between Britain and Argentina are begun on Nov. 4th.

1968 Memorandum of Understanding reached between the two governments, then dropped after Lord Chalfont's visit to the islands.

1971 Agreement reached between Britain and Argentina on trade ties between Falklands and the mainland.

1972 Argentina, as part of the agreement, constructs the first airstrip at Port Stanley.

1973 Juan Peron elected Pres. of Argentina. Talks on the Falklands break down over sovereignty issue.

1974 Britain proposes condominium government for the Falklands; the islanders refuse.

1975 Air travellers from Falklands to mainland are now required by Argentina to obtain clearance from the Argentine Foreign Ministry. Diplomatic relations between Britain and Argentina are broken.

1976 Argentine destroyer fires on British research ship near the Falklands. New talks between Britain and Argentina. U.N. Res. 31/49 continues to urge negotiations on sovereignty issue. Argentina establishes weather and research station on Southern Thule in South Sandwich Islands.

1977 British Minister of State Edward Rowlands visits Falklands to obtain islanders' views on negotiations; two rounds of talks held.

1978 A draft agreement on scientific activities in the Falkland Dependencies reached, but is rejected by Falklands government.

1979 Margaret Thatcher elected Conservative Prime Minister of Britain. Nicholas Ridley is sent to the Falklands to obtain islanders' views.

1980 Gen. Leopoldo Galtieri appointed Commander-in-Chief of the Argentine Army (Jan. 1st). New talks held between Britain and Argentina on Falklands question in April. Rex Hunt named Gov. of Falkland Islands.

1981 Falkland Islands Councils protest to Parliament over negotiations. Gen. Roberto Viola becomes Pres. of Argentina in Mar., but is deposd in Dec. Argentina protests to U.N. in Sept. Galtieri becomes Pres. of Argentina in Dec.

1982 FEBRUARY: Talks between Britain and Argentina result in agreement for further negotiations. Argentine newspapers threaten military action if talks do not produce results soon. MARCH: 3rd— Thatcher orders contingency plans developed in the event talks break down; 8th—Lord Carrington writes American Secretary of State Haig, requesting help in ending the developing crisis; 19th—Constantino Davidorf, a scrap metal dealer, lands a work party on South Georgia Island in violation of British regulations, and raises Argentine flag; 20th—British Commander at Grytviken ordered to remove Davidorf; 22nd—Davidorf party is reportedly withdrawn; 25th— Argentine naval ships sent to South Georgia; 26th—Argentine ships leave supplies at South Georgia; 29th—British submarine ordered to Falklands area; 30th—massive Argentine labor strikes are directed at military government; 31st—British informed by intelligence sources that Argentine invasion of Falklands imminent. APRIL: British Cabinet decides not to reinforce British garrison in Falklands, but to seek U.S. help; 2nd—Pres. Reagan urges Galtieri in phone conversation to use restraint. Argentine soldiers land at Port Stanley, and take the capital after brief fight. British troops and Gov. Hunt repatriated through Uruguay. The Falklands are officially renamed Islas Malvinas, the capital Puerto Argentino; 3rd—in a major debate in British Parliament, Thatcher announces that a task force will be sent to retake the islands. U.N. Res. 502 adopted, calling for an end to hostilities. South Georgia taken by Argentina; 5th—Lord Carrington resigns; 6th—Brig. Gen. Mario Benjamin Menendez appointed Gov. of Malvinas and Dependencies; 7th—Britain declares 200-mile Exclusionary Zone around Falklands and freezes $1.4 billion in Argentine assets held by British banks. European Economic Community imposes sanctions against Argentina; 8th—Secretary Haig arrives in London in attempt to negotiate crisis, talks collapse on April 30th; 22nd—Galtieri visits Falklands; 24th—British fleet put on battle alert as it nears Falklands; 25th—Britain recaptures South Georgia Island; 26th—O.A.S. adopts resolution supporting Argentina; 30th—total Exclusionary Zone around Falklands established by British. Haig announces U.S. support for Britain and sanctions against Argentina. MAY: 1st—British planes bomb airstrip at Port Stanley and Darwin/Goose Green; 2nd—Argentine cruiser *General Belgrano* sunk by British submarine *Conqueror* outside Exclusionary Zone, with loss of 368 men. Argentine tug sunk; 4th—British bomb Port Stanley; British detroyer *Sheffield* sunk by Argentine Exocet missile; 6th—two British Sea Harriers lost in bad weather; 7th—Exclusionary Zone is widened by British to within twelve miles of Argentine coast; 8th—Argentina rejects peace proposal by Peru; 9th—Argentine fishing vessel *Narwal* seized; 11th—Argentine supply ship sunk in Falkland Sound; 14th—British raid on Pebble Island destroys Argentine supplies and eleven planes; 14th—Britain presents final negotiating position to U.N. Sec.-Gen. Perez de Cuellar; 19th—Argentina presents its own proposals; 20th—both governments reject the other's proposals; 21st—Britain invades Falklands at San Carlos Bay, landing 5,000 troops; British frigate *Ardent* sunk; 23rd—British frigate *Antelope* sunk; Britain claims many Argentine planes shot down; 25th—massive Argentine air attacks sink British destroyer *Coventry* and freighter *Atlantic Conveyor*; 26th—U.N. adopts Res. 505 urging negotiated settlement; 28th—British attack Darwin and Goose Green; Argentines surrender on 29th, with 250 Argentine dead, 1,400 captured; 31st—British soldiers reach outer portions of Argentine defense perimeter at Port Stanley. JUNE: 2nd—British occupy hills near Port Stanley; 4th—U.N. Res. calling for ceasefire vetoed by U.K.and U.S.; U.S. later says it should have abstained; 6th—British troops completely encircle Argentine positions at Port Stanley, and begin shelling Argentine emplacements there; 7th—Pres. Reagan pays official visit to U.K.; British landing ships *Sir Tristram* and *Sir Galahad* badly damaged by Argentine bombs; 10th—Peru sends ten Mirage jets to Argentina to replenish losses; 11th—Pope John Paul II visits Argentina, denounces all wars as "unjust"; 13th—British ship *Glamorgan* damaged by land-based Exocet; British forces advance to within two miles of Port Stanley; 14th—British offensive breaks through Argentine line; Argentine forces surrender effective 9:00 P.M. Falklands time; British take over 11,000 prisoners; 16th—British war toll set at 255 dead; 17th—Pres. Galtieri of Argentina forced to resign; 18th—Britain begins repatriating Argentine prisoners; 19th—British forces take South Sandwich Islands; 20th—European Economic Community lifts economic sanctions against Argentina; 22nd—Argentine army assumes full power, the Air Force and Navy withdrawing from the junta; 23rd—Thatcher flies to Washington to confer with Reagan; 25th—Sir Rex Hunt returns to Falklands as Civil Commissioner; JULY: 1st—Reynaldo Bignone sworn in as Argentine Pres.; 2nd—Argentine war toll set at 645 dead and missing; British task forces and ground forces commanders replaced; 7th—European Economic Community agrees to provide financial aid to Falklands; 14th—final Argentine prisoners of war repatriated; 22nd—Britain lifts Exclusionary Zone around Falklands; 26th—Brig. Gen. Menendez dismissed from Argentine army. AUGUST: British lengthen airfield at Port Stanley to accomodate a squadron of Phantom jets.

1983 JANUARY: A bipartisan panel exonerates the Thatcher government; Mrs. Thatcher visits the Falklands for the first time. APRIL: British relatives of the war dead visit their graves. Ex-Pres. Galtieri is arrested after charging military bungling in the war. MAY: British Parliament dissolved. JUNE 9th: Thatcher is reelected with largest majority of any government since 1945. Michael Foot announces his intention to resign as head of Britain's Labour Party.

I
Invitation to a Tea Party
The Falkland Islands/Las Islas Malvinas;
Colonial Land Claims;
The British Occupation of the Islands

1. The Falkland Islands/Las Islas Malvinas

Deep within the South Atlantic Ocean, about 300 miles off the tip of the South American mainland, lie the Falkland Islands, or Las Islas Malvinas, as the Argentines call them [we have used the name "Falkland Islands" throughout this book for convenience; this does not, however, imply acceptance on our part of British sovereignty over the islands]. The nearest mainland point in Argentina is the town of Rio Gallegos. About 800 miles due south of the Falklands lie the South Shetland Islands, perhaps a hundred miles north of Graham Land, the northernmost tip of Antarctica. To the southeast of the Falklands are South Georgia Island, the South Sandwich Islands, the Shag Rocks, and the South Orkneys, all except the South Orkneys part of the Falkland Islands Dependencies. These subsidiary islands are uninhabited save for research stations; all are occupied by Great Britain, but claimed by Argentina (including the British Antarctic Territory).

The Falklands proper consist of perhaps 200 islets and two main islands, called East Falkland (Isla Soledad to Argentina) and West Falkland (Isla Gran Malvina), with a total area of about 4,700 square miles. The terrain consists of rolling hills and small mountains, interspersed with rocky outcroppings, peat bogs, and some plains. The soggy, irregular landscape makes vehicular traffic beyond Port Stanley (the capital) almost impossible, except with four-wheel-drive trucks; the only permanently paved roads stop a few miles outside of town. Most travel in the islands is conducted with light aircraft or (less frequently) by boat. The two main islands are separated by a long strait, the Falkland Sound (Estrecho de San Carlos), and include many fjords, inlets, and natural harbors. The Choiseul and Grantham Sounds nearly divide East Falkland Island at its midpoint, leaving a land bridge no more than four or five miles wide. The highest point on the islands is Mt. Usborne (Mt. Alberdi), at 2,312 feet, on East Falkland.

Although the surrounding ocean has a somewhat moderating effect on the Falklands' climate, the islands remain a cold and dreary place to live. The highest temperature ever recorded on the islands is 75 degrees F., the lowest 12 degrees. Frost has been recorded in every month of the year. During the summer month of January the mean daily maximum temperature is only 56 degrees; about 28 inches of rain fall annually, much of it as mist or light drizzle, with an average of more than 200 days of precipitation annually. Humidity ranges from 75-90 percent, depending on the season. Snow falls about 50 days a year, but rarely persists. The most pervasive and disagreeable feature of the islands' weather is the constant wind, averaging 15-20 miles per hour daily, with frequent gales, and very few calm days. The winds are particularly vicious and unpredictable during the winter months, which coincide with the northern hemisphere's summer. Such variable conditions caused great problems for both Britain and Argentina during the course of the war.

Due to the cool climate and a strongly acidic soil, no large plants exist on the islands except for a few dwarf fruit trees planted by the Kelpers themselves. The natural vegetation of the Falklands consists primarily of coarse grasses, heath, various weeds, and some small shrubs. The uplands are spotted with bare patches of rock and eroded land gulleys. Large mammals were completely absent from the islands before 1764, when the first human settlement was founded, except for a single species of indigenous fox, now extinct. The settlers introduced cattle, which quickly went wild when the first attempts at colonization were abandoned; these later provided food for pirates and settlers alike. Sheep were introduced by the British in the 1840s, and proved ideally suited to the chilly climate and low, grassy hills; the herds had grown to over 800,000 head by the 1890s. Overgrazing of native grasses, however, has reduced their numbers in the twentieth century to a stable population that hovers around 650,000 head. Production of wool is the main industry on the islands, and virtually the only one which produces overseas income.

In recent decades, some attempts have been made to find oil beneath the waters between the Falklands and Argentina, with no certain results. Such discoveries would, of course, vastly increase the economic value of the islands; in the absence of any sure indications, the islands remain and shall always remain economically marginal, requiring some outside financial support in perpetuity for any sustained development. While the roughly 1,800 permanent residents are remarkably self-sustaining, they do not possess a sufficiently large economic base to maintain more than a stark and drab existence at best, with all of the attendant social ills that that implies (alcoholism, for example, is a major problem on the islands).

2. Colonial Land Claims

At the heart of the Falklands dispute, and at the base of both the Argentine and British claims to the islands, are a series of inconsistently-documented colonial and precolonial visits by Spanish, Dutch, French, and English explorers, as well as piratical nationals of these and other countries. The arguments have been vehement on both sides, the legal and historical opinions learned and erudite, and the results completely negative, in terms of making any real progress toward settlement of such mutually incompatible views. The known facts, with attendant speculations, are these:

The Argentine claims to the Malvinas date back to 1493, when Pope Alexander VI drew an arbitrary line through the South American continent, awarding all territories on the right side of the line to Portugal, and those on the left side to the Spanish Empire. The new world had been little explored at this time, so no one really knew what the division gave each of these two world naval powers (England's navy was insignificant at this time). As it happened, Spain received most of South America, while Portugal only colonized the eastern part of Brazil. Included within the Spanish sphere of influence were the Falkland Islands. What power did the Pope actually have to grant these lands? In theory, the popes of this time claimed temporal powers over the entire known and unknown world; in actual fact, the Pope's real temporal powers were confined to a portion of central Italy, the Papal States. But the popes wielded enormous political and social influence, particularly in a dispute of this kind—Spain and Portugal accepted the demarcation, at least until Portugal began expanding its territories westward a hundred years later. Of course, once the protestant movement began, twenty years later, the formerly Catholic countries of northern and western Europe actively began to oppose the claims of the Catholic Church, as well as those countries still supporting the Papacy. Thus England has never accepted the Spanish claims to the Falklands based upon Pope Alexander's division.

The first European to explore the waters near the east coast of South America was Amerigo Vespucci, at that time in the service of the Portuguese, who sailed from Lisbon in 1501 (1). During the spring of 1502, as he was tacking southeast, away from the coast, he " . . . sighted new land, . . . and found it all barren coast; and we saw in it neither harbor nor inhabitants" (2). Most of the experts agree that there is insufficient evidence to determine precisely what Vespucci saw, or where this "new land" actually was. Indeed, both Magnaghi and Levillier hold that the letter which includes the above passage is, in fact, a fabrication, and that Vespucci actually sailed north after reaching a point on the coast somewhere between the 47th and 50th parallels (3).

Another early explorer was Magellan (Fernando de Magalhaes), who explored the east coast of South America late in 1520, in the course of his famous round-the-world voyage. Twenty years later, Alonso de

Santa Cruz described the voyage in these terms: " . . . leaving this bay [San Julian Bay], some islands were discovered east thereof at a distance of some eighteen leagues which they called Yslas de Sanson y de Patos, because they found there many fat penguins . . ." (4). Arce contends that maps prepared after the Magellan expedition demonstrate conclusively that these islands *were* the Falklands (5); however, the distances between the mainland and the islands cited by Magellan's successors are much too short, and the position of the islands on contemporary maps vary several degrees up and down the coast. There is thus no conclusive evidence supporting Arce's contentions. Arce also notes the expedition of Simon de Alcazaba in 1535, who reported discovering several islands south of the 45th parallel (6); here again, no real evidence is offered.

A more probable candidate for discoverer of the Falklands is Francisco Camargo, who sailed from Sevilla in August, 1539, and reached the tip of South America in January, 1540. One of the three vessels in the expedition was driven back from the Strait of Magellan by a gale that blew fiercely from the south. On February 4th, they sighted a group of mountainous islands, with long bays and inlets, no woods whatsoever, filled with fowl, sea lions, and foxes, a description which matches very well with what is known of the islands' early appearance. The explorers stayed six months before returning to Spain; the descriptions above are taken from their fragmentary published log (7). Most historians seem to regard Camargo's claims as the strongest among these early explorers, although none of them rule out the possibility that Vespucci, Magellan, or some other voyager found the islands first. The maps included in Santa Cruz's official survey of the world's islands, *Islario* (1541), incorporate material from all of the above expeditions, but rely particularly on the data reported by Camargo's surviving vessels (8).

John Davis was the first English explorer to sail near the eastern tip of South America, as part of Sir Thomas Cavendish's expedition. Davis commanded the ship *Desire*. On May 21, 1592, Davis lost sight of Cavendish's vessel off Puerto Deseado; after fruitless searching, Davis stopped at Penguin Island, then headed south toward the Magellan Strait, where he hoped to locate his commander. On August 9th, the *Desire* was buffeted by storms, and on the 14th, "we were driven in among certain isles never before discovered by any known relation lying fifty leagues or better from the shore east and northerly from the straits" (9). No further description is provided, and no attempt was made to land on the islands—Davis immediately returned to the Strait of Magellan when conditions bettered.

A year later, Richard Hawkins sailed from England, reaching the South American coast in February of 1594. On February 2nd, he sighted land, "next of anything in 48 degrees" of latitude, where he saw fires, noted rivers or inlets with discolored runoff, and described the land as being largely flat. The Falklands are actually located between 51-53 degrees of latitude, and many of Hawkins's descriptions seem at variance with the known geography of these islands; however, his account is sufficiently vague as to allow almost any interpretation. Goebel and Arce regard his claims as spurious, Goebel believing Hawkins actually sighted part of the Patagonian coast; Cawkell *et al.* tend to give his observations more weight, in line with prevailing British opinion (10). It should be emphasized that Hawkins wrote his memoirs in prison more than twenty years after the events narrated, without access to his papers and logs; this may account for some of the discrepancies in his story.

Sixteenth century sightings of the Falklands were concluded by Sebald de Weert, a Dutch master of the *Geloof*, one of five vessels under the overall command of Jacob Mahu. In April of 1599, Mahu's company were halfway through the Strait of Magellan when they were hit by a series of storms so fierce that the ships were separated. The *Geloof* turned back. On January 16, 1600, "three little islands were sighted, hitherto neither noted nor drawn on any map. These were given the new name Sebaldes. These islands are distant from the continent sixty leagues toward the east and southeast in 50 degrees, 40 minutes latitude" (11). Most geographers now believe that de Weert sighted the Jason Islands, lying northwest of the Falklands group. In any event, no landfall was made. Le Maire and Schouten confirmed de Weert's discovery in January of 1616.

The next known sighting was in January, 1684, by the English buccaneers, Cowley and Dampier, who recorded visiting the Sebalds, and discovering a new island at 47 degrees south latitude, which they named Pepys. Six years later, in January of 1690, John Strong, Captain of the pirate vessel, the *Welfare*, found himself near the Sebalds; he then sailed south into a long strait which he named Falkland Sound (the Argentines call it San Carlos), apparently after Viscount Falkland (1659-1694), then a Commissioner of the Admiralty (later First Lord). Strong noted penguins, fresh water, an absence of woods, seals, fowl, and an abundance of kelp. Although he landed on the islands, he made no attempt to take possession of them in any formal sense (12).

French sailors visited the islands and their environs in 1701, 1703, and 1708, resulting in a new map being produced in 1716 by the French cartographer, Amedee Frezier. Delisle called the islands Iles Malouines on a map of 1722, after the port of St. Malo, from which most of these ships had sailed (13). "Malouines" was later corrupted by the Spanish into Islas Malvinas. The name Falkland was first applied to the islands by the English in 1708, when Captain Woode Rogers, a privateer, labeled them "Falkland's Land" (14). John McBride called them by their full name in 1766, and renamed the Sebalds the Jasons at the same time (15).

What are we to make of these early sightings, randomly recorded over a 200-year period? Some are undoubtedly genuine; however, separating the fictitious from the real is very difficult in these early accounts, as is often the case when dealing with documents dating from this period. Many of these sailors were minimally educated, took little care with their sightings, were forced to used primitive instruments in making measurements, and sometimes had political or other considerations in mind when publishing their memoirs or logs. Their accounts were adjusted accordingly. There appear to be no recorded instances of the islands actually being specifically claimed by either the British or the Spanish, despite landfalls at irregular intervals by nationals or pirates of both nations. Any objective observer must come to the conclusion that the islands, being both unoccupied and unclaimed, essentially remained at this point open to the first nation to establish a colony on their shores.

So it was that the Frenchman, Antoine de Bougainville, who had served with Montcalm in the French and English wars in Quebec, proposed to his government that he undertake at his own and his relatives' expense a colonization of the islands, which had the potential of providing a safe harbor and way station for ships rounding the Horn. In September of 1763, two ships sailed from St. Malo, reaching the Jasons on January 31, 1764. Several days later, on February 3rd, Bougainville discovered Berkeley Sound (which he named French Bay), on East Falkland, where Fort St. Louis (later Port Louis) was erected; the islands were formally claimed for King Louis XV on April 5, 1764, under the name Les Malouines. Three days later, Bougainville left for St. Malo, but returned in January, 1765, with new settlers and additional supplies. with no trees to provide wood for construction materials, peat, sod, and earth were used in building the fort and dwelling places (tents were also erected). The surviving stock, including horses and cows, had been released in very weakened condition upon landing; they were gradually rounded up and placed in newly-constructed stables. G. de Bougainville Nerville was appointed first Governor. The thriving colony was visited for a third time in 1766 (16).

By this time, however, Spain had officially protested the presence of a colony in what it considered to be its sphere of influence, claiming that the Malvinas belonged to it by right of territorial proximity, a somewhat dubious legal principle. Since its claim rested on uncertain ground, it agreed to purchase the colony from Bougainville, reimbursing him for his investment; the French Government agreed, rather than create a diplomatic incident, and the colony was officially ceded to Spain on April 1, 1767 (17).

The English had not been idle during this period. Having been notified of Bougainville's plans, they mounted an expedition under the command of Captain John Byron, grandfather of Lord Byron, who sailed with two ships on June 21, 1764, arriving at the Falklands on January 12, 1765. Byron landed on Saunders Island, off the northwest coast of West Falkland Island, taking formal possession of the islands in the name of the Crown on January 23, 1765 (18). The landfall on Saunders was named Port Egmont, in honor of the then First Lord of the Admiralty,

John Egmont, Earl of Egmont. Byron planted a vegetable garden, but left the islands shortly thereafter. Later that year John McBride was sent to the Falklands by the British Government with instructions to remove any foreign settlements, if possible, and to establish an English base; or to set up a joint settlement if these other unnamed foreigners refused to leave. McBride reached the islands on January 8, 1766.

McBride surveyed the islands per his instructions over the next year, finally discovering the French colony at Port Louis on East Falkland on December 2nd. The Englishman delivered his formal warning, which the French dutifully rejected, and sailed for home the following month, a year after he had arrived. The French in the meantime had fortified their position, but turned their settlement over to the Spanish in April. At this time, according to McBride's description, Port Louis consisted of only seventeen houses, mostly built of sod (only the Governor's was made of stone), with perhaps 130 settlers (19). Most of these colonists returned to France when the Spanish Governor, Felipe Ruiz Puente, arrived. East Falkland became Isla Nuestra Senora de la Soledad, Port Louis being renamed Puerto Soledad (20).

The problem of ownership of the islands now became paramount. The Spanish claimed the Malvinas by right of first discovery, and by right of cession from the first colonists, the French, who had formally taken possession and built a settlement in 1764. The English claimed the Falklands by right of first discovery, by virtue of its proclamation of 1765, and through actual occupation in 1766; they further held that the Spanish had not arrived until 1767, after the British had already established their fort. On balance, the Spanish claim seems stronger, if one discounts the original voyages of exploration, and considers only the actual settlement of the isles, and the legal continuation from the French to the Spanish, all of which is supported by extant documents. However, one can also take the position that both claims were valid, if applied only to that portion of the Falklands upon which settlement was actually made—in other words, awarding East Falkland Island to the Spanish, West Falkland to the British. In any event, the English Captain Hunt, master of the *Tamar*, encountered a Spanish vessel from Puerto Soledad on November 28, 1769. The Capitan-General of Buenos Aires had already been instructed by Madrid on February 25, 1768 that "no English establishments are to be permitted, and you are to expel by force any already set up if they do not obey the warnings, in conformity with the law" (21). So both Governors immediately exchanged notes warning the other to leave immediately. Hunt stated:

". . . the said islands belong to his Britannic Majesty, by right of discovery as well as settlement, and that the subject of no other power whatever can have any right to be settled in the said islands without leave from his Britannic Majesty . . . I do, therefore . . ., warn you to leave the island . . . (within) six months from the date thereof . . ." (22). Hunt's letter prompted a series of warnings and counterwarnings between Port Egmont and Puerto Soledad, and notes between the

Governors and their respective masters, in Buenos Aires and in England (Hunt sailed for home in March, leaving the vessel *Favourite* on station, under command of Captain George Farmer). Francisco Bucareli, the Spanish Capitan-General in Patagonia, immediately ordered Don Juan Ignacio de Madariaga to evict the British, by force if necessary (23). Madariaga's expedition consisted of four frigates, a xebec, artillery, and 1,400 marines, including some 300 seasoned troops. They anchored off Port Egmont on June 4, 1770.

The two English Captains, Farmer and William Maltby, were asked to evacuate or face military action. Fifteen minutes were allowed for a reply. Farmer refused to capitulate, and ordered the *Favourite* to move closer to shore. Madariaga fired two shots across the ship's bow, put his marines on shore, and opened fire on the blockhouse, where he English artillery had been installed. On June 10th, the British surrendered, and were allowed to remove their settlement peacefully. Departure of the English vessel was delayed until the Spanish had had a chance to notify their masters in Buenos Aires and Madrid; the *Favourite* finally set sail for England on July 14th (24).

England at first seriously considered going to war with Spain over the Falklands, but ultimately demured. Although the islands might be valuable as a way station round the Horn, they were also a dreary, expensive venture to maintain so far from home. Still, the outcome was in doubt until the very end of the negotiations. The Spanish were swayed, among other things, by a letter from King Louis XV of France stating that he would not necessarily support a Spanish war with the British. Prince Masserano, the Spanish negotiator, agreed to allow the British to resettle their base, supposedly subject to a secret agreement: "As they assure us they will evacuate the Falklands later, and that we should rely on their promise, the King has determined to concede that which is to save his honor and leave for later the negotiation on the evacuation of the island, accepting their offer although it be merely verbal" (25). The existence of a secret agreement has always been denied by the British Government.

Masserano's official declaration was dated January 18, 1771, and stated: ". . . The Prince de Maserano declares . . . that things shall be restored in the Great Malouine at the port called Egmont, precisely to the state in which they were before the 10th of June, 1770 . . . at the same time, he declares that the engagement of his said Catholick Majesty, to restore to his Britannick Majesty the possession of the port and fort called Egmont, cannot nor ought in any wise to affect the question of the prior right of sovereignty of the Malouine islands, otherwise called Falkland's Islands . . ." (26). The British in their acceptance document failed to acknowledge the last section of the Spanish declaration. There was much debate in the English body politic about the wisdom of accepting this statement, particularly concerning the ability of the Crown to hold any territories without exercising full sovereignty over them. Lord Camden noted at the time: "The right of sovereignty becomes absolute *jure coronae* from the moment the restitution takes place. Nor does it seem to me the King's title is abridged or limited; inasmuch as the reservation neither denies the right on one side nor asserts it on the other. The question remains as it stood before the hostility; the King of Spain declaring only that he ought not to be precluded from his former claim by this act of possessory restitution" (27). Whether Camden's views are in accordance with international law is a question which remains unanswered to this day, and concerning which the British and Argentine governments hold vastly different views.

The order for restoring the status quo was issued on February 7th, and a new British expedition was outfitted, arriving at Port Egmont on September 13, 1771. The British flag was raised by Captain Stott, commander of the small force, on the 15th. The Spanish restored the confiscated artillery and provisions the following month. According to Goebel (28), Masserano immediately had difficulties following the signing of the order in securing a firm commitment from the British for a timetable for withdrawal. Dates of 1772-1773 were mentioned by the English, when Masserano had understood that no more than a few months might be involved. Finally, the Spanish Government decided to take no action, and a potential second crisis was averted. The British post was reduced in size in 1773, and finally abandoned on May 20, 1774, ostensibly for economic reasons. A plaque was affixed to the blockhouse which read: "Be it known to all nations that the Falkland Islands, with this fort, the storehouse, wharfs, harbors, bays, and creeks thereunto belonging are the sole right and property of his Most Sacred Majesty George the Third, King of Great Britain, France, and Ireland, Defender of the Faith, etc. In witness whereof this plate is set up, and his Britannic Majesty's colors left flying as a mark of possession by S. W. Clayton, commanding officer at the Falkland Islands, A.D. 1774" (29).

In 1775 Captain James Cook, the noted explorer, discovered South Georgia Island, landing there at three different places. This uninhabited, perpetually ice-bound isle lies approximately 1,200 miles southeast of the Falklands. Cook took possession of the territory in the name of King George III, naming it the "Isle of Georgia" (30). A later British explorer, Captain Waddell, revisited the island in 1823, and also formally claimed it for England.

The Falklands were included by the Spanish in the Viceroyalty of Buenos Aires, set up in 1776. A year later, the Governor was ordered to destroy the remaining traces of the British settlement; the plaque was sent to Buenos Aires, where it remained until 1806; at that time, the British General Beresford, who was in command of the English occupying army, removed it to England (31). On October 25, 1790, Britain and Spain signed the Nootka Sound Convention, which had resulted from a dispute over possession of a portion of Vancouver Island that was claimed by both countries. In this agreement, both sides ". . . agreed with respect to the eastern and western coasts of South America and the islands adjacent, that the respective subjects shall not form in the future any establishment on the parts of the coast situated to the south of the parts of the same coast and of the islands adjacent already occupied by Spain; it being understood that the said respective subjects shall retain the liberty of landing on the coasts and islands so situated for objects connected with their fishing . . ." (32). Goebel states: "The terms of the sixth article by inference forbade any landing at the Falklands as they were a place already occupied by Spain" (33).

In June of 1806, notified that Buenos Aires had been captured by the British, the Governor of the islands abandoned his post; four years later, in 1810, revolution broke out in Buenos Aires against the Bonaparte government of Spain, resulting in the erection of a provisional government loyal to the Bourbons. On July 9, 1816 the Viceroyalty was transformed into the independent United Provinces of the Rio de la Plata. The Falklands had been abandoned by the old government on March 18, 1811. The United Provinces systematically began to assert its claim over the entire region between the Plata River and Cape Horn, including the Magellan Strait and Tierra del Fuego, but made no immediate attempt to occupy the islands. During the decade following abandonment, the islands were used by whalers, sealers, fishermen, and pirates. On November 6, 1820, Colonel David Jewitt took formal possession of the Malvinas in the name of the United Provinces, and officially warned the fifty whaling and sealing ships that no fishing or hunting would be allowed on or near the islands without appropriate licenses. Pablo Aregusti was appointed Governor in 1823; later that year the Provinces granted Jorge Pacheco and Louis Vernet thirty leagues of land, with attendant fishing and ranching rights. Vernet abandoned this venture a year later, but returned in 1826. In 1828 Vernet was awarded exclusive fishing rights in the Malvinas. On June 10, 1829 the United Provinces issued a decree affirming its rights to the Falklands, stating that they had inherited the islands from Spain, by virtue of the revolution of 1810, and by proximity of the islands to the mainland; the islands were now to be placed under a Military and Political Governor, to reside at Soledad. Vernet was made the new Governor. As possessor of the sole fishing rights on the islands, Vernet used his new powers aggressively to pursue and punish any ships infringing on his territory. He notified all sealers and whalers in the area to pay the required taxes, or to leave the area immediately. As an example to the others, Vernet ordered Matthew Brisbane, skipper of the British schooner *Elbe*, to seize three offending American ships, the *Harriet*, the *Superior*, and the *Breakwater*, on July 30, 1831. The *Superior* reached an accomodation with Vernet, paying him 1,000 skins for duties; it then promptly sailed to Buenos Aires, lodging a complaint with the American embassy there (34). The *Breakwater* managed to escape from Vernet's control several days after its seizure, and sailed for the United States. The *Harriet* agreed to abide by a decision of the courts in Buenos Aires; Vernet himself (with his family) accompanied the ship to Argentina. There, the inexperienced junior United States consul, George Washington Slacum, who had unexpectedly become temporary head of the United States mission upon the untimely death of his superior, filed a virulent protest with the Provinces' government, and ordered a passing American warship, the *Lexington*, to proceed at once to the Falklands to protect American rights and citizens (35). Commander Silas Duncan and his ship reached the islands on December 28, 1831, where he promptly seized by deception Vernet's seconds-in-command, destroyed the fort's guns and powder, sacked the houses, seized a packet of seal skins, arrested a number of the settlers, scattering the rest, and declared the islands free of all government (36). This precipitated a major diplomatic crisis between the two American republics, with several exchanges of harsh letters from Washington to Buenos Aires and back again, and multitudinous filings of claims and counterclaims for damages. Vernet demanded reimbursement from the United States for the destruction of his fort and goods, but never received it; the American ships demanded recompense for their losses. The correspondence on this subject continued until March of 1886, when the United States State Department officially informed Argentina that it would not discuss the matter further until Britain's claims of sovereignty had been settled (37).

The United Provinces appointed as replacement for Vernet a new Governor, one Juan Esteban or Jose Francisco Mestivier (sources vary), who arrived in the Malvinas on October 10, 1832; two months later he was murdered by his own men, leaving the government in chaos. The Commander of the Argentine ship *Sarandi*, Jose Maria Pinedo, assumed authority as acting Governor (38) in mid-December. It was then that the British arrived.

3. The British Occupation of the Islands

The English became interested again in the naval importance of the Falklands in the late 1820s. Woodbine Parish, British Consul-General in Buenos Aires, systematically began accumulating information on the islands, which he then forwarded to the Home Office in London. Among others, he examined government archives in Buenos Aires dealing with the Falklands, and interviewed Vernet in 1829 just before he was appointed Governor. In July of that year, a man named Buckington wrote the British Government, urging that a colony be reestablished on the islands. Less than a month later, on August 8, 1829, the Earl of Aberdeen instructed Parish to protest against actions "done without reference to the validity of the claims which His Majesty had constantly asserted to the sovereignty of the islands" (39). This Parish did in November. General Juan Manuel de Rosas' government acknowledged the protest, but never officially responded to it. Meanwhile, Vernet had begun flirting with Parish, apparently with the idea that the British might assume control of the Falklands, providing Vernet with the power to back up his title. The American intervention left the colony in a shambles, half-deserted, half-destroyed, without any effective governance.

Henry Fox, the new British consul, arrived in Argentina in December of 1831. He was immediately ordered by Lord Palmerston to demand Vernet's removal; Fox wisely decided to let the Americans fight their own battles. In a letter to Palmerston dated October 15, 1832, Fox recounted a conversation with the American *charge*, Francis Baylies, in which the American had stated that the United States had no intentions of claiming the Falklands, but was willing to acknowledge British sovereignty, so long as American vessels had free fishing rights there (40). Baylies further indicated that the Americans would not countenance piracy (i.e., intervention by the Provinces' government) or the deliberate harassment of American vessels; and that the British, if they indeed claimed to own the islands, should take steps to control the depredations of pirates and Argentines alike (41).

By this time, however, the die had been cast. On August 29, 1832, the British Admiralty submitted to Viscount Palmerston, the British Prime Minister, the draft of an order instructing Admiral Baker, Chief of the Naval Division operating out of Rio de Janeiro, to take whatever steps might be necessary to "exercise periodically British sovereignty over the Falklands." The order was approved on August 31st; Baker was told that "the King would look with pleasure upon the dispatch to Port Egmont of a vessel of the South Atlantic Fleet authorized to perform acts of sovereignty" (42). The warships *Clio* and *Tyne*, under command of Captain J. F. Onslow, were ordered by Baker on November 28th to occupy the Falklands, reestablishing British control by force, if necessary. Onslow arrived at the deserted ruins of Port Egmont on December 20, 1832. The fort was partially rebuilt, and the official notice of sovereignty restored. On January 1, 1833, the *Clio* arrived at Puerto Luis (renamed by Vernet from Puerto Soledad); the following day, Onslow boarded the *Sarandi*, and handed Acting Governor Pinedo an official letter:

"On board H.B.M.'s sloop *Clio*. Berkeley Sound, January 2, 1833. I have to acquaint you that I have received directions from his Excellency and Commander-in-Chief of His Britannic Majesty's ships and vessels of war, South American station, in the name of His Britannic Majesty, to exercise the rights of sovereignty over these islands. It is my intention to hoist tomorrow the national flag of Great Britain on shore, when I request you will be pleased to haul down your flag on shore and withdraw your force, taking all your stores belonging to your Government" (43).

Pinedo protested bitterly the next morning, refusing to lower his flag; he finally agreed to withdraw, however, without bloodshed, appointing Juan Simon Acting Governor of the colony. The British landed several boats at 9:00 A.M., erected a flagpost at the home of the senior British resident, lowered the Provinces' flag (which was dispatched by boat to the *Sarandi*), and hoisted the Union Jack. The *Sarandi* sailed on the 5th. Onslow himself returned to Britain a few days later, leaving William Dickson, the senior British resident, in charge, with orders to raise the flag whenever foreign ships arrived. In his official report, Onslow recommended that a permanent military base be established on the Falklands, to preserve order and to protect whalers and settlers alike (44).

The *Sarandi* arrived in Buenos Aires on January 15th; the following day, Manuel V. de Maza, Provinces' Foreign Minister, delivered an official letter of protest to Philip Gore, British *charge*, who knew nothing of the affair, and could only wait for instructions from his government. Manuel Moreno, the United Provinces' ambassador to Great Britain, sent a letter to Lord Palmerston on April 24, 1833, asking, in effect, whether Onslow had been ordered to evict Pinedo, or had been acting on his own initiative. Palmerston replied on April 27th that Onslow had acted under the full authority of the British Government. On June 17, 1833, Moreno officially protested the British occupation; relying primarily on a history drawn up by Vernet some years before, the ambassador restated the Provinces' case, which, he said, was based upon legal succession to the established rights of Spain. These included initial discovery, initial occupation, purchase from France, and ultimate abandonment of the English settlement (45). The British delayed six months before replying on January 8, 1834; in his letter, Palmerston ignored most of Moreno's points, and instead mentioned Parish's protest of 1829, which, he said, had been ignored by the United Provinces. Britain's claim to sovereignty, he said, had been repeatedly asserted in the discussions with Spain in 1770-1771, the result of which had been restoration of the British presence in the Falklands. He added: "The Government of the United Provinces could not reasonably have anticipated that the British Government would permit any other state to exercise a right as derived from Spain which Great Britain had denied to Spain itself" (46). Palmerston further stated that no secret understanding had ever been found recorded in published proceedings of the earlier discussions between Spain and Britain.

Meanwhile, on the islands themselves the situation remained chaotic. The result of the American and British adventures had been devastating; most of the already ramshackle houses were destroyed or in disrepair, the permanent colony had shrunk to less than thirty individuals, and no attempt was made by the British to control the numerous sealers of various nationalities that used the islands as a temporary base. Matthew Brisbane returned from Buenos Aires in March of 1833 to manage Vernet's property, but met opposition from the former convicts that comprised much of his labor force. Their dissatisfaction resulted in the murders of Brisbane, Simon, Dickson, and two others on August 26, 1833. Antonio Rivero and his gauchos, the killers, scattered into the interior. On January 8, 1834, H.M.S. *Challenger* arrived off the islands as part of its long voyage to map the coasts of South America; Lieutenant Henry Smith was installed as first British administrator of the Falklands on January 10th (47). Using a force of marines and officers, Smith systematically searched out the plotters, eventually returning them for trial to England. However, since the murders had been committed before the British government on the Falklands had been officially installed, they could not be held, and were eventually returned as free men to South America.

Moreno protested again on December 29, 1834; the British did not respond. In January, 1838, Britain rejected a suggestion by General Rosas that the Provinces would accept British sovereignty over the Falklands if Britain would forgive a loan dating back to 1824. On December 18, 1841, Moreno protested for a third time, on this occasion stressing the inaccuracies of Palmerston's position, and stating that, in any case, Britain had never owned the island of Soledad (East Falkland). Lord Aberdeen responded on December 29th that the Provinces could not alter an agreement made forty years before between Britain and Spain, and that the British Government considered that agreement final (48). Moreno replied on March 5, 1842:

"The undersigned . . . is compelled to declare . . . that the United Provinces cannot accept, and will never be able to accept, the Resolution of H.B.M.'s Government of the 5th instant, as it is, in their opinion, unjust and contrary to their evident rights; reproduces the protests by them made on June 17, 1833 and on December 19, 1834, against the assumption by the Crown of Great Britain of sovereignty over the Malvinas and against the seizure of, and ousting from the settlements in Port Louis, also known as Puerto Soledad, by H.B.M.'s sloop *Clio*, reparations for which (the seizure and the ousting) is due them, as well as against all other actions from said occupation resulting; the Government of the United Provinces, therefore, deposits these protests, conferring upon the full value they may have at the present, or at any other time" (49). A further protest was made by Moreno on July 3, 1849, after Palmerston, in a debate in the Commons on July 27th, had stated: "England had occupied the Falklands because she had found them unoccupied; it would not be wise to reopen an exchange of correspondence which had been concluded by the consent of one of the parties and the perserverance of the other" (50).

Smith restored order to the islands in the five years of his administration, although there were only a handful of permanent residents, numbering at any one time no more than 20-30 persons, including children. The wild horses and cows that roamed the islands were corralled and domesticated, a few at a time. Gardens were planted, the adminstrator's house refurbished. Smith was replaced by Lieutenant Robert Lowcay in the middle of 1838. Lowcay spent most of his time surveying, allowing the improvements Smith had made to deteriorate. He was in turn replaced by Lieutenant John Tyssen in the fall of

1839 (51). Tyssen rebuilt the corrals, and increased the number of tamed horses and cattle. However, sealers still roamed the islands outside the immediate vicinity of Port Louis unchecked, and something would obviously have to be done if the British presence were to be maintained.

G. W. Whitington had been granted 6,400 acres of land on East Falkland Island by Captain Langdon, who had in turn been given the land by Vernet. Whitington formed the Falkland Island Commercial Fishery and Agricultural Association in 1834, obviously hoping to follow Vernet's lead in establishing a commercial monopoly on the Falklands. The British declined to recognize Whitington's acquisition, realizing that by doing so they would be giving Vernet's own land claims legitimacy [Vernet pursued his claims against the British Government for nearly twenty years after the original British occupation, finally winning a small award in a London court], thereby tacitly acknowledging that the United Provinces had had the legal right to sell Vernet the land in the first place—in other words, that the Provinces had sovereignty over the islands. Whitington was not to be deterred by this refusal, and instead applied for a new grant of land from London, agreeing to pay all expenses for a settlement expedition to the islands, with himself to be named civilian Governor. Again the British refused. In 1842, Whitington sent his brother, J. B. Whitington, to the Falklands, with two ships, about twenty settlers, livestock (including sheep), and supplies (52). Upon his arrival in November, he established himself at Port Louis, built a large house, and started a fish salting business; he also requested cession of a ten-square-mile tract on the island.

By this time, the British Government was finally beginning to move. The first civil administrator, Lieutenant Richard C. Moody, was appointed Lieutenant-Governor on August 2, 1841, being inaugurated at Port Louis on January 22, 1842 (53). Previously, the Naval officers who had administered the island did so under military law, without the pretense of any civilian government, and without any civilian title. Now the first beginnings of a colonial adminstration were being established. Port Louis (renamed Anson) was unsuitable as a center of governance for the Falklands, since ships often had to wait weeks to enter Berkeley Sound during bad weather. A new town was planned in the Port William area, which had a harbor secure from bad weather, with several safe anchorages. Moody called the settlement Port Stanley. By the end of 1844, almost all the settlers except for Whitington and his workers had made the move. On June 23, 1843, Letters Patent were officially issued by the Queen for establishment of "Her Majesty's Settlements in the Falkland Islands and their Dependencies" (54). Moody's title was changed to Governor and Commander-in-Chief, the same title used by all of his successors until the Argentine Invasion of 1982. An Executive Council was inaugurated on April 2, 1845, and a Legislative Council on November 13, 1845. Moody finally settled at Port Stanley on July 18, 1845.

The first effort to attract settlers was conducted by Samuel Fish Lafone of Montevideo, Uruguay, who in January, 1844 proposed to the Government that he domesticate the wild cattle roaming the islands, and use them to entice buyers from overseas. In an agreement signed in London on March 16th of that year, Lafone was given the right to sell land on Lafonia Peninsula, with rights to the wild cattle there, for a period of six years. Due to troubles in Uruguay, Lafone was unable to start his venture until May of 1847. Despite further concessions from the British Government, the venture was a complete financial failure. In 1851 Lafone sold his holdings to the Falkland Islands Company Ltd., a British corporation established specifically to acquire Lafone's interests; the Company remains the major landholder and commercial enterprise on the islands to this day. Moody set up his own licensing scheme for the wild stock in 1847 (expanded by Rennie in 1849), giving purchasers of 160-acre lots the right to graze cattle on surrounding Crown lands (55). George Rennie succeeded Moody as Governor in 1848.

The result of this policy was gradual colonization, with a systematic extermination of the wild cattle—by the 1870s they had all been killed. West Falkland Island was colonized directly from Britain by the arrival in 1867 of the ship *Diane*; within two years, the entire land area of West Falkland had been leased to just eight settlers. Inhabitants on East Falkland had the right during this period to bring five laborers out from England at government expense. The first sheep were introduced in 1841, but all died of disease. In 1852 J. P. Dale, first manager of the Company, introduced a new flock of Cheviots that thrived in the Falklands' climate.

The government experienced great difficulties in establishing control over the numerous islands and inlets, and over the hundreds of whalers, sealers, and fishermen of all nationalities who used them as temporary refuge. Port Stanley benefited, however from the California gold rush of 1849, and the subsequent influx of vessels sailing around the Horn. During the 1850s and '60s, the population slowly grew, and order was gradually imposed over the entire island span. In May of 1853 Governor Rennie asked the British government to send an official note to the United States government, complaining of the destruction caused by American sealers in the islands. On January 9, 1854, reports were received in Stanley of an American whaler, the *Hudson*, which had unlawfully killed a number of animals on New Island. Rennie at once sent for a British brig, the *Express*, to restore order. The resident American agent, W. H. Smyley, in turn requested the presence of an American warship, the *Germantown*. The commander of the American vessel confronted the Governor on March 3, 1854, refusing to acknowledge British sovereignty over the uninhabited portions of the islands. Meanwhile, the *Express* had seized the *Hudson*, and returned with it to the capital. The American commander protested both verbally and in writing; the masters of the American ships later filed claims against the British government. Ultimately, the claims were settled in the Americans' favor many years later by an international tribunal; but the British government, while paying the settlement, refused to allow any challenge to its sovereignty: "The British Government would not discuss the right of sovereignty with another Power, but would continue to exercise in and around the islands of the Falkland group the right inherent under the laws of nations in the territorial sovereignty, and to prevent all possibility of mistake would not allow the wild cattle on the Falkland Islands to be destroyed or other depredations to be committed on the islands by any foreigner to whatever nation they may belong" (56).

By 1873 Port Stanley included some 800 individuals, several rows of cottages, and a large Government House. In 1881 the Falklands became financially independent of Britain; two years later, a Land and Tenement Tax was imposed upon residents of Port Stanley.

The Argentines had not forgotten their dispute during this period. The December 15, 1884 issues of the Buenos Aires newspapers carried an announcement by the Argentine Geographic Institute of the forthcoming publication of a new map of Argentina on which the Malvinas appeared as part of Argentine territory. The British ambassador immediately questioned the official status of the map. Francisco Ortiz, Argentina's Foreign Minister, replied that he could not comment on the status of the publication, but that in any event, the question was irrelevant when considering the matter of sovereignty over the Falklands; he hinted that Argentina would welcome an official discussion on the latter question. On December 27, 1884, the British Government filed an official protest. Ortiz replied on January 5th that the question of sovereignty was by no means settled; he also summarized the political history of the islands from the Argentine point of view. The British reply on January 8th stated that as far as the British Government was concerned, the controversy over the islands was a closed matter (57); the actions of 1833 were justified by the Argentine failure to respond to Parish's protest of 1829. There the matter remained for two years.

Argentina reminded Britain in 1887 that it had received no reply to its last protest; the British stated in turn that they had replied orally in 1886, again saying the matter was closed. Norberto Quirno Costa, Argentina's Foreign Minister, replied on January 29, 1888 that his government had no record of an 1886 conversation, and that the British had no right unilaterally to settle the matter. The British *charge* in Buenos Aires then stated in a letter dated April 13, 1888 that the British "refused to enter into a discussion of H.B.M.'s rights to the Falkland Islands, a right which, in the opinion of that government, left no room for doubt and did not present any difficulty, of any nature whatsoever" (58). On June 8th Quirno Costa issued a final response, stating that the refusal of the British to discuss the matter did not affect the rights of Argentina, and that Argentina "maintained, and would always maintain, its claim to sovereignty over the Malvinas, of which it had been deprived by force in time of peace" (59). The official status of the Falklands was raised to that of a Colony on February 29, 1892.

A major battle was fought between British and German naval forces off the Falklands on December 8, 1914, in which the German fleet was virtually destroyed. A similar battle was fought in World War II near the South American coast. In both wars Port Stanley was used as a British naval base. Income taxes were instituted in 1939. By 1948 the islands had internal air service. In 1949 universal suffrage was promulgated. The Executive Council was enlarged in 1947, again in 1954, and again in 1957, to increase representation by the islanders, who now have a permanent majority. These changes gave the islanders self government in all but name. New constitutions were inaugurated in 1964 and 1977 (60). The Governors during this period continued to be British civil servants, usually career Foreign Service officers who served one term of 3-7 years, and then moved on.

Some mention should be made in this section of the Falkland Islands Dependencies and the British Antarctic Territory, also claimed by Argentina. As we have already seen, Captain James Cook discovered South Georgia Island on January 17, 1775, although an earlier claim had been made by Englishman Anthony de la Roche in 1675. Cook also discovered the South Sandwich Islands on January 31, 1775. naming them Sandwich Land after the then First Lord of the Admiralty. The South Shetland Islands were discovered by English Captain William Smith on February 18, 1819; revisiting the islands in October of that year, he formally claimed them in the name of King George III, naming them New South Britain. A few months later, on January 16, 1820, Edward Bransfield also landed, and again claimed the islands for Britain. The South Orkney Islands were discovered by a British sealer, Captain George Powell, on December 6, 1821. The following day he landed on the largest of the islands and formally claimed them for King George IV, calling the isle Coronation Island. Graham Land, the northernmost part of Antarctica, was discovered on January 30, 1820, also by Bransfield; he called the territory Trinity Land. In 1829, Captain H. Foster landed there, and formally took possession in the name of King George IV. On February 21, 1832, another British sealer, John Biscoe, landed in the Palmer Archipelago, believing it to be part of the mainland, and took possession in the name of King William IV, calling it Graham Land, a name which was later applied to the whole territory (61).

The Dependencies were included under the jurisdiction of the Falklands Government from 1843, when the administration was first established. Beginning in the 1890s, licenses were issued by the British government to whalers and sealers in these Dependencies, including licenses to Argentine nationals and companies. Argentina never officially mentioned or claimed these territories until the twentieth century. In 1903, a man named Bruce transferred administration of a small meteorological station on Laurie Island in the South Orkneys (Islas Orcadas) to Argentina, which accepted the station on January 2, 1904.

The Argentine government regarded this as a transfer of sovereignty, and correspondingly erected a radio station there in 1925. The British protested, saying that any communications on the islands would have to be regulated by the appropriate British and Falkland laws. When Argentina applied for radio call letters directly to the International Telegraph Bureau at Berne, the British protested. Argentina replied that the actions of the Argentine government, within Argentine territory, were limited only by the provisions of the international conventions it had signed (62). Two years later, on September 14, 1927, Argentina officially asked the International Postal Union to accept that Argentine jurisdiction, "*de facto* and *de jure*, comprised the continental area, the territorial waters, the islands situated off the main coast, a portion of Tierra del Fuego, the archipelagos of Staten Island, of New Year, of South Georgia, and of the South Orkneys" (63). On January 28, 1928, the Argentine Ministry of Foreign Affairs stated that Argentine sovereignty over the Orkneys was the result of "the first actual and continued occupation of the islands" (64). Nine years later, on June 1, 1937, the Argentine ambassador to London stated that the Dependencies were under the jurisdiction of the Falkland Islands government, and that Argentina therefore reserved rights over all of them (65).

During the 1940s and '50s, both Argentina and Britain continued the war of words over both the Falklands and the Dependencies (the southern portion of which later became part of the British Antarctic Territory), as well as embarking upon a systematic policy of establishing bases throughout the dependent islands and Antarctic regions. Britain made no effort to remove the Argentine facilities, but did patrol them on various occasions with British warships and icebreakers. Argentina for its part established post offices at some of the bases, and in every way acted as if it owned the territories. On January 3, 1947 the British Government protested against issuance of stamps by Argentina for use in the Malvinas and its "Dependencies." After restating Britain's case concerning the Falklands themselves, Ambassador Cooke further indicated that the Argentine claim to the Falklands Dependencies could not be substantiated by the evidence, and that British claims to these lands were based upon initial discovery and annexation, the final act having been the Letters Patent of March 28, 1917. Argentine Foreign Minister Bramuglia replied on February 15th that Argentina did not recognize Britain's rights to the Argentine Antarctic Territory; unilateral declarations, he said, did not necessarily confer sovereignty over a region; Argentina could hardly accept British claims over the Dependencies when the Falklands themselves belonged to Argentina; the Patents of 1908 and 1917 were invalid, since they included Patagonia, recognized internationally as part of Argentine territory; Argentina in any event was the first actual settler of the Dependencies, having maintained a meteorological station on Laurie Island continuously since 1904. Argentina, he said, did not need officially to annex the area to own it (66).

In 1955 Britain attempted to place adjudication of the Dependencies issue before the International Court of Justice, but Argentina refused to accept its jurisdiction (67). Here the matter stood until March 6, 1957, when President Pedro Eugenio Aramburu of Argentina issued a decree formally incorporating into the Territory of Tierra del Fuego the Falklands, South Georgia Island, the South Sandwich Islands, and the Argentine Antarctic Territory.

II
A Simmering Brew
The Argentine Government;
A Period of Negotiations; Impasse

1. The Argentine Government

A history of the Falklands Conflict would not be complete without at least a cursory look at Argentine government, society, and history, which together have fostered a kind of super-nationalism or *machismo* common to central and South America, but particularly strong in Argentina. The myth of Argentina as a new-world earthly paradise, a country of destiny, has been so drummed into successive generations of Argentine school children that its truth is no longer questioned. But the dream soured in the middle years of the twentieth century, leaving a fragmented political and social structure sadly in need of repair. Ironically, Argentina is indeed blessed with abundant natural resources, a favorable climate, an educated society largely descended from European immigrants, and the highest per-capita income in Latin America. The romanticized image of the gaucho—independent, arrogant, self-sufficient, even belligerent—is the national paradigm of Argentina. However, it is the legacy of Spanish colonialism, with its corrupt, inefficient, artificial, self-destructive, stratified social and governmental structures, which has eaten away at the underpinnings of Argentina, poisoning the body politic to such an extent that Argentina as presently constituted may well be ungovernable. Moreover, the tendency of the Argentine people to seek scapegoats for their problems in the Jews or other minorities or nationalities, and to portray their Latin American neighbors as culturally and inherently inferior, bespeaks a national *machismo* that clouds every public and governmental act. As Jorge Luis Borges has said: "I don't think we are worthy of democracy. When we choose, we choose Peron or someone of that ilk. I want to be charitable; I do not profess to understand this country." Beginning in 1930, Argentina has seen a continuous and continuing cycle of military usurpation, civilian demagoguery, and left-wing revolution. The result of this constant political and social uproar has been the systematic

94913 LIBRARY
COLBY-SAWYER COLLEGE

fragmentation of Argentina, with politicians matched against the military, the labor unions against big business, the landed against the landless, the left against the right. Each uses the national myths against the others, seeking to win absolute domination of its own ideas or influence. In such a game no one wins. The Argentines themselves have a saying: *"No hay salida"*—"There is no way out."

The pattern was set in Argentina from the very beginning. British General William Beresford invaded the provinces on his own initiative, seizing Buenos Aires on June 27, 1806. After a series of battles, and after reinforcements were sent from London, the British expeditionary forces were defeated by a peasant militia army on July 5, 1807, and forced to withdraw. The internal chaos caused by the British incursion, combined with the unsettled situation in Spain itself (Napoleon had deposed King Fernando VII in 1808, and had placed his own brother, Joseph Bonaparte, on the Spanish throne), created an untenable situation for the Spanish Viceroy. The masses gathered in Buenos Aires on May 25, 1810 (thereafter celebrated as the greatest Argentine national holiday, Veinticinco de Mayo), demanding deposition of the Napoleonic viceroy. A junta was installed to rule in the name of the Bourbons; in 1812 junta member General Manuel Belgrano defeated the royalists at Tucuman, marking an end to Spanish rule forever. The United Provinces of the Rio de la Plata were proclaimed an independent state on July 9, 1816 (68). The next forty years provided interminable episodes of civil war, military usurpation of government, and massive internal unrest as the gauchos of the inland provinces resisted control by the educated aristocrats of Buenos Aires. President Bernardino Rivadavia, elected in 1826, was followed in 1833 by General Juan Manuel de Rosas, who established a dictatorship that lasted until 1852. A constitution proclaimed in 1853 changed the name of the country to Argentina, and reestablished a democratic form of government, although the aristocrats actually retained much of the power.

During the later years of the nineteenth century and the early part of the twentieth century, the stabilization of the government allowed phenomenal economic growth, which, combined with a large influx of immigrants from Italy (General Galtieri, for example, is descended from Italian immigrants), Spain, and other European countries, created a general sense of promise, prosperity, and even destiny. The economic hardships of the Great Depression prompted a *coup d'etat* by General Jose Uriburu in 1930, thus establishing a pattern of military intervention which has continued to this day. The British, who had invested heavily in Argentina's rail network, and who had established other close economic ties that were threatened by a potential Argentine collapse, forced upon Argentina the Roca-Runciman Treaty (ratified in 1933), which froze import duties for goods shipped from Argentina to Britain, and provided humiliating reciprocal terms for Argentina, which now had to reduce tariffs on British imports, pay its debts to Britain in pounds sterling, and give special treatment to British investors working in

Argentina itself. The treaty was greatly resented in Argentina. President Ramon Castillo was overthrown by another military coup in 1943; a third military revolt brought to power Colonel Juan Peron in 1944. Peron was elected President in February, 1946, in a campaign which featured the popular political slogan: "Englishman, give us back the Malvinas!" (69).

The ascendancy of Peron marks the beginning of modern Argentine history, a period notable primarily for its revolving-door governments, immense social and political unrest, constant military coups, and a faltering economy. Peron promulgated a new constitution in 1949 to replace that of 1853; among its features was a clause allowing him to succeed himself as President. A Peronista Party was established later the same year. Also in 1949, Chile, Britain, and Argentina reached an agreement freezing all claims in the Antarctic, and keeping all naval and military forces out of an area south of 60 degrees south latitude (an area including the South Orkneys). Peron tried to expand the industrial base of Argentina very quickly in the late 1940s; when the economy failed to grow as rapidly as projected, and when his immensely popular wife, Evita, died prematurely in 1952, Peron began to lose his support among the masses. A military coup in 1955 failed to oust the President, but undercut his political support; later that year Peron was forced into exile, and General Pedro Aramburu was named President by the new ruling junta.

Peronismo remained the strongest political force in Argentina, even without the physical presence of its titular leader. Peron's primary contribution to modern Argentine political life was an almost total polarization of the basic elements in Argentine society, which split into fragmentary groups that have never seemed able to reach a consensus on a solution to the myriad problems affecting Argentine life and economy. Further, Peron's xenophobic attitude toward the United States and Europe, and toward his Latin American neighbors, as developed in his writings and speeches, built Argentine nationalism from an already strong force in Argentine life to almost rabid levels. He used the Malvinas as a diversionary issue to maintain his own power and position, a pattern followed by later Argentine governments. This systematic breast-beating over the "lost islands," has permeated Argentine education, mass media, and public myth during recent decades, exacerbating an already tense situation, and contributing greatly to the sense of unreality which pervaded the Argentine government and public just prior to the outbreak of the war.

The constitution of 1853 was restored in 1957, leading to new presidential elections. Dr. Arturo Frondizi was elected President in 1958. When Frondizi legalized the Peronista Party, allowing it to field candidates in the 1962 congressional elections, he was overthrown by still another military junta, which named Jose Guido the new President. New presidential elections were held in 1963; the Peronistas were prohibited from fielding a candidate. A liberal, Dr. Arturo Illia, was elected. Peron attempted to return to Argentina in 1964, but was turned back at the border. Civil and economic unrest continued to mount over the next few years, resulting in the deposition of Illia in 1966 by another military junta. General Juan Carlos Ongania, a right-wing conservative, was named President (70). The legislature was dissolved, several guerrilla movements began operating in the inland provinces as well as in the cities, press censorship was instituted, and political parties were forbidden. Oppression failed to solve the country's problems, however, and the junta deposed the unpopular president in 1970, replacing him with another general, Roberto Levingston. Increased terrorist bombings led to Levingston's fall just a year later; General Alejandro Lanusse took office as President under a reform program. Peron returned to Argentina in 1972, but declined to run for president in the 1973 elections. Dr. Hector Campora, the Peronista candidate, won the contest, but promptly resigned to make way for Peron's return. Peron was formally elected President in a landslide victory in September of 1973, with his wife, Isabel, as Vice-President. Peron died of old age less than a year later, in July of 1974, Isabel succeeding as President in his place.

The administration of President Isabel Peron was a disaster for Argentina, as she staggered from one calamity to another. By the time she was deposed in 1976, in another military coup, urban terrorism had reached appalling proportions, the economy showed signs of failure, and the body politic had divided into dozens of warring political factions. The new junta named General Jorge Videla as President of Argentina, and immediately set out to destroy the terrorists by whatever means necessary, including torture, imprisonment, summary execution, massive press and personal censorship, terror, and military campaigns. The urban assassins were themselves assassinated, but the price paid by society as a whole was terrifying. Thousands of men and women were arrested or simply disappeared; many were discovered in later years buried in mass graves. Others have never been found. The numbers of *"los desaparecidos,"* as they are called in Argentina, may total 20,000 persons. Only in the last few years has there been any attempt in Argentina to force the government to account for these killings; each week the mothers and relatives of the missing march silently in front of the Presidential Palace on the Plaza de Mayo, or file missing persons reports with appropriate government agencies.

Videla served exactly five years as President, longer than any other military man in modern Argentine history. Having come into power allegedly to solve Argentina's two great problems of terrorism and economic inflation, he succeeded with the first, and tried to cope with the latter through ever-increasing financial controls. The trade unions and political parties were abolished, the legislature dissolved, and a tight clamp placed on spending. Inflationary levels, which had been running at 300 percent annually, dwindled to bearable levels. By 1981, however, inflation was rising again; Videla, as government figurehead, had to go. Videla's administration had been so repressive, however, that handing the government back over to the abolished political parties could have resulted in prosecution of members of the military regime; therefore, Videla insisted upon a guarantee of amnesty before turning power back to civilians; he also demanded a constitutional clause giving the military the unilateral right to "supervise" any future government. These terms were unacceptable to the leaders of the different political factions in Argentina, and have remained so to this day; as an interim solution, Videla resigned, and the junta named a new military president, General Roberto Viola, on March 29, 1981 (71).

Viola survived in office for only eight months; as inflation continued to rise and the economy to worsen, Viola was gradually discredited in the eyes of the Argentine people. Following several interim presidents, General Leopoldo Galtieri was named to that office on December 22, 1981. Galtieri survived the debacle in the Falklands by only a few days; on June 19, 1982, General Alfredo Saint-Jean became interim president, and on July 1st, General Reynaldo Bignone was named permanent Chief of State. Civilian elections for the presidency have been promised for fall or winter of 1983; the days of the military regime may finally be numbered. In the long term, however, the military must be considered the power behind the throne in Argentine politics; no administration, civilian or military, will be able to govern without the collective approval of the Army, Navy, and Air Force commanding officers. Moreover, the government has still not solved the problems inherent in the Argentine economy; lopping three zeros off the currency, as it did early in 1983, may make financial life more manageable for the *hoi polloi*, but it scarcely addresses the problem of a runaway inflation amounting to 150 percent annually. Until Argentina is willing to make fiscal and political compromises agreeable to all major segments of the population, to remove the military from the governing process forever, to reform its social, financial, and political charters in a way that is perceived to be fair by all, and to elect governments that address the problems of state without stooping to demagoguery or usurpation of power, there is little possibility of a solution to the Falklands crisis, or indeed, to the crisis of Argentina itself.

2. A Period of Negotiations

By the early 1960s, Britain, overburdened with the legacies of several world wars and a declining economy, had begun divesting itself of many of its colonial possessions and pretentions. The cost of defending and maintaining order in each of these overseas territories was proving impossible to justify in the light of changed world realities. One by one, the colonies were either given independence or abandoned (as was the case with Aden/South Yemen). The Falkland Islands had long since lost any military or strategic value to either Britain or Argentina; in any event, Britain had reduced the size of its navy to a few dozen small- and medium-sized ships designed to patrol in local waters only. The naval base at Port Stanley was abandoned shortly after World War II.

In September of 1964 an Argentine pilot flew his craft to Port Stanley, landing in a nearby field [the only airstrip on the islands capable of handling jets and larger craft was built in 1972; some grass and dirt strips do exist near the larger settlements outside of Port Stanley], and taking possession of the islands in the name of Argentina. The Argentine Government dissociated itself from this incident, but during the same year brought the Falklands issue before The Committee of 24, a special group set up by the United Nations to discuss the granting of independence to colonial countries and peoples. The Committee recommended that the two governments negotiate their differences. Britain initially refused, but later reconsidered, after the General Assembly voted on December 16, 1965 to support the Committee, in the form of Resolution 2065, which urged both Britain and Argentina to "proceed without delay with the negotiations recommended" (72). This time the British acquiesced, perhaps seeing the United Nations resolution as a face-saving opportunity to rid itself of yet another troublesome and expensive overseas territory.

In January, 1966, the Argentine Government formed El Instituto y Museo Nacional de las Islas Malvinas y Adyacencias, under control of the Ministry of Foreign Affairs; its charter defined its purpose as stimulating the national conscience, demanding return of the islands to Argentina, and collecting and publishing books, articles, and propaganda films on the subject. During the same month, Michael Stewart, the new British Foreign Secretary, made an official visit to Buenos Aires, where he agreed to the Argentine request to begin serious negotiations as soon as the details could be arranged (73). In February a group of Argentines formed La Junta de Recuperacion de las Malvinas, whose stated aim was "to seek a rapid solution of this long-standing dispute" (74). Initial talks between the two governments began on July 18, 1966, between Dr. Alejandro Lastra, Argentine Ambassador to Britain, and H. A. F. Hohler, Assistant Under-Secretary of the Foreign Office. Lastra immediately submitted a letter demanding return of the Falklands to Argentina, a demand rejected by Britain, which refused to consider the question of sovereignty. Instead, Hohler stated, the talks should concentrate on such issues as easing travel restrictions between the Falklands and Argentina, and promoting trade between the two territories. Undoubtedly it had already occurred to the British that promotion of such ties might be an easy method of getting the islanders accustomed to dealing with Argentina, and might, over the long term, make them more tractable on the subject of possible Argentine sovereignty. However, nothing could be agreed upon except the desirability of continuing the discussions at a later date; the talks were suspended on July 22nd.

On September 28, 1966, a group of twenty Argentine nationals belonging to El Movimiento Nueva Argentina hijacked an Argentine airliner in an incident that became known as Operacion Condor; after forcing the plane down on a racetrack near Port Stanley, the commandos stuck an Argentine flag in the ground, and read a proclamation that all the islanders were now Argentine citizens. Five islanders were seized as hostages, but later released. On the same day, five shots were fired at the British Embassy in Buenos Aires, where the Duke of Edinburgh was staying on an unofficial visit. President Ongania denounced the "invasion," while reaffirming Argentina's claims to the Falklands. Britain had ordered the frigate *Puma* to the Falklands, but accepted on September 30th a proposal that would return the airline passengers and commandos to Argentina aboard the Argentine naval transport, *Bahia Buen Suceso*. The hijackers were charged by the Argentine government with air piracy, although they were received as heroes by the Argentine people (75).

Talks between Britain and Argentina began on November 4th, upon the arrival of the new Argentine Ambassador, General Eduardo McLoughlin. Britain proposed a freeze on the sovereignty question for a period of thirty years, to allow normalization of relations between Argentina and the Falklands; at the expiration of that period, the islanders would then be free to choose Britain, Argentina, or independence. Argentina rejected the idea. Britain then stated formally that it would be prepared to relinquish sovereignty under certain specified conditions, provided the islanders' wishes were respected. When Sir Cosmo Haskard, Governor of the Falklands, reported on the progress of the talks to his Executive Council, the Unofficial (that is, the elected) Members immediately drafted a letter of protest to Parliament, warning that negotiations currently in progress could result in the cession of the islands at any moment, and adding: "the inhabitants of the islands have never been consulted regarding their future. They do not want to become Argentines. They are as British as you are, mostly of English and Scottish ancestry, even to the sixth generation. Five out of six were born in the islands. Many elderly people have never been elsewhere. There is no racial problem; no unemployment; no poverty; and we are not in debt. The people of these islands do not wish to submit to a foreign language, law, customs, and culture, because for 135 years they have happily pursued their own peaceful way of life—a very British way of life, unique in fact, when you consider that the islands are 8,000 miles from the country which they still call 'home.' Lord Caradon said to the General Assembly of the United Nations in 1965: 'The people of this territory are not to be betrayed or bartered. Their wishes and interests are paramount and we shall do our duty in protecting them.' British Ministers have said the same until 1967, since when there has been silence. Is our tiny community to be used as a pawn in power politics? . . . We need your help!" (76). A British Foreign Office spokesman replied on March 12, 1968 that the negotiations with Argentina were confidential, but repeated a statement made in December, 1967 by Governor Haskard, who said he had been reassured by the British Government that it was being "guided by a strong regard for the interests of the people of the Falkland Islands, and in any event . . . will see that there is the fullest consultation with them" (77). In the House of Lords on the following day, Lord Chalfont, the Minister of State for Foreign Affairs, was strongly prodded by other members of Parliament to state without equivocation that Britain had no intention of ceding sovereignty to the Argentines. Goronwy Roberts, Minister of State at the Foreign Office, was similarly questioned in Commons on March 18th, and said: "We shall proceed on the principle of full consultation and of consent" (78). Michael Stewart, the Foreign Secretary, stated before Commons on March 26th: "We have no doubt at all that sovereignty is now legally ours" (79). Also in March, as a result of this controversy, The Falkland Islands Emergency Committee was formed in Great Britain to make the public and government in England aware of the islanders' wishes. The Committee changed its name in 1973 to the United Kingdom Falkland Islands Committee.

A Memorandum of Understanding was reached by the two governments in August, 1968. It included a passage which stated: "The Government of the United Kingdom as a part of such a final settlement will recognize Argentina's sovereignty over the Islands from a date to be agreed. This date will be agreed as soon as possible after (i) the two governments have resolved the present divergence between them as to the criteria according to which the United Kingdom Government shall consider whether the interests of the Islanders would be secured by the safeguards and guarantees to be offered by the Argentine Government, and (ii) the Government of the United Kingdom are then satisfied that those interests are so secured" (80). Publication of this statement was to include a cover letter issued by Britain stating that no transfer would take place unless the inhabitants of the islands agreed to it.

This memorandum was followed by the official visit of Lord Chalfont to the Falklands between November 23rd-28th, 1968, to advise the islanders of the Government's negotiations and policies concerning their future. On November 23rd, he stated that Britain "very soon [hoped] to come to an amicable and agreed position with Argentina, [but] there will be no sovereignty change against your wishes" (81). On November 24th, he met with Governor, Sir Cosmo Haskard, and with the Executive Council. The following day, he met with the unofficial members of the legislative Council. During the latter meeting, one islander stated that the British had originally promised the Kelpers that no pressure would be exerted on them to accept Argentine rule, but that in fact such pressure had been applied during the preceding three years. In his reply, Chalfont pointed out that failure to reach agreement could result in life for the islanders becoming "less pleasant and even less safe" "If you wish to stay under British sovereignty," he said, "you must remember that the British Government has this responsibility for you. . . .Great Britain is not the great imperialist power of the nineteenth century . . . . When you say 'Keep the Falklands British' make absolutely certain that you know in your own minds what this means. It means something different to what it meant in 1900'' (82).

Chalfont was closely questioned in Parliament upon his return on December 3rd. Subsequently, the British Government decided at a cabinet meeting on December 11th that attempts to reach an agreement between Britain and Argentina on the basis of the Memorandum of Understanding would be dropped, due both to public and governmental outcries, and to Argentina's stated objections to the British position that sovereignty would not be transferred if the islanders disapproved. That same day, Michael Stewart stated in the Commons: "There is a basic divergence [between Britain and Argentina] over H.M. Government's insistence that no transfer of sovereignty could be made against the wishes of the Falkland Islanders . . . . H.M. Government could only consider the solution of this dispute by a cession of sovereignty to Argentina, first, as part of an arrangement which would secure a permanently satisfactory relationship between the Islands and Argentina, and second, if the Islanders themselves regarded such an arrangement as satisfactory to their interest and it accorded with their wishes. It is on this basis that H.M. Government propose to continue to negotiate with the Argentine Government in order to overcome the obstacles which now exist to a normal relationship between the Islands and the mainland . . . ." (83).

On December 12th, Sir Alec Douglas-Home, Leader of the Opposition, forced a vote on the issue, to demonstrate clearly that, "should the Conservatives inherit a continuing negotiation, they would exclude from the talks the subject of sovereignty." The Government prevailed by a vote of 293-234. Dr. Nicanor Costa Mendez, responding for Argentina to the public discussion of these issues, stated on the same day that Argentina could not "accept in any way" Britain's insistence on "subordinating recognition of Argentine sovereignty to the desires of the inhabitants" (84). However, since Britain was now willing to discuss the issue after 150 years of silence, that "itself was motive enough to continue the negotiations and to believe that they will reach their logical conclusion, the recognition of Argentine sovereignty over the Malvinas Islands. This Britain has not conclusively rejected" (85).

To provide an impetus for both the islanders and British to reach an accomodation, Argentina relaxed its policy of harassment, and instead began making serious attempts for the first time to open new lines of communication between the Falklands and the mainland. The talks between the two governments continued, even after Edward Heath's election as Conservative Prime Minister in June of 1970; all discussions were held without prejudice to the sovereignty question. On July 1, 1971 agreement was reached on sixteen points: 1) a special consultative committee, comprising representatives of the Argentine Foreign Mission and the British Embassy in Buenos Aires, would be set up to deal with questions arising from the establishment of communications between the Islands and the mainland; 2) Argentina would issue white cards to residents of the Falklands for easy travel to and from Argentina;

3) residents of the Falklands visiting Argentina would be exempt from military service and payment of taxes there; 4) luggage travelling between the two territories would be exempt from duties; 5) any Falklander moving permanently to the mainland would be allowed, for one time only, to bring his personal belongings (including car) into Argentina duty-free; 6) both Governments would facilitate transit, residence, and work of persons present in the Falklands or Argentina for the specific purpose of improving communications; 7) the British would arrange a regular shipping service between the islands and the mainland; Argentina would do the same for air travel; 8) Argentina would provide temporary air service to Port Stanley by amphibious plane until an airport could be constructed; 9) both Governments would simplify travel procedures between the two territories; 10) persons born in the Falklands would be exempt from military service in Argentina; 11) both Governments would study means of improving communications between the Falklands and Argentina; 12) postal, telephone, and telegraph connections between the two would be expedited; fees would be based upon prevailing charges at point of origin; 13) postage stamps issued at point of origin would be accepted on mail in either direction; 14) Argentina would provide technical, health, educational, and agricultural assistance to the islands, and provide educational facilities on the mainland for the islanders, with some scholarships; 15) conversations between the governments would continue through normal diplomatic channels; and 16) the agreement could be terminated with six months' notice by either government (86).

The Exchange of Notes added: "Since divergence remained between the two Governments regarding the circumstances which should exist for a definite solution to the dispute concerning sovereignty over the Falklands, nothing contained in the Joint Statement and approved by both Governments on August 5th should be interpreted as: (a) a renunciation by either Government of any right of territorial sovereignty over the islands, or (b) a recognition of or support for the other Government's position with regard to such sovereignty. Furthermore, no acts or activities taking place as a consequence of the implementation of the Joint Statement and during its operation should consitute a basis for asserting, supporting or denying the position of either Government with regard to territorial sovereignty over the Falklands" (87). Under a separate agreement ratified in May, 1972, Argentina began building a temporary airport at Port Stanley; it was opened in November of that year. As it happened, however, this was the last major breakthrough in working toward a negotiated settlement of the Falklands issue; thereafter, relations between Britain and Argentina began a long, slow decline.

3. Impasse

1973 proved to be a turning point in British-Argentine negotiations over the Falklands. Talks held in April and May of that year broke down when Argentina reiterated its demands for substantive discussions on the sovereignty question. Juan Peron took office as President of Argentina on October 12th. Less than a month later, on November 5, 1973, Argentina sent a note to United Nations Secretary-General Kurt Waldheim demanding an end to British colonialism in the Falklands, accusing Britain of paralyzing the negotiations, and adding that the United Nation's policy of respecting self-determination would have been better served if applied retroactively to the Argentine colonists evicted by the British in 1833. In response to Argentina's note, the General Assembly passed another resolution (#3160) in December, urging both parties to "arrive at a peaceful solution of the conflict of sovereignty between them," and "to put an end to the colonial situation" (88). Upon election of Harold Wilson as Prime Minister in March of 1974, the new Labour Government broached to Argentina the idea of a condominium (joint administration), with self-rule for the islanders. However, the Falklanders refused to participate, and the idea was dropped in August, 1974. James Callaghan, Labour Foreign Secretary, met his Argentine counterpart in New York in September, concluding two minor agreements for the Falklands on trade and oil. Opposition members in the Argentine Congress called on their government to cut off all trade and communication links with the Falklands on November 5, 1974; the Argentine press then mounted a campaign bolstering the idea of an armed invasion of the islands. One of the newspapers was shut down by the government. Argentina's Foreign Minister, Alberto Vignes, stated on December 20th that there would be no invasion while a negotiated solution remained viable (89). In January, 1975 Argentina unilaterally required all air travellers going from the Falklands to the mainland to obtain clearance first from the Argentine Foreign Ministry, a direct violation of the agreement of 1971. Britain protested vigorously.

Minister Vignes was warned by the British Ambassador to Argentina in April of 1975 that any invasion of the Falklands by Argentine forces would be met with a military response. It should be noted here that Britain throughout this period only maintained a small force of Marines at Port Stanley, numbering at any one time no more than 20-30 soldiers, under the titular command of the Falklands Governor (who also bore the title Commander-in-Chief of the Falklands). British intelligence assessments during these years rated the possibility of an invasion from Argentina as minimal (90). Britain proposed in July of 1975 that discussions be held for joint Argentine-British development of the South Atlantic. Vignes countered with a suggestion that sovereignty over the Falklands could be ceded to Argentina with a simultaneous leaseback arrangement, similar to that in effect in British-controlled Hong Kong, with total cession taking place at some future time. He also suggested that Britain cede immediately to Argentina (or that Argentina unilaterally occupy without opposition) the islands of South Georgia and South Sandwich. Further talks on economic or communications issues were rejected by Vignes. Britain again warned that unilateral military action on Argentina's part would be met with force (91).

Concerned over the gradual decline in the islands' population and economy, Britain announced in October that Lord Shackleton would be sent to the Falklands to conduct an economic and fiscal survey, at the request of the Islands' Executive Council. Argentina immediately warned that Shackleton's mission would be a violation of the agreement of 1964, in which both sides had agreed "to abstain from unilateral innovations in fundamental aspects of the question" (92). The Argentine Ambassador to London was recalled on October 28, 1975. On December 8th the Argentine representative to the United Nations stated in a speech to that body: "We are prepared to continue our efforts, but the limits of our patience and tolerance should not be underestimated if we should have to face an obstinate and unjustified refusal to negotiate by the other party" (93). Shackleton arrived in Port Stanley on January 4, 1976. On January 13th Argentina advised Britain to recall its ambassador to Buenos Aires. Coincidentally, an Argentine work force arrived at Port Stanley on January 16th to begin extension of the temporary landing strip there, under terms of a previous agreement; the work was carried on without incident, and completed in June. On February 4th the Argentine destroyer *Almirante Storni* fired on the British research ship *Shackleton* at a point seventy-eight miles south of Port Stanley, several months after the British naval *attache* in Buenos Aires had been warned that that vessel would be intercepted if it entered Argentine waters. The Argentines later claimed the British ship was searching for oil.

A military assessment made for the Prime Minister at this time (February, 1976) pointed out that reinforcement of the Falklands by air was impossible, due to the primitive condition of the main airport at Port Stanley, the unpredictable weather conditions, the distance to Port Stanley from Ascension Island (the nearest British base), and the unlikelihood that any South American airfields would be available in a military emergency for British planes. The Chief of Staffs concluded that a determined Argentine attempt to evict the British would probably succeed, and that only a major amphibious force of Brigade Group strength, utilizing all of the Navy's amphibious resources, could retake the islands (94). Callaghan therefore ordered a major review of the Government's Falkland Islands policy in March of 1976, and decided to seek new negotiations with Argentina, including discussion of the sovereignty question. Initial talks were held in secret in July and August. Meanwhile, Lord Shackleton's report was published on July 20th. In it he stated that the Falklands' resources and population were gradually declining, and that, "in any major new developments of the islands' economy, especially those relating to the exploitation of offshore resources, co-operation with Argentina—even participation—should, if possible, be secured" (95). The United Nations General Assembly on December 1, 1976, approved a new resolution (#31/49) expressing "its gratitude for the continuous efforts made by the Government of Argentina . . . to facilitate the process of decolonization and to promote the well-being of the population of the islands" (96). It again urged both parties to "expedite the negotiations concerning the dispute over sovereignty."

On December 20th, a helicopter from the H.M.S. *Endurance* discovered an unauthorized Argentine military station on the island of Southern Thule in the South Sandwich Islands. The British protested what they regarded as a violation of their sovereign rights in these islands, but Argentina maintained its base until the outbreak of the war in 1982.

Two months later, on February 2, 1977, Anthony Crosland, British Foreign and Commonwealth Secretary, announced in Parliament that Edward Rowlands, Minister of State at the Foreign and Commonwealth Office, would visit the Falklands a few weeks later to "hear from the islanders at first hand how they view their future," and would then stop at Buenos Aires. "Any such discussion," he said, "which would inevitably raise fundamental questions of the relationship between the islands, Britain, and Argentina, would take place under the sovereignty umbrella—that is, Her Majesty's Government would wholly reserve their position on the issue of sovereignty, which would in no way be prejudiced." Further, "any changes which might be proposed must be acceptable to the islanders . . . nothing will be done behind their backs" (97). Rowlands reached the Falklands on February 17th, and arrived in Buenos Aires on the 21st. The Governments later announced that negotiations on the islands' future would take place in mid-1977. While the February talks were in progress, a British task force consisting of ten ships was sent to the mid-Atlantic, ready to be used in the Falklands if the Argentines threatened military force during the discussions.

In March of 1977 press reports indicated that several Argentine businessmen had made attempts to purchase the Falkland Islands Company Ltd. The offer was refused, since Falklands law prevents the sale of land to non-citizens without a license from the Governor and the approval of his Executive Council. A new round of talks between Britain and Argentina took place in Rome between July 13-15, 1977, in which the British sought a solution based upon a leaseback arrangement, after a period of time during which the islanders could become accustomed to the idea. Britain proposed for the first time separating the issue of sovereignty over the Falklands from that of its Dependencies. The latter were apparently considered expendable. A second series of discussions took place between December 13-15th, in New York City, amid reports that Argentina had seized seven Soviet and two Bulgarian ships fishing in Falkland waters during September and October (98). While the talks were talking place, a British submarine and two frigates were secretly deployed around the Falklands. At New York, agreements were reached setting up two working groups which would prepare reports on the sovereignty question and on economic cooperation. The committees met for the first time in February, 1978. On May 10th the Argentine Foreign Ministry declared that Southern Thule Island was an integral part of Argentine territory. A ministerial level meeting between Britain and Argentina was held between December 15-17th, 1978, in Lima, Peru, resulting in the drafting of an agreement on scientific activities in the Falklands Dependencies; this was rejected by the Falkland Islands Council, and Britain was thus forced to return it unsigned at the next meeting, in March of 1979 (99). Two months later James Callaghan, Labour Prime Minister, lost the British General elections. His replacement was Margaret Thatcher, the so-called "Iron Lady."

III
The Pot Boils Over
Ominous Mutterings;
The Argentine Invasion
War!

1. Ominous Mutterings

The Conservative government of Margaret Thatcher took office in May of 1979. The Foreign and Commonwealth Office presented the new Minister of State, Nicholas Ridley, with a series of options relating to the Falklands question: 1) break off negotiations immediately and be prepared to defend the islands; 2) give up the islands, offering to resettle the islanders without charge in New Zealand or elsewhere; 3) pretend to negotiate, postponing any effective action as long as possible; or 4) negotiate in good faith with Argentina to find a solution palatable to islanders, Parliament, and Argentina. Lord Carrington, the new Foreign and Commonwealth Secretary, suggested that Ridley visit the Falklands and Argentina before making a decision. Subsequently, Ridley met with Argentina's Deputy Foreign Minister, Comodoro Carlos Cavandoli, on June 12th, who told Ridley that his government would require the issue of sovereignty to be part of any negotiations (100). Ridley then visited the Falklands in July, where he discussed with the Kelpers the advantages of cooperation with the Argentines, but also stated that no cession would be made without the Falklanders' approval. The Legislative Councillors indicated a clear preference for a freeze in negotiations, and expressed a decided coolness toward the idea of leaseback condominium.

Ridley returned to Argentina, where the two governments agreed to restore normal ambassadorial relations. Just before his departure, however, he was given an *aide memoire* expressing Argentina's dissatisfaction with the results of the March, 1979 meeting, and indicating that, in Argentina's view, negotiations should proceed "at a more dynamic pace." Further, the letter continued, while the interests of the Falklanders surely must be taken into account, they must not become third parties to an agreement. Ridley responded by reiterating Britain's position that no settlement was possible without the islanders' approval (101).

Lord Carrington presented a list of options on the Falklands' question to the Prime Minister and members of the Defence Committee on September 20, 1979, basically restating the proposals given to Ridley in June. Carrington himself recommended that Britain proceed with substantive negotiations on sovereignty, suggesting the leaseback option as a possible solution. Such negotiations, he said, would make a military solution by the Argentines less likely in the foreseeable future. Before negotiations could proceed, he would require support from both Parliament and the Falklanders. The following week Carrington met with General Carlos Pastor, Argentine Foreign Minister, in New York. Pastor proposed a series of weekly contacts between the Argentine and British ambassadors, followed by regular meetings between junior and senior ministers, with an established advance agenda. Carrington could only give a nebulous reply, since he had not yet received instructions from his Government (102). Carrington pressed for a definition of policy upon his return to London on October 12th, pointing out in his memorandum the dangers of ending negotiations with Argentina, including the threat of invasion. If the Argentines concluded, he said, that there was no real prospect of a negotiated transfer of sovereignty, Britain ran a high risk of direct military attack on the islands. Argentina, he added, clearly had the capability to capture the Falklands (103). Mrs. Thatcher decided, however, to postpone action on the Falklands question until the Rhodesian crisis had been settled; subsequently, Ridley was forced to decline an invitation from Argentina to further exchange views. Carrington's assessment of the situation was seconded by the Joint Intelligence Committee in its report of November, 1979. Argentina, it concluded, was determined to regain the islands, by force, if necessary, but preferably through peaceful means.

On December 5, 1979, General Leopoldo Galtieri was appointed Commander-in-Chief of the Argentine Army and member of the ruling junta, replacing General Roberto Viola in both positions. The appointments were effective January 1, 1980. Galtieri, age fifty-three, was described by many commentators as a political moderate who had consistently supported a return to democratic rule in Argentina. Simultaneously with his appointment, three hard-line generals were retired: Carlos Suarez Mason, the Army Chief of Staff; Diego Urricarriet; and Santiago Omar Riveros. On December 19th, the junta published a series of proposals entitled "Political Bases of the Armed Forces for the Process of National Reorganization," a guide for discussions with political and social leaders on an eventual return to civilian rule (104). "Subversive" and "corrupt" citizens would be excluded from the political process, however, as would communists. These proposals envisioned a semi-democratic state based on Christian principles, stressing family virtues, private property, and a political system with an elected president and two elected chambers of a legislature. Concerning the military, the document stated: "The armed forces, in an institutionalized intervention in the Government, will have a role in making decisions on the conduct of national strategy, national security, and defense of the Constitution" (105). Peronists were specifically excluded from the list of acceptable political parties.

Carrington again advised his government on January 24, 1980 to sanction exploratory talks with the Argentines. The Defence Committee decided on January 29th that negotiations could go forward, but not under guidelines established by the Labour Government; instead, Carrington was instructed to secure the approval of the Falkland Islands Legislative Council before proceeding. This he did. The new round of discussions between Britain and Argentina took place between April 28-30, 1980, New York City. For the first time a Falklands Councillor took part in the proceedings. Argentina restated its position on sovereignty, but agreed to hold further talks on development of resources in the Southwest Atlantic. The Defence Committee agreed in July to seek a solution to the Falklands issue based on a leaseback arrangement, and instructed Ridley to visit the Falklands in November to gauge the islanders' reactions to the idea. The response of the Falklanders was mixed, a vocal minority denouncing any potential change in their status, a majority apparently undecided (106). When Ridley reported on his trip to Parliament on December 2nd, he was received with outright hostility.

The Falkland Islands Joint Councils issued a statement on January 6, 1981 which said: "While this House does not like any of the ideas put forward by Mr. Ridley for a possible settlement of the sovereignty dispute with Argentina, it agrees that Her Majesty's Government should hold further talks with the Argentines at which this House should be represented and at which the British delegation should seek an agreement to freeze the dispute for a specified period of time" (107). The Defence Committee decided on January 29th, at the recommendation of Carrington, to seek further talks with the Argentines, with a long-term aim of reaching a leaseback agreement while trying to educate the islanders in the interim. At these new discussions, held in New York in February, Ridley proposed a freeze on the sovereignty question, an idea which was rejected outright by the Argentines. Carrington reported to the Prime Minister and Defence Committee on March 13th, saying that the talks had perhaps enlightened the two island Councillors who had attended them. He saw, however, little point in continuing negotiations until the Falklanders demonstrated more flexibility. He also stated that, should the islanders insist upon maintenance of the status quo, Britain would need to make preparations for defense of the Falklands.

General Roberto Viola took office as President of Argentina on March 29, 1981, and was forced to devalue the Argentine peso by 23 percent three days later, following a 10 percent devaluation that had taken place just six weeks earlier. The Argentine economy was showing serious signs of unravelling at the edges. In May the British Ambassador to Argentina urged his government to resume negotiations at the first opportunity, including discussion of the sovereignty issue, to avoid deterioration in British-Argentine relations. An Assistant Under-Secretary of State was sent to the Falklands to urge the Councils to reach a decision. On May 29th, General Galtieri stated: " . . . Neither are we prepared to allow those who are discussing with us the return of the island territories that are Argentine by historical inheritance and legal right to interfere in the slightest way with the search for and exploitation of the wealth of our continental shelf. Nobody can or will be able to say that we have not been extremely calm and patient in our handling of international problems, which in no way stem from any appetite for territory on our part. However, after a century and a half they are becoming more and more unbearable" (108).

Ridley chaired a meeting at the British Foreign and Commonwealth Office on June 30, 1981 to review Britain's Falklands policy. J. B. Ure, Superintending Assistant Under-Secretary of State of the South America Department, prepared a paper based upon his visits to Argentina and the Falklands the previous month. The Argentine Foreign Affairs personnel, he said, were "reasonably relaxed about progress—or lack of progress—on the Falklands negotiations and well disposed towards the leaseback idea," but the military leaders were "less patient and might require a more 'forward' policy at any time" (109). Opinion in the islands had not hardened irrevocably against leaseback, he said, but more needed to be done to educate both the Falklanders and the British public about the options facing them, and the danger of inaction. The British Ambassador to Argentina also contributed his views: ground had been lost since February, he stated, in both Argentina and in the Falklands; the British public should be shown the potential costs of the alternatives to serious negotiations. He also warned of the risk of Argentina using Britain as a scapegoat for its domestic problems before the end of the year. The Falklands Governor stated that the islanders wanted nothing to do with the Argentines, and did not believe that any terms governing a leaseback arrangement could provide them with sufficient guarantees for preservation of their way of life. The Defence Council decided to seek a delay in further negotiations while mounting a public education campaign; the new Falklands Councillors, when elected, should be persuaded to allow the talks to continue; contigency plans, both civilian and military, should be prepared (110).

Ridley reported to Lord Carrington on July 20th, pointing out what he regarded as a gradually deteriorating stalemate on the Falklands question. The new Councillors, he said, would undoubtedly be more hostile to substantive sovereignty talks than had the previous Falklands government. If Argentina concluded, he continued, that Britain was unwilling or unable to negotiate seriously, retaliatory actions should be expected, perhaps as early as 1982. Three options were available: to negotiate without the islanders' participation; to mount a public education campaign in the Falklands and in Britain; to break off negotiations, and prepare contingency plans. He recommended the second course.

A general strike took place in Argentina on July 22nd, the first since the last military coup. President Viola resumed talks with leaders of the banned political parties over the possibility of resuming democratic government. Behind the scenes, however, the hardline position of the junta was strengthened when Admiral Jorge Isaac Anaya, an ardent nationalist, was appointed on September 11th Commander-in-Chief of the Argentine Navy, and a member of the junta. On July 27th, the Argentine Foreign Minister, Dr. Oscar H. Camilion, handed the British Ambassador a formal note expressing Argentina's dismay at the lack of progress since the last round of talks in February. It was not possible, he said, "to postpone further a profound and serious discussion of the complex essential constituents of the negotiations—sovereignty and economic co-operation—in a simultaneous and global fashion with the express intention of achieving concrete results shortly. A resolute impetus must therefore be given to the negotiations. The next round of negotiations cannot be another mere exploratory exercise, but must mark the beginning of a decisive stage towards the definitive termination of the dispute" (111).

At a meeting on September 7, 1981 Lord Carrington discussed the Falklands problem with the Lord Privy Seal (Sir Ian Gilmour), Ridley, and other Foreign and Commonwealth Office officials; a draft paper was prepared indicating the necessity of finding a solution soon, and suggesting again that an educational campaign be mounted, both in Britain and in the islands. Later in the month, however, on September 23rd, Carrington reversed himself, as explained in a letter from one of his subordinates to the British Ambassador in Argentina: "Domestic political constraints must at this stage continue to prevent us from taking any steps which might be interpreted either as putting pressure on the Islanders or as overruling their wishes" (112). Carrington also mentioned in a letter sent to the Prime Minister on September 14th that he still regarded the leaseback option as the most viable solution, but increasingly despaired of getting the Falklanders to approve this or any other arrangement. Without their acquiescence, he said, continued negotiations with Argentina would be difficult or impossible. He further suggested the possibility of asking Argentina to provide a list of alternative solutions to the problem.

Dr. Camilion, Argentina's Foreign Minister, addressed the United Nations on September 22nd, again pointing to Britain's "present illegal occupation" of the Malvinas, and expressing his hope that he "would be able to report in due course to the General Assembly that this series of negotiations concerning the Malvinas, South Georgia, and South Sandwich Islands, which we hope will begin soon, was the last one" (113). Carrington met with the Argentine minister the following day, stating that Britain would never coerce the islanders into accepting Argentine sovereignty, and suggesting that Argentina come forward with new proposals. Camilion replied that Argentina was only interested in sovereignty, which was strictly a matter of negotiation between Britain and Argentina—the Falklanders could not be allowed to veto negotiations, or to dictate terms. Following the meeting, the Argentine press quoted the Ambassador as having been satisfied with the progress of the discussions: "Lord Carrington advanced to the point of saying that the present status quo is difficult to sustain today" (114).

Meanwhile, the British envoy in Buenos Aires replied to the letter previously sent to him, criticizing the lack of policy on the part of his superiors, and stating that it was unlikely in his view that the islanders would ever agree to any transfer of sovereignty. The longer the delay, he said, the sooner the Argentines would conclude that negotiations were a waste of time. If the British Government had decided to abandon negotiations, they should say as much directly to Argentina, and prepare for the consequences, which might involve military action (115). Camilion met with the British ambassador on October 14th, assuring the envoy that Argentina recognized the complexity of the issue, and was prepared for lengthy negotiations, provided that the ultimate goal was transfer of sovereignty. On the same day, the results of the Falkland Islands Legislative Council elections were announced, giving an increased majority to opponents of negotiations with Argentina. The new Council promptly issued a statement saying it would agree to new talks only if they did not include the issue of sovereignty on the agenda. A new round of negotiations with Argentina was proposed for December 17-18th in Geneva, Switzerland; these were later postponed until January, 1982, and again to February, due to civil unrest in Argentina and various scheduling conflicts.

Meanwhile, the Ministry of Defence had been asked by the Foreign and Commonwealth Office in May of 1981 to assess the military situation on the islands, and finally reported their findings to the Chiefs of Staff on September 14, 1981. Few options were noted. The Falklands' defense force consisted of forty-two lightly-armed Royal Marines under the overall command of the Islands' Governor, Sir Rex Hunt; and the H.M.S. *Endurance*, an armed icebreaker operating during the summer months in the British Antarctic Territories, a vessel which had been scheduled for permanent withdrawal from the region in March of 1982. The short length of the runway at Port Stanley, the lack of other airstrip facilities, the foul and unpredictable weather of the islands, precluded reinforcement of the marines quickly or in sufficient numbers to make any practical difference to a developing military confrontation. Essentially, the Falklands were defenseless, and likely to remain so in the foreseeable future. Any British military response must necessarily be a naval one, requiring a minimum of twenty days' transit time for surface ships, plus whatever additional time might be required to assemble support ships, troops, supplies, reinforcements, etc. (116). The cost of extending the airfield at Port Stanley to accomodate large military craft would exceed sixteen million pounds for a surface length of 12,000 feet. Military options available to Argentina included harassment of British shipping, occupation of the Dependencies, hit-and-run raids on the islands, and/or occupation and invasion of the Falklands. A force sufficient to prevent a full invasion would require at the minimum an aircraft carrier, four destroyers, a submarine, supply ships, and marines or other manpower to reinforce the land garrison. Such a force would be expensive to maintain, would siphon away ships needed for other purposes, and might precipitate the very action it had been sent to deter. Faced with an Argentine occupation, there would be no certainty of retaking the islands. A British counter-invasion would require large naval and land forces with corresponding air support; the supply problems would be enormous (117).

On November 9, 1981 President Viola of Argentina suffered a moderate heart attack, and was hospitalized in stable condition. His absence precipitated a power struggle in the junta. An interim President, General Horacio Tomas Liendo, took office on November 21st. Regarded as a moderate supporter of Viola's polcies, Liendo resigned when the junta confronted Viola on December 11th, forcing his permanent resignation as President, ostensibly on grounds of ill health (118). The hardliners had won the day. Vice Admiral Carlos Alberto Lacoste assumed office as new interim President. Meanwhile, Brigadier General Basilio Arturo Lami Dozo was named Commander-in-Chief of the Argentine Air Force on December 17th, thereby strengthening General Galtieri's position. Galtieri was named President of Argentina on December 22nd. Included in the new cabinet were Dr. Nicanor Costa Mendez, a strongly anti-communist supporter of the United States, as Foreign Minister; and Dr. Roberto Alemann, a free-market advocate, as Minister of Finance. Alemann immediately allowed the peso to "float" (i.e., be devalued), and cut salaries for all public employees, including those of the armed services. Galtieri made an initial effort on assuming office to be more publicly visible than his predecessor; he released a statement outlining his net personal financial worth, assumed civilian clothes (although he retained his military position), attempted to mingle with common citizens, sponsoring barbecues and other social activities, generally catered to what he perceived to be public needs and desires (119).

In the final months of 1981 a continuing debated raged in Parliament over the projected withdrawal of the *Endurance* from the South Atlantic. The House of Lords discussed the issue formally on December 16th. Several Argentine newspapers reprinted a story originally published by the *Daily Telegraph* that asserted Britain was "abandoning the protection of the Falkland Islands" (120). A British intelligence report in September, 1981 suggested that Argentina viewed the withdrawal of the *Endurance* as a deliberate political gesture, rather than a result of economic cutbacks (the real reason for its termination). Carrington attempted to persuade the Secretary of State for Defence to reinstate the *Endurance*; in a letter dated January 22, 1982, he stated that withdrawal of that vessel was being construed both by Argentina and by the Falklanders as part of a deliberate British policy of reducing support for the islands. Prime Minister Thatcher supported the Defence Office decision, which was reaffirmed on February 3rd. Carrington again expressed his concern on February 17th.

The British Ambassador in Buenos Aires submitted his annual report to the Foreign Office on January 1, 1982. In it he noted that the cabinet chosen by Galtieri was a vast improvement over the ministers in the previous government. He also indicated that, while a confrontation had been avoided in 1981, "the Argentines and the Islanders (are) more on each other's nerves than a year ago" (121). The Foreign Office reply, dated January 28th, said that Britain would be fortunate to avoid a confrontation during the coming year, unless attitudes changed on the Falklands. Governor Hunt submitted his annual report on January 19th, noting that relations with both Britain and Argentina had deteriorated during 1981, and that island opinion had hardened against the lease-back proposal. Further, the Falklanders' suspicions concerning British government intentions had been deepened by passage in London of the British Nationality Bill, which excluded the islanders from British citizenship. The elected members of the Legislative Council were unanimously opposed to leaseback. Hunt saw no way out of the impasse, but did not expect overt Argentine military action. A formal reply to the Governor was made by J. B. Ure on March 4, 1982: "We are now perilously near the inevitable move from dialogue to confrontation" (122). Ure also pointed out that the options open to Argentina were far greater than withdrawal of services, and that Britain would have difficulties finding the money or the resources to defend the islands adequately. Thus, the islanders should be under no illusions as to the consequences of a breakdown in negotiations.

Argentina delivered an official paper to the British Ambassador in Buenos Aires on January 27th, 1982, again restating the Argentine case for sovereignty. British recognition of Argentine sovereignty over the Falklands and its Dependencies (South Georgia and the South Sandwiches) remained a necessary precondition to any final settlement of the question—Argentina would never relax or abandon its claims. It called for serious negotiations "within a reasonable period of time and without procrastination" that would result in British recognition of Argentine sovereignty. Argentina would respect the interests of the islanders, but could not include them as a party to any settlement. As a mechanism to resolve the impasse, Argentina suggested formation of a permanent commission, comprised of representatives of both governments, to meet in the first week of each month alternatively in each capital, to work for one year or less on resolving all of the outstanding issues; either government could withdraw from the commission at any time without warning. The British response, delivered February 8th, restated its position that Britain had sovereign rights over the Falklands, its Dependencies, and the surrounding continental shelves and maritime regions; that it could not accept the Argentine position, but was willing to negotiate further, to find "an early and peaceful solution to this dispute which can be accepted by all concerned, namely the British and Argentine Governments and the people of the Falkland Islands" (123). A private message from the British Ambassador to his government dated February 3rd stated that "Admiral Anaya, probably with President Galtieri's full agreement, had got into the driving seat in regard to the Malvinas negotiations and had ruled, in effect, that a test period should be allowed to see if negotiations got anywhere" (124). He further speculated that this test period might run until January, 1983, the 150th anniversary of Britain's occupation of the Falklands.

During this period the partially-controlled press in Argentina was filled with speculative or even sensational articles on the Malvinas problem. A January 24th story in *La Prensa* predicted that Argentina would set conditions for continuation of the talks; if these were not accepted, the newspaper indicated, negotiations would immediately cease. The article also indicated that Argentina would undoubtedly receive United States support for any action taken to recover the islands. "A military attempt to resolve the dispute cannot be ruled out when sovereignty is at stake" (125). A follow-up article dated February 7th stated that, failing serious negotiations with Britain on the islands' future, Argentina reserved "the right to take other action, which might by no means exclude the recovery of the islands by military action" (126). A third article, published on February 9th in the English-language newspaper, *Buenos Aires Herald*, indicated that the new government in Argentina would accept any risks to recover the islands, but thought an invasion would be "utterly unnecessary" (127). A fourth article, published on February 18th, justified military intervention in the Malvinas on three grounds: Argentina's isolation from the western world's strategic and military planning operations; failure of negotiations to settle the border dispute with Chile over the Beagle Channel islands, which had included Papal mediation; and Soviet designs on the South Atlantic area, and expansion of the Soviet fleet into the waters near Argentina.

A new round of discussions between Argentina and Britain were scheduled for late February. In advance of the talks, Lord Carrington, Britain's Foreign Minister, wrote the Prime Minister and other members of the Defence Committee, suggesting that Argentina's proposal for establishment of working discussion groups to settle the crisis, while attractive, was based upon an unrealistic time frame; any agreement reached would necessarily require ratification by the Falklanders through an islands-wide referendum. The tough attitude of the new Argentine government, he said, combined with the intransigence of the islanders, made any such agreement exceedingly difficult to attain. Lord Buxton, Chairman of Anglia Television, met privately with Dr. Costa Mendez in Buenos Aires on February 23rd, and later reported to the British Ambassador that Costa Mendez had emphasized the issue of sovereignty, and had stated that some alternative would need to be found to the leaseback proposal; he discounted the idea of invasion. Buxton stated that he was under the impression that Costa Mendez was being pressured by the Argentine junta (128). The talks themselves were held at New York on February 26-27th, 1982. The British delegation was led by Richard Luce, Minister of State at the Foreign Office; also participating were two members of the Falklands Legislative Council. The Argentine delegation was headed by Dr. Enrique Ros, Undersecretary for Foreign Affairs.

Britain opened the meeting with presentation of a working paper outlining its position on Argentina's proposal for a permanent negotiating commission to solve the Falklands question. Any such body, it said, could be presided over by ministers from both governments. The British delegation would include representatives of the Falklands government. The commission would examine all aspects of the question during its one-year life, and recommend an overall settlement. Either party could terminate discussions at will. Meetings would be held alternatively in both capitals. Argentina agreed to the proposals, and the talks were adjourned cordially, with issuance of a joint *communique* (129). Upon return to Buenos Aires, the Argentine negotiators issued a press release, stating: "Argentina has negotiated with Great Britain over the solution of the sovereignty dispute over the Islands with patience, loyalty, and good faith for over fifteen years, within the framework indicated by the relevant United Nations resolutions. The new system consitutes an effective step for the early solution of the dispute. However, should this not occur, Argentina reserves to terminate the working of this mechanism and to choose freely the procedure which best accords with her interests" (130).

According to Calvert, citing an April 15, 1982 issue of *The Times*, which in turn quoted from "classified official reports," General Galtieri had already decided before this meeting to prepare "for the effective occupation of the islands east of Cape Horn," and "to define by force the situation pending with Great Britain," in the event the negotiations produced no immediate results (131). This allegation is unverifiable. The Argentine press, in commenting on the February negotiating session, quoted Government sources as saying that parallel plans had been formulated in case the proposed commission failed to produce immediate progress toward a solution. In another article, *La Prensa* speculated that such action might include withdrawal of air and other services. Britain would have no more than three or four months to demonstrate its good faith. After that, the story continued, much more drastic action, including a possible invasion, might be taken by the end of the year (1982). A military invasion, *La Prensa* claimed, would be "understood" by the United States, to whom Argentina would offer joint military facilities (132).

Luce wrote Ros on March 3rd, expressing his concern at Argentina's official *communique* of March 1st, which contravened the understanding reached in New York that all proposals made at that meeting would remain confidential. He regarded the implied threats contained therein as "disturbing." Ros, in a meeting with the British Ambassador to Argentina on March 4th, assured him that it was an unfortunate incident—the Ministry of Foreign Affairs, he stated, accepted no responsibility for attributions made to it by the Argentine press (133). Costa Mendez, in a meeting with the Ambassador the following day, expressed his dissatisfaction at the progress of the discussions, but denied any intention on his part to threaten the British government. He emphasized the need for monthly meetings between the interested parties.

Luce met with Thomas Enders, United States Assistant Secretary of State for Latin American Affairs, in Washington following the New York negotiating session, and asked him to encourage the Argentine government to "keep things cool" during Enders' forthcoming trip to Buenos Aires. Enders was in Argentina between March 6-8th, where he met with Galtieri and Costa Mendez, among others; Enders later advised the British Ambassador to Washington that he had raised the matter with Costa Mendez, expressing his government's concern. On March 3rd, the British Ambassador to Uruguay reported to his government that he had been told by a leading Uruguayan that Argentina was adopting a much tougher negotiating attitude toward the Falklands, and might be contemplating military action. That same day, Luce was questioned in Parliament about the Falklands talks. He stated there would be no agreement without consent of the Commons and of the Falklanders. When asked about preparations being made in the event of military acton, he stated: "We have no doubts about our sovereignty over the Falkland Islands, and no doubt about our duties to the Islanders" (134). Two days later, Carrington met with Luce, J. B. Ure, and P. R. Fearn, and agreed on the following actions: messages would be sent to Ros and Costa Mendez, urging that talks resume; Carrington would draft a personal message to American Secretary of State Alexander Haig; a statement would be prepared concerning the United Nations resolutions; a draft paper would be prepared for the Defence Committee, outlining the various alternatives, and the Foreign and Commonwealth Office should immediately begin considering initiatives to be taken if the talks broke down irrevocably.

Intelligence reports made to the British government during early March of 1982 discounted reports of overt military action against the Falklands, at least until the next southern summer, beginning in the latter part of that year. There would be no invasion, these reports said, unless negotiations broke down completely (135). The British military *attache* in Buenos Aires reported March 2nd on a visit he had made to the Falkland Islands in January to assess the military position there. He stated that the most likely threat to the Falklands was posed by the Argentine Navy, which might of its own accord seize one of the outlying islands, or stage a twenty-four-hour raid. If Argentina came to believe that negotiations were fruitless, invasion was the likely alternative. The Argentine military prided itself, he said, on its ability to conduct a swift coup and seizure action. On March 10th the Defence Intelligence Staff of the British Ministry of Defence also pointed to the Argentine Navy as a possible inciter of military action should negotiations fail, stating that the Navy favored a military solution, although the other services preferred continuation of diplomatic efforts so long as there was some hope of success.

On March 3rd Prime Minister Thatcher ordered contingency plans prepared in the event negotiations broke down. Accordingly, a note was sent to Lord Carrington on March 8th, instructing him to prepare a list of alternatives for the next meeting of the Defence Committee. Also on the 8th, Thatcher spoke to John Nott, Minister of Defence, asking him how soon Royal Navy ships could be sent to the Falklands. The Minister replied on March 12th that a small fleet of relatively fast frigates would require twenty days' passage to reach the islands. On March 8th, Carrington sent a draft of a proposed message to Costa Mendez to the Falkland Islands Councillors for their consideration. The draft expressed pleasure at the agreement reached in New York, but dissatisfaction at the subsequent press reports from Buenos Aires. It sought agreement on two points: the commission would examine all aspects of the sovereignty issue without prejudice to either side; but negotiations could not be held against a background of threats. The Councillors approved the draft, with an added clause stating that there could be no negotiations, in their view, on the sovereignty question; that any future talks should only strive to convince the Argentines that Britain had a stronger claim; and that, in any event, the Falklanders were determined to stay British at whatever cost (136). The draft was never actually sent, being superseded by subsequent events. However, by March 18th, Foreign Office officials had already judged the probable Argentine response to the draft as negative, and had decided to prepare contingency plans, in accordance with Mrs. Thatcher's instructions. Carrington was instructed to seek Nott's agreement for maintenance of the *Endurance* on its South Atlantic station indefinitely.

Carrington wrote to Secretary Haig on March 8th, expressing Britain's increasing concern over events in Argentina, particularly the threats in the Argentine Press to use force if negotiations failed. Carrington also stated that he hoped the United States would use whatever influence it had to urge the Argentines to ease existing tensions; he further hoped that Haig would help insure a peaceful solution to the crisis based upon the democratically-expressed wishes of the islanders. Haig's reply of March 15th was noncommittal, saying America would continue to urge a constructive approach to the problem for all interests concerned.

Intelligence reports made to the British government during mid-March showed no consistent patterns. Some, quoting various Argentine military sources, stated that no invasion or overt military action was contemplated in the near future; others indicated that the junta was displeased with the developments in New York, particularly with the failure of the Argentine representatives to secure a starting date for the monthly series of commission meetings. Should the British fail to set a date by the end of March, the intelligence reports indicated, air and sea services between Argentina and the Falklands might be withdrawn. An invasion was not seriously contemplated, but could not be completely discounted, due to the unpredictability of the junta members and other senior officers in the Argentine armed services (137).

At this point, the developing diplomatic crisis was suddenly over-shadowed on March 19th by the events on South Georgia Island. Within two weeks, Britain and Argentina would find themselves at war.

2.   The Argentine Invasion

The battle over the Falklands/Malvinas was precipitated by a seemingly minor incident on South Georgia Island. Constantino Davidoff, an Argentine businessman specializing in reclamation of scrap metal, had secured a contract in 1979 from Christian Salvesen, the Edinburgh-based company which managed the Crown leases on South Georgia for the abandoned whaling stations there. The agreement gave Davidoff an option to purchase the remains of the stations, and dispose of them as salvage. The option was exercised in 1980; under the terms of the contract, the scrap had to be removed from the island by March of 1983. Davidoff then contacted the British Embassy in Buenos Aires on several occasions in 1980 and 1981, but apparently never secured the proper permits. Davidoff visited the station at Leith on December 20, 1981, aboard the Argentine icebreaker, *Almirante Irizar*; the British Commander of the survey base at Grytviken on South Georgia reported the un-authorized presence of that vessel to Governor Hunt on December 31st. The British government ordered Hunt to issue a permit to Davidoff if he applied for one, and to avoid any provocative incidents; he was further told to order Davidoff off the island if he attempted to make another unauthorized landing. Britain filed a formal protest in Buenos Aires on February 9, 1982; it was rejected by Argentina on February 18th (138). Davidoff called at the British Embassy in Buenos Aires on February 23rd, and apologized for the mixup; he then requested full instructions on obtaining the proper permits. Before securing those permits, however, he notified the Embassy on March 9th that he was sending forty-one workmen to South Georgia two days later on the Argentine naval support vessel, *Bahia Buen Suceso*, and would remain on site for four months.

The Base Commander at Grytviken notified Hunt on March 20th that the *Bahia Buen Suceso* had been observed in Leith Harbor, and that a large number of workers had been put ashore; further, the party had raised the Argentine flag, and had fired a number of shots into the air.

Hunt ordered the Commander to have the Davidoff expedition report to Grytviken and lower the Argentine flag; if they refused, he said, they should be evicted. The British Embassy in Buenos Aires notified the Argentine Ministry of Foreign Affairs that Britain regarded Davidoff's actions as a serious incident. The *Endurance* was immediately dispatched to South Georgia. On March 21st the Base Commander reported to Hunt that the Argentine flag had been lowered, but the party remained on shore. On the same day, Argentina expressed hope in an official note to the British Ambassador that the incident would be minimized. On March 22nd the Commander confirmed that the *Bahia Buen Suceso* had left the area, and that the workers had been withdrawn. The Argentine government in a second note again stressed that Davidoff had acted on his own initiative, and that the incident did not reflect deliberate action to put pressure on Great Britain. Britain withdrew the sailing orders to *Endurance* (139). The Base Commander at Grytviken transmitted a second message on March 22nd, later in the day, stating that Argentines had been spotted on shore, and that a French yacht, *Cinq Gars Pour*, had made contact with them. Argentine Naval Headquarters congratulated the *Bahia Buen Suceso* on its successful mission, and directed it to return home. The British government then ordered the H.M.S. *Endurance* to return to South Georgia, and to remove the remaining Argentines, by force, if necessary.

On March 23rd the Captain of the *Endurance* reported to his superiors that the *Bahia Buen Suceso* had observed radio silence during its foray, a clear indication to him that that vessel had been operating under the direct instructions of the Argentine Navy. That same day, Dr. Costa Mendez summoned the British Ambassador to his office, and expressed his surprise that such a minor incident was escalating so rapidly, without resort to possible diplomatic solutions. He suggested that if the party on South Georgia was removed by force, those in the Argentine Foreign Ministry who were trying to moderate events would lose control of the situation. Military action might provoke a military response. He did agree to examine the possibility of the *Bahia Buen Suceso* returning to South Georgia to remove its landing party, as an alternative to forcible removal by the *Endurance*. Subsequently, the latter vessel was ordered to stand off Grytviken; Carrington agreed to the return of the Argentine ship, provided action was taken immediately. Carrington sent a note to the British Prime Minister and other members of the Defence Committee on March 24th, outlining the deteriorating political climate of the preceding month, and saying that an early confrontation with Argentina now seemed to be a real possibility. He referred to the draft message he was preparing for Costa Mendez (and which had been in preparation since the February negotiation session), saying it would now require amendment to take into account the South Georgia incident. He felt, however, that it might not be acceptable to Argentina; given the state of Argentine public opinion, which had been led to believe by sensational newspaper reports that

Britain was on the verge of ceding sovereignty of the Falklands to Argentina, a rejection by the Argentine government could lead to commercial, political, or military reprisals. He therefore urged the Defence Committee immediately to prepare contingency plans. He also wrote Defence Minister Nott on the same day, urging him to maintain the *Endurance* on station indefinitely (140). Costa Mendez informed the British Ambassador, also on the 24th, that he was having difficulties persuading Admiral Anaya, Commander-in-Chief of the Argentine Navy and a member of the junta, to desist from military reaction to the deployment of the *Endurance*. Anaya had previously been identified in British intelligence reports as the most "hawkish" member of the junta; new reports suggested that he might force the junta's hand by taking unilateral naval action against the meager British forces. The British military *attache* in Buenos Aires reported on the 24th that any attempt to remove the Argentines at Leith by force would be met with force, and that such action could easily escalate into a military occupation of the Falklands (141).

Intelligence reports indicated that Argentine ships were dispatched to South Georgia on March 25th; the nearest of these, the *Bahia Paraiso*, reached Leith Harbor later that day, with several landing craft and helicopters. Carrington reported to the British Cabinet that evening that the *Endurance* was standing by at Grytviken, but would not be used immediately, due to the dangerous increase in tensions. Should the Argentines threaten military action against the Falklands themselves, he said, Britain could not easily defend them at such long range and on such short notice (142). There were hurried exchanges back and forth between London and Buenos Aires throughout the day: Costa Mendez said Argentina could not now withdraw from South Georgia without having appeared to succumb to British pressure; Britain suggested a way out of the crisis by having the Argentines' passports stamped at Grytviken, thereby allowing them to continue their work at Leith Harbor. Argentina was also told, "we are committed to the defence of British sovereignty in South Georgia as elsewhere" (143). Intelligence reports again indicated the Argentine Navy was taking a very hard line on the crisis, while the Argentine Foreign Ministry was seeking a more conciliatory solution.

On March 26th, *Endurance* reported that the *Bahia Paraiso* had left Leith after depositing large quantities of supplies on shore. There were no signs of a military build-up, however. Carrington decided at this point to evacuate the Argentines as previously planned with the *Endurance*, but to transfer them willingly to any Argentine vessel that challenged the action. Also, the arrival at Port Stanley of replacement troops for the small garrison there gave the Government the opportunity to leave the old garrison in place, thereby effectively doubling the number of marines available to defend the colony to about eighty soldiers. A Defence Ministry assessment of the military situation on this date emphasized that, should the Argentines take the islands by force, there were no assurances British forces could retake them by amphibious assault. Also on the 26th, Costa Mendez issued a public statement stating that Argentina would give all necessary protection to the men on South Georgia. The British military *attache* in Argentina reported intense activity at the naval base at Puerto Belgrano, including the embarkation of marines, and the sailing of several ships, including at least one submarine.

Costa Mendez gave the British Ambassador a formal reply to the British protests on March 28th. It stated: "The British Government has reacted in terms which constitute a virtual ultimatum backed by the threat of military action in the form of the despatch of the naval warship *Endurance* and a requirement for the peremptorily immediate evacuation of the Argentine workers from the Island . . . [this] constitutes a disproportionate and provocative response [which has] received wide diffusion in the press [and] has had a negative effect on developments and which is not the responsibility of the Argentine Government. . . . In the light of this attitude my Government can only adopt those measures which prudence and its rights demand. In this context the Argentine workers in South Georgia must remain there since they have been given the necessary documentation to do so" (144). That evening, Carrington sent Alexander Haig a message asking that the United States help mediate the dispute.

On Monday, March 29th, Mrs. Thatcher ordered a nuclear submarine sent to the Falklands area; Nott also ordered a supply ship to South Georgia to replenish the depleted stores of the *Endurance*. Nott then ordered Rear Admiral Sir John Woodward, the Flag Officer of the First Flotilla in Gibraltar, to be prepared to detach a force of frigates and destroyers if and when they were needed in the South Atlantic. The British Ambassador in Argentina noted that Argentine press reports avidly supported the junta's actions; he warned that the junta might take further action simply to gain political popularity. Haig sent messages to both governments urging restraint, and insisting that the United States would remain neutral in any dispute; he offered his services as mediator. The Argentine *charge* in London told the British Foreign Ministry that the only way the dispute could be resolved at this juncture would be through British acceptance of the proposals put forward in New York a month earlier (145). He did not receive an encouraging reply. Intelligence reports in Britain suggested that some sort of military action short of full-scale invasion would take place in or near the Falklands shortly, probably consisting of occupation of one of the outlying islands in the group. Also on this day, most of the Argentine fleet sailed from Puerto Belgrano for previously-scheduled joint naval maneuvers with Brazil.

Carrington sent a message to Costa Mendez on March 30th, proposing a visit of a Foreign and Commonwealth Office minister to Argentina, and the resumption of negotiations on the Falklands issue once the situation on South Georgia had been defused. Carrington stated in the

House of Lords on the same day that *Endurance* would remain on station as long as necessary; Luce said in the House of Commons that the islanders' wishes were paramount, and that Britain was prepared to defend the Falklands, if necessary. Later that day, Carrington summoned the United States *charge* to express his displeasure at Haig's message. In the afternoon, the Defence Ministry convened a meeting of the Defence Operations Executive, an emergency executive agency that acts on behalf of the British Chiefs of Staff to provide central direction during actual military operations. It noted the positioning of Argentine ships within a thousand miles of the Falklands, and suggested that Argentina would probably take some action in April against one or more of the islands. No changes had been noted in Argentine Air Force readiness, however. The Executive recommended against the deployment of a surface fleet, noting the cost factor and the impending onset of the southern winter. Carrington sent a note to the Prime Minister saying that a second nuclear submarine was being sent to the South Atlantic. He also noted there were no signs at present that Argentina was preparing an invasion of the Falklands. Preparation of a British surface fleet would be highly provocative, he added. That evening, the British Ambassador delivered a note from Carrington to Costa Mendez saying that a confrontation would have serious consequences, and suggesting that defusion of the incident would provide grounds for resumption of the overall talks.

That same day, the Argentine junta was shaken by massive labor union demonstrations in Buenos Aires against the government's austerity measures, resulting in massive arrests of the protestors; further demonstrations took place on the 31st. Also on the 30th, Argentina rejected attempts by the United States to mediate in the dispute, stating that there would be no confrontation on South Georgia so long as Britain left the workmen there alone. The only possible solution to the dispute, Costa Mendez said, was negotiations without delay on the sovereignty question. British intelligence reports received on the 30th stated that a peaceful solution to the South Georgia problem was possible, but, should an Argentine be killed or injured, Argentina would initiate military invasion of the Falklands. Another report indicated that Argentina might well occupy one of the outlying Falkland Islands during April (146).

On March 31st, the British military *attache* in Buenos Aires reported that the entire Argentine fleet was at sea, but without its fleet commanders. That evening, Nott was informed by military intelligence that Argentina had set the early morning hours of April 2nd as the time for military intervention in the Falklands. Nott immediately sought a meeting with the Prime Minister, Mrs. Thatcher, which was attended by Luce and other Foreign and Defence Ministry officials (Carrington was in Israel). A formal message to President Reagan was drafted and sent at 9:00 P.M., indicating that an invasion of the Falklands might be imminent, and stating that Britain could not acquiesce to occupation of the islands by Argentina. Reagan was asked to contact Galtieri, and seek assurances that no military action would be taken unilaterally by the Argentines. Thatcher also ordered the Chief of Naval Staff to prepare a task force capable of retaking the islands should the need arise (147). The British Ambassador in Buenos Aires and the Governor of the Falklands were officially informed of developments; Hunt was ordered to notify only his garrison commander for the present. The H.M.S. *Endurance* was ordered back to Port Stanley. Intelligence reports later in the day indicated that Costa Mendez was being used only as an adviser by the junta on the South Georgia affair; it was also reported, without confirmation, that the Argentine Navy had asked for a forecast of voting in the United Nations General Assembly in the event of an Argentine invasion. A marine brigade was reportedly being prepared by Argentina for disembarkation.

The British Cabinet met on the morning of April 1, 1982. The Prime Minister noted that the best hope of defending the Falklands lay in possible United States mediation of the dispute. Further intelligence reports presented at this meeting indicated a landing target of Port Stanley for the Argentine Expeditionary Forces. However, the reports emphasized that there was yet no firm indication that the junta had made up its mind to invade the Falklands, although the preparation of an amphibious task force was certainly a disturbing factor. A very large British fleet would be required to retake the islands in the event of an invasion. For the moment, however, there was no alternative but to seek a diplomatic solution to the crisis. It was agreed not to attempt reinforcement of the garrison at Port Stanley, since too few soldiers could be landed by the 2nd to make any difference in the resolution of the crisis. A message from American Secretary of State Alexander Haig indicted that the United States Ambassador to Argentina had asked Costa Mendez to take no steps to aggravate the situation. America maintained its neutrality, however. A later message from President Reagan stated that America would do all in its power to dissuade Argentina from military action.

Later that day Dr. Costa Mendez responded to previous messages from the Britons by saying: "Since the matter raised is disregard of Argentine sovereignty: I judge pointless the despatch of a person to examine the events in the Georgias since Argentina considers this incident resolved. In fact the workers there are carrying out their tasks under normal lawful conditions without any breach of the agreement previously reached between our two countries. Bearing in mind the antecedents and course of the negotiations from 1964 to today, we would have accepted the despatch of the representative proposed by Great Britain if his task had been to negotiate the modalities of transferring sovereignty over the Malvinas Islands and their Dependencies to the Argentine Republic, which is essentially the central cause of the present difficulties. I cannot omit to draw attention to the unusual British naval deployment towards our waters reported in the international press which can only be interpreted as an unacceptable threat of the use of military force. This obliges us to refer to the UN organisation where Argentina will circulate a note on the antecedents of this case" (148). Shortly thereafter, the British military *attache* in Buenos Aires reported that Argentine Air Force planes were transporting troops to the southern part of that country.

The evening of April 1st, the British Ambassador to the United Nations appealed to the Secretary-General to issue a statement urging both sides to resolve their difficulties through diplomatic means. This he did. The President of the Security Council also urged restraint. The British Foreign and Commonwealth Office informed Governor Hunt of the Falklands and the British Ambassadors in Washington, New York, and Buenos Aires that it had reliable information indicating an Argentine task force would assemble near Port Stanley the next morning, on Friday, April 2nd. The United States Ambassador to Argentina met with President Galtieri that evening, and delivered a letter from President Reagan; Galtieri was noncommittal, but discussed the need of the British to transfer sovereignty. The American Ambassador judged from this conversation that an invasion was likely. Governor Hunt began deploying his small force of marines. Further intelligence reports received that evening suggested that the junta had previously decided on the military option during the last days of March, if no concrete proposals for serious discussions on the sovereignty question had been received from the British by the end of the week (April 2nd). Finally, late Thursday evening, at a meeting attended by Mrs. Thatcher, Lord Carrington, and Mr. Nott, it was decided to put troops on immediate notice for deployment to the Falklands. A naval task force had begun to assemble in British ports; this would join up with the British fleet stationed in Gibraltar, and could set sail within forty-eight hours, if necessary (149). Calvert quotes an April 6th article in the British newspaper, *The Guardian*, in stating that some Argentine forces came ashore on the remoter sections of the Falklands archipelago just before midnight (150).

President Reagan attempted to call Galtieri the evening of the 1st, but was refusd; he finally made contact with Galtieri in the early morning hours of April 2nd; but the Argentine President stood firm, and gave the impression of having already decided on the military option. Reagan told Galtieri that any invasion of the Falklands would have damaging effects on Argentine-American relations. Intelligence reports received by Britain at about the same time indicated that orders had been issued by the junta on April 1st calling for an Argentine occupation of the Falklands and its Dependencies. About 6:00 A.M. local time, some 2,500 Argentine troops began disembarking at Port Stanley.

Governor Hunt had not been idle since being notified the previous day of the impending invasion. Major Mike Norman, who had taken command of the eighty marines in Port Stanley just two days before, immediately set about preparing a defense. He had a small stock of barbed wire stretched along York Beach, and divided his men into six squads, ordering them to withdraw gradually toward Government House, where a final stand would be made. The soldiers had only limited numbers of small arms and ammunition. That night Hunt went on islands-wide radio to inform the population of the Argentine threat. The only other defenders available were the volunteer Falkland Islands Defence Force, consisting of 120 ill-trained islanders. Resident Argentines on the islands were rounded up and locked away in the Town Hall. At 4:25 A.M. on April 2nd, Hunt declared a state of emergency (151). The first Argentines landed by helicopter at Mullett Creek. At 6:00 A.M. sixteen amphibious landing boats were spotted entering the bay. Very shortly, the Argentine troops launched an attack on Government House, which was vigorously defended by the marines. Two hours later, about 8:00 A.M., the Argentine forces proposed surrender terms to the British. Since Hunt had no alternative, he readily agreed to lay down arms, and formally surrendered to the temporary military Governor, General Oswaldo Jorge Garcia, and to the Commander of the Argentine marine force, Admiral Carlos Busser. The Britons claimed seventeen Argentines killed and five wounded; Argentina admitted to one soldier killed and two wounded. The British suffered no casualties. Hunt was driven to the airport, immediately flown to Argentina, and thence allowed to cross the border into Uruguay; the British marines were similarly repatriated, although several remained in hiding on the Falklands until April 5th, when they were captured without incident.

The Foreign and Commonwealth Affairs Office issued meaningless statements throughout the day, essentially saying it had no information to give the press; finally, at about 6:00 P.M. London time, Carrington and Nott confirmed the Falklands invasion, indicating that the Governor had been taken prisoner, and placing the strength of the Argentine fleet at one aircraft carrier, one cruiser, four destroyers, three corvettes, and three troop ships. An emergency cabinet meeting was held at 7:30 P.M. in London, including the heads of the British armed forces. Mrs. Thatcher ordered the British task force assembled as planned. A major debate was held in the British Parliament the following morning, on April 3rd. Much criticism of the British government's handling of the crisis was expressed in the popular British newspapers published that morning, and some of this carried over into the Parliamentary debate. The Prime Minister, Mrs. Thatcher, opened the proceedings with a statement of the facts as she then knew them (she had just talked with ex-Governor Hunt, who had now arrived in Uruguay), stating emphatically that "the Falkland Islands and their dependencies remain British territory. No aggression and no invasion can alter that simple fact. It is the Government's objective to see that the islands are freed from occupation and returned to British administration at the earliest possible moment"; to this end "the Government have now decided a large task force will sail as soon as all preparations are complete; the H.M.S. *Invincible* [an aircraft carrier] will be in the lead and will leave port on Monday, June 5th" (152). She added: "The people of the Falkland Islands, like the people of the United Kingdom, are an island race. They are few in number, but they have the right to live in peace, to choose their own way of life and to determine their own allegiance. Their way of life is British; their allegiance is to the Crown. It is the wish of the British people and the duty of Her Majesty's Government to do everything that we can to uphold that right. That will be our hope and our endeavor, and, I believe, the resolve of every member of the House" (153).

In response Michael Foot, Leader of the Opposition Labour Party, stated that the islanders "are faced with an act of naked, unqualified aggression, carried out in the most shameful and disreputable circumstances. Any guarantee from this invading force is utterly worthless—as worthless as any of the guarantees that are given by this same Argentine junta to its own people" (154). He concluded: "The Government must now prove by deeds—they will never be able to do it by words—that they are not responsible for the betrayal and cannot be faced with that charge" (155). The administration of Mrs. Thatcher was criticized by many members of the Commons for not foreseeing or anticipating Argentine military action, for not taking countermeasures at an earlier date, when they might have proved a deterrent to Buenos Aires, and for deciding to send an ill-prepared task force that might well meet with disaster in the face of entrenched Argentine positions and air attacks. After assurances by Nott that the task force could indeed perform its assigned tasks, the three major parties agreed to support the Government and the expeditionary force, and the House was adjourned.

That same day Peter, Lord Carrington offered his resignation to Mrs. Thatcher, who at first rejected it, but then accepted it on April 5th. Carrington's assistants, Richard Luce and Humphrey Atkins, also resigned. Francis Pym was appointed Carrington's successor. John Nott, the Defence Minister, also offered his resignation, but was refused by the Prime Minister, who indicated that he was needed to manage the war effort during this time of crisis. Meanwhile, Sir Anthony Parsons, Britain's Ambassador to the United Nations, introduced Resolution 502 in the Security Council, which was adopted by a vote of 10-1, with four abstentions, also on April 3rd. Only Panama supported the Argentines. The Resolution called for an immediate end to hostilities, withdrawal of Argentine forces from the islands, and for a diplomatic settlement of the crisis in accordance with Article 2 (4) of the United Nations Charter, which prohibits the use of force against the territory of any state (156).

On South Georgia Island, where the small British research station at Grytviken had been monitoring the Port Stanley radio broadcasts, the British officer in charge, Lieutenant Keith Mills, assumed the worse, and began preparing for an Argentine invasion force. He had some twenty-two Royal Marines under his command. Mills received instructions on April 3rd to defend his position as long as possible. Early that morning, an Argentine corvette appeared off shore, and began offloading troops via helicopters. Mills opened fire with small arms weapons. One helicopter was downed. The corvette began returning fire from offshore, and then moved forward into the bay, at which point the British soldiers hit the vessel with antitank shell, causing some structural damage. Seeing he was heavily outnumbered, Mills agreed to surrender his force shortly thereafter. The Argentines had suffered several killed and an unknown number wounded; the British soldiers had one wounded (157). They were repatriated with their fellow marines from Port Stanley to Uruguay. A permanent Argentine Military Governor for the Malvinas and Dependencies was appointed on April 6, 1982, in the person of General Mario Benjamin Menendez, commander of the occupation forces. He would remain in those positions for just over two months. Port Stanley was renamed Puerto Argentino, Spanish was made the official language of the islands, and British citizens were threatened with up to sixty days in jail for "disruptive activities." All private radio transmitters were confiscated. Falklands currency and stamps were declared invalid.

3. War!

The course had now been set for a shooting war, unless last-minute negotiations could somehow alter the sweep of events. The British side was headed by Prime Minister Margaret Thatcher, first woman head of government in an English-speaking nation. Having been elected in the Conservative Party sweep of May, 1979, Thatcher was fifty-five years old. She had become active in Conservative politics during her days at Somerville College, Oxford University, where she took a degree in chemistry. Her first portfolio was a term as Secretary of State for Education and Science in Edward Heath's government (1970-74). After Heath's defeat in the two 1974 British elections, his days as Party leader were clearly numbered, and he was forced to resign from that position in 1975. Margaret Thatcher narrowly beat out several opponents to be named Leader of the Opposition in February of that year. Upon her election as Prime Minister, Thatcher took a hard line against Soviet adventurism, and adopted an equally tough posture on the declining British economy, choosing to accept high unemployment as the price for controlling inflation. During 1981-82 unemployment reached its highest level in Great Britain since the Great Depression, and Thatcher's popularity plummeted. The "Iron Lady," as she likes to call herself, refused to bend, however, on this issue or on the Falklands question. Her Minister of Defence, John Nott, was fifty years old in 1982, a former army officer who studied law at Cambridge University, and later served as Minister of State for the Treasury in Heath's government(158).

The Argentine triumvirate was headed by General Leopoldo Galtieri, fifty-five years of age in 1982, a career Army officer born of working-class parents who later studied at the Argentine Military College, the traditional shaper of the Argentine military officer. He studied army engineering in the United States in 1960-61. Galtieri participated in the internal war fought by Argentina against urban terrorists and guerrilla insurgents during the 1970s, eventually commanding the Third Army Corps and the First Army Corps, successively. He was known as a "soldier's soldier." Politically, he was considered a moderate by Argentine military standards, a pivot between the views of his brother officers on the junta. His fellow junta members, Admiral Jorge Isaac Anaya and Brigadier General Basilio Lami Dozo, shared similar ages and backgrounds with Galtieri, Anaya being regarded as a hardliner politically, Lami Dozo as a comparative liberal. Lami Dozo was an experienced officer who had fought against the guerrillas during the 1970s; Anaya had no active combat experience, the Argentine navy not having fought a significant action in a hundred years.

The armed forces of both nations faced potentially serious difficulties. On the Argentine side, the Army consisted of a few battalions of elite, highly-trained, well-supplied special forces, and tens of thousands of ill-trained, poorly-supplied raw recruits and draftees; the Argentine officer corps was almost an establishment unto itself, with special quarters, privileges, and powers. The Argentine Air Force had available a mixture of about 250 old and new planes, including a handful of French-made Super-Etendard jets armed with air-to-ship Exocet missiles, slow, propeller-driven Pucaras, specially designed and built by Argentina to combat the guerrillas, American-made Skyhawks, and Israeli-made Daggers. Not all were serviceable. The Argentine Navy also possessed this curious mix of old and new, its major capital ships, a carrier and a heavy cruiser, being forty-year-old obsolete hand-me-downs from previous wars and combatants; several of the destroyers and frigates, however, were modern ships incorporating the latest in missile and electronic technology. The Navy also had four diesel-powered submarines, two of them ex-American vessels.

Britain possessed a large number of highly-trained elite forces accustomed to fighting under adverse conditions of the kind to be expected in the Falklands. Its air and naval forces, however, had been severely impacted by budgetary cuts during the 1970s, leaving only two small carriers still active (one had already been sold to Australia, and the other was already headed for the scrapheap), a number of modern frigates and destroyers, and 15-20 nuclear-powered submarines. The only jet aircraft that could be accomodated by the carriers were Sea Harriers, a relatively slow-moving VTOL design that had been approved with great controversy in the 1960s, but had never actually seen combat conditions. Most military analysts regarded them as greatly inferior to the Skyhawks and Mirages possessed by the Argentines.

Britain would have to send a large fleet 7,800 miles from home, keep it supplied and defended in adverse weather conditions, and attack well-fortified Argentine positions. Argentina did not have enough time to extend the airstrip at Port Stanley to accomodate bombers or heavily-loaded jet fighters, and so would have to provide air cover for its thousands of troops from bases on the Argentine mainland. The Skyhawks and Mirages, comprising a majority of Argentine's effective air fleet, had a fuel range of 700-800 miles, thereby limiting combat time over the islands for any one plane to no more than a few passes. Further, Argentina's two large ships both lacked effective defenses, being technologically obsolete, and were thus extremely vulnerable to both air and submarine attack. The absence of clear military superiority by either side, and the large number of military variables, including the unpredictable weather, gave heart to the leadership of both countries throughout the campaign.

At a meeting of the Privy Council of Great Britain on Monday, April 5, 1982, an order was issued empowering the government "to requisition for Her Majesty's Service any British ship and anything on board such ship wherever the ship may be" (159). The British had no large troop or supply ships, and so had to convert merchant and passenger vessels for the Falklands expedition. Among the ships commandeered were the liners *Canberra* and *Queen Elizabeth II*, to be used as troop transports, and the container ship *Atlantic Conveyor*, to be used as a weapons supply ship and as an additional parking strip for the Sea Harriers. The fleet was built around two anti-submarine aircraft carriers, the H.M.S. *Hermes*, which the government had already marked for the scrapheap, and H.M.S. *Invincible*, which had recently been sold and was now awaiting delivery to the Australian Navy (out of courtesy, Australia later cancelled the arrangement). In addition, the *Fearless*, an amphibious assault ship, was just saved from being scrapped; her sister ship, *Intrepid*, was also sent. The fleet included five destroyers: *Sheffield*, *Antrim*, *Glamorgan*, *Glasgow*, and *Coventry*; twelve frigates: *Alacrity*, *Rhyl*, *Aurora*, *Battleaxe*, *Euryalus*, *Lowestoft*, *Broadsword*, *Plymouth*, *Yarmouth*, *Brilliant*, *Ariadne*, and *Dido*; two landing ships: *Sir Galahad*, and *Sir Geraint*, three tugs: *Salvageman*, *Yorkshireman*, and *Irishman*; three chartered oil tankers; *Esk*, *Tamar*, and *Tay*; a medical ship (converted from a cruise ship), the *Uganda*, a troop ship, *Norland Ferry*; and many other minor vessels. Rear Admiral John Woodward was given command of the fleet. Several nuclear-powered submarines were also sent to the South Atlantic on separate patrols. Ascension Island, about halfway between London and the Falklands, was used as a forward base—the ships were ordered to converge there for assembly into a fleet. Ascension was leased from Britain by the Americans, who maintained an airbase there accessible to British aircraft.

During the early days of the war, Britain was also not idle on the diplomatic front. On April 7th, the British government declared that, effective at 5:00 A.M. British time on April 12th, Britain would establish a 200-mile exclusionary zone around the islands. Initially, the zone excluded only Argentine ships, but it was later broadened to cover aircraft as well. Any Argentine vessel spotted in this zone after the effective date was subject to attack and/or sinking on sight. Argentina promptly declared its own exclusionary zone around the Falklands and its Dependencies, but had no effective means of enforcing its orders. Britain also immediately froze $1.4 billion of Argentine assets in British banks, thereby causing enormous financial problems for an already devastated Argentine economy. Several large international loans and credits under negotiation collapsed under the financial pressures. Argentina at that time owed $7 billion in short-term loans, but possessed liquid assets of only half that amount (160). Germany, France, and other members of the European Common Market were pressured by Britain to suspend all arms shipments to Argentina, and to impose a ban on Argentine imports; Argentina immediately reciprocated.

Argentina, on the other hand, immediately set about reinforcing the islands, using C-130 transports landing at twenty-minute intervals to ferry large supplies of food and military materiel, and to increase the size of the occupying force to 9,000 troops, most of them members of the 9th Infantry Brigade. The demonstrations against the government of General Galtieri abruptly changed into outpourings of support, as thousands of Argentines flocked into the square opposite the Presidential Palace in the days following the occupation. Every political party and labor union, every newspaper and broadcast station, endorsed the seizure. For once, the Argentine body politic united behind its leaders. Army enlistments increased dramatically, and Argentine newspapers ran stories about soldiers preparing for war and about the occupying forces in the Malvinas. Some 80,000 draftees were called back into uniform. President Galtieri told a cheering crowd of 150,000 Argentines that Argentina would "inflict punishment on anyone who dares to touch one meter of Argentine territory" (161). The 2,000 demonstrators arrested on March 30-31st were released as a gesture of good will. The Argentine position was backed by many of the Latin American countries, although some publicly deplored the invasion itself.

Into this chaos stepped American Secretary of State Alexander Haig in the role of mediator. Within a few days after the April 2nd invasion, it was apparent that Britain was seriously preparing to send a fleet to the South Atlantic; but it was also clear that this fleet, restricted to the speed of its slowest ships, would take at least two weeks to reach the Falklands, possibly longer. This gave all the parties a certain amount of time and space in which to rethink their positions, and to decide whether they really wanted to go to war. The United States, as a close ally of both powers, was, with its self-proclaimed neutrality, an obvious candidate for intermediary. On April 7th President Reagan, with the agreement of Costa Mendez, formally presented the Secretary of State with his difficult task. Haig arrived in London on April 8th. Foreign Minister Pym stated Britain's position forthrightly: Britain would not negotiate until the Argentines left the islands; if, however, the invaders were willing to withdraw, he could promise substantive talks on the sovereignty question, subject, as always, to veto by the islanders themselves. Haig then flew to Buenos Aires on April 9th. Although Costa Mendez proclaimed in public that the danger of war was receding, in private President Galtieri was as inflexible as his British counterparts, stating that Argentina would never withdraw from its national territory. He reinforced his comments by pointing to the crowd of 150,000 Argentines gathered outside the Presidential Palace, the Casa Rosada. In a speech made to this gathering after Haig's departure, he stated: "The dignity and honor of the Argentine nation is not negotiable by anyone" (162). Haig then returned to London.

He resumed discussions with the British government on April 12th, presenting them with proposals either made by Argentina or suggested by himself. These included simultaneous withdrawal from the islands of the Argentine military forces and the British fleet, with the Argentine flag left in place; the islands would then be patrolled by Argentine police until the sovereignty issue could be settled. The British rejected this plan, but made proposals of their own: withdrawal of all forces, Argentine and British; and temporary establishment of a tripartite administration consisting of Argentina, Britain, and the United States, with the latter having final decision over any conflicts that might arise, until such time as the sovereignty issue could be decided by all parties, including the islanders. Argentina would restore air and sea links previously in service to the Falklands. This plan was promptly rejected by Costa Mendez (163). Haig then returned to Washington on the 13th to report to President Reagan.

Mrs. Thatcher stated in the Commons on April 14th that Britain would regard any breach of the exclusionary zone as a sign of the junta's intentions; for its part, the junta withdrew all naval vessels from the area, relying completely on its nine C-130 transports to resupply the islands, and making no attempt to break the embargo. On April 15th Galtieri informed President Reagan that Argentina was prepared to comply with United Nations Resolution 502, and to withdraw its forces from the Falklands if the British would first withdraw their approaching fleet. Haig talked with Costa Mendez and with the three members of the ruling junta between April 16-19th, and received a number of counterproposals. These included withdrawal of all forces to their home bases, with interim administration of the islands under the aegis of a government council comprised of equal numbers of Argentines and Falklanders, with United Nations supervision. This arrangement would end on December 31, 1982 with sole Argentine sovereignty. Meanwhile, Argentines from the mainland would have the right to buy land on the Falklands, and to settle there if they desired. Britain discussed this plan over the next few days, in public (the Commons) and in private. During one parliamentary debate, Margaret Thatcher said: "The issue here is one of international order. We are dealing with the basic charter of the United Nations, of which self-determination forms a part. It is a wide issue which has associations and connotations for many countries and peoples, not just, as in this case, the wishes of the islanders. Therefore, that is an important issue. The Government has made their position clear on all those central issues" (164). On the 22nd, Galtieri visited the Malvinas for the first time, stating: "I am convinced that the blue and white flag of Argentina will never come down from the Malvinas. We really want a peaceful settlement . . . We have warm hearts but what is needed now is cool heads. The British may defeat us; but they cannot break our spirits. Our material things may be destroyed, but our spirits cannot be broken" (165). Costa Mendez was quoted as saying: "The English reaction is so absurd, so disproportionate, this seems like a chapter in a science-fiction novel" (166).

The British ships sailed from Portsmouth and other harbors as they were readied; some of the destroyers and frigates were dispatched immediately from Gibraltar. On board the *Invincible* was Prince Andrew, Queen Elizabeth's second son, serving as a helicopter pilot. Time was beginning to run out for any real possibility of a negotiated settlement. The fleet included about a thousand soldiers from the Royal Marines and from the Parachute Regiment, the so-called "Paras," many of whom had served in Northern Ireland during the civil unrest there. These were bolstered by another 4,000-5,000 troops sailing later in the month on the converted troop ships. While many of the soldiers had experienced combat duty in various corners of the world, the naval forces were relatively untested—Admiral Woodward, for example, had never commanded a ship under fire, having been primarily a desk-bound officer prior to this new assignment. Of great concern to the British forces was the uncertain weather situation in the South Atlantic during this season of storms, and the effects which bad weather might have upon men, materiel, and tactics—one helicopter was, in fact, lost during training exercises on the way south. Because the weather was expected to deteriorate gradually as the winter season advanced for the southern hemisphere, the British forces were under enormous tactical pressure to proceed with their plans immediately upon their arrival near the Falklands. This they did.

During the interim period between the Argentine invasion and the outbreak of actual fighting, both Argentina and Britain were receiving clandestine intelligence reports from the Soviet Union and the United States, respectively, regarding disposition of opposing forces. The Russians launched several spy satellites in its Cosmos series into Polar orbit, so they would overfly the South Atlantic region several times daily; unfortunately for Argentina, such reports did not often prove very useful, due to cloud cover and bad weather. The British fleet was also shadowed constantly by Soviet trawlers and spy planes. United States satellites enabled Britain to maintain constant contact between the appropriate war offices and their South Atlantic forces; in addition, British planes and ships were being serviced and fueled by the American airbase on Ascension Island, as required by the leasing agreement which first allowed the United States to construct the facility. Later in the war, the Americans provided KC-130 air tankers to help refuel British bombers and fighters flying out of Ascension Island.

This was the situation on April 24, 1982, when the British forces were officially put on battle alert as they neared the Falkland Islands and its Dependencies. Rear Admiral Woodward declared that he intended to make the Falklands blockade "air and sea tight" (167). On Sunday, April 25th, Britain made its first military move by recapturing South Georgia Island. In fact, a small reconnaissance team had been landed there on April 21st, with the loss of two helicopters forced down in severe winds. These intelligence parties reported that Argentine troops on the island numbered only about 100 soldiers, and seemed poorly commanded and deployed. As helicopters began landing additional British patrols on the island Sunday morning, they spotted the Argentine submarine *Santa Fe*, which was entering Grytviken harbor to resupply the Argentine garrison there. The boat was immediately attacked with machine-guns, rockets, and depth charges, damaging the hull and conning tower, and starting a small fire that forced it to beach itself near the jetty. One crewman was injured. Meanwhile, British troops had landed *en masse*, and British destroyers and frigates began laying down an artillery barrage around the Argentine garrison, without actually trying to hit it. The Argentines surrendered before the British ground forces approached close enough to their fortifications to engage in small-arms fire. The Argentine garrison at Leith, where the conflict had first begun, also surrendered the next day without firing a shot. Some 156 military and thirty-eight civilian prisoners were taken (168). Costa Mendez responded to the British actions by stating that Argentina was "now technically in a state of war" with Britain (169).

At a meeting of the Organization of American States in Washington on April 26th, Costa Mendez pressured the members for support of his proposal to take collective action against Great Britain. While the members were generally supportive, many were privately disturbed at Argentina's overt invasion of the Falklands. The resolution finally passed by the Organization of American States, on a vote of 17-0 with three abstentions, called on Britain to cease hostilities, while Argentina was asked only "to refrain from any act that might exacerbate the situation." Secondly, the resolution urged both parties "to call an immediate truce that will make it possible to resume and develop normally the negotiations aimed at a peaceful settlement of the conflict, bearing in mind the rights of sovereignty of the Republic of Argentina over the Falklands and the interests of the islanders." Thirdly, it deplored "the adoption by members of the European Economic Community and other states of coercive measures of an economic and political nature which are prejudicial to the nation" (170).

On April 27th Michael Foot, Leader of the opposition Labour Party in Britain, urged Mrs. Thatcher to send Francis Pym, her Foreign Secretary, to meet with the United Nations Secretary-General, Javier

Perez de Cuellar, before any further military actions were taken. This was the first crack in the unified support for the government exhibited by either of the British opposition parties (Labour and the Social Democrats/Liberal Alliance) since the Argentine invasion. [The divergence between the Conservative and Labour views on the Falklands has in fact widened over the last year, finally culminating in the June, 1983 British elections, in which the official Labour Party Platform included a clause mandating negotiations on the Falklands question should Labour be elected.] Haig's attempts to mediate the crisis had faltered on April 26th, when Costa Mendez, on instructions from his government, refused to meet with the American Secretary of State, although they did exchange views during the Organization of American States meetings later that week. Out of frustration, Haig made one final proposal of his own, suggesting that both forces withdraw from the Falklands area; that the Falklands be governed for a five-year period by locally-elected representatives and officials, under the aegis of a tripartite commission operated by Britain, Argentina, and the United States; that any Falklands resident who wished to leave be granted adequate compensation; and that a framework be established to negotiate a final settlement of all governmental and personal claims. This proposal was rejected and made public by Argentina, despite pledges of secrecy; it was neither rejected nor accepted by the British.

Events hereafter moved rapidly toward war. On April 29th Great Britain announced that, effective at 11:00 A.M. Greenwich Mean Time on April 30th, British forces would establish a Total Exclusionary Zone around the Falklands, applying to all ships and aircraft of any nation attempting to aid the Argentines, covering a radius of 200 miles from the islands; permission to transit the zone could only be given by the Defence Ministry in London (171). On April 30th, Secretary Haig announced Argentina's rejection of his proposals, and simultaneously announced the end of American neutrality: "Argentina's position remains that it must receive an assurance now of eventual sovereignty or an immediate *de facto* role in governing the islands which would lead to sovereignty. For its part, the British Government has continued to affirm the need to respect the views of the inhabitants in any settlement. The United States has thus far refrained from adopting measures in response to the seizure of the islands that could have interfered with our ability to work with both sides in the search for peace. The British Government has shown complete understanding for this position. Now, however, in the light of Argentina's failure to accept a compromise, we must take steps to underscore that the United States cannot and will not condone the use of unlawful force to resolve disputes" (172). A few days earlier, Haig had castigated Argentina during the Organization of American States meeting for having taken military action against the islands. The United States House of Representatives voted the same day to approve a nonbinding resolution expressing "full diplomatic support for Great Britain in its effort to uphold the rule of law''; the Senate simultaneously passed its own resolution on a vote of 79-1, urging that America ''use all appropriate means to assist the British government'' (173). Haig also announced limited military and economic sanctions against Argentina, including suspension of arms shipments, and halting Export-Import Bank credits and loan guarantees and United States Commodity Credit Corporation loan guarantees. These had relatively minor impact, since Argentina was neither receiving extensive military aid nor using many of the loan guarantees. Haig further indicated that the United States would provide war materiel to Great Britain as requested; America would not, however, in any way become directly involved in the war. He concluded: ''The United States remains ready to assist the parties in finding that settlement. A strictly military outcome cannot endure over time. In the end there will have to be a negotiated settlement acceptable to the interested parties. Otherwise, we will all face unending hostility and insecurity in the South Atlantic'' (174). Costa Mendez immediately responded at the United Nations by stating that Argentina was ''always willing'' to comply with United Nations Resolution 502, but that Argentina's claims of sovereignty were ''non-negotiable'' (175). Francis Pym noted: ''To have the world's most powerful state on our side must make Argentina see that aggression cannot pay'' (176).

During the early-morning hours of May 1st, a long-range British Vulcan bomber made a surprise attack on the Puerto Argentino airstrip, cratering it with twenty-one 1,000-pound bombs. The Vulcan, an obsolete twenty-year-old nuclear bomber, had been converted to handle non-nuclear ordnance, flown to Ascension Island, and then refueled three or more times during the 7,500-mile trip to the Falklands and back again. The destruction of the only long runway on the islands was vital to the British plans for invasion, making difficult the resupply of the Argentine garrison, and preventing the Argentines from stationing modern jet fighters anywhere on the Falklands. With the Port Stanley airstrip unserviceable, the Argentine Skyhawks and Mirages would have to fly their missions from the mainland, leaving them with only a few minutes of flying time over the Falklands before they would have to return to their home bases or run out of fuel. The British immediately followed up the surprise attack with strafing and bombing runs by the twenty Sea Harriers based on the two British aircraft carriers, now on permanent station about ninety miles east of the Falklands coast. The Harriers also hit the short dirt runway at Goose Green, where a number of the propeller-driven Pucaras were based. Some of these craft were damaged or destroyed on the ground. The British suffered no casualties in this first day of active fighting (177). Later that day Sea King helicopters attacked Port Darwin with rockets and machine-gun fire, and the destroyers and frigates off the northeast coast of the Falklands shelled military fortifications near Port Stanley. The Argentines struck back by attacking the fleet with Skyhawks, Mirages, and Canberra bombers, but inflicted only minor damage on two warships.

Britain claimed one Canberra bomber downed and another damaged, and three Israeli-built Dagger fighters destroyed and one damaged; Argentina claimed two Harriers destroyed and others damaged, and the *Hermes* destroyed (many of the Argentine claims were later discredited as the war progressed).

Argentina immediately set about restoring the Port Stanley airstrip, filling in the bomb craters and repairing damaged hangars. In fact, Argentina was able to use the strip haphazardly throughout the campaign, primarily for resupply, despite the best efforts of the British bombers to close it down permanently. After each bombing attack, the damage was carefully and tenaciously repaired. The last C-130 flew out of Puerto Argentino (Port Stanley) the day before the Argentines surrendered. But Argentina was never able to risk basing any of its fighters at Stanley, thus reducing the nearly 10-1 advantage of Argentine planes over their British counterparts to much more even odds. Argentina undoubtedly expected to establish air superiority over the British relatively early in the campaign; in actual fact, the British held their own from the very first day, gradually whittling down the Argentine fighters through constant harassment by the Harriers, land- and sea-based rocket fire, and shipboard defenses. By the end of the war, the Argentine Air Force had been decimated, with relatively few air losses by the British, although the British had paid a terrible price at sea defending against the Argentine air attacks.

Galtieri made a speech later the same day in which he said: "Attempts have been made to portray us as bloody aggressors, when the truth, as everyone knows, is that in recovering unredeemed territory we prefer to die than kill; and so, in an unprecedented military operation, neither the adversary nor the Malvinas population suffered a single casualty . . . Now the British Empire, emboldened by the supposed results of its campaign of pressure, is resorting to the direct and overt use of force. There remains no other recourse but to respond with military action to this violence" (178).

The next day, on May 2nd, the British submarine *Conqueror*, cruising submerged near the Isla de los Estados, about 240 miles southwest of the Falklands, spotted a small Argentine fleet comprising the heavy cruiser, *General Belgrano*, with several accompanying destroyers. Judging that the *Belgrano* was attempting to make a southerly run around the exclusionary zone to attack the British fleet, the *Conqueror* fired several wire-guided Tigerfish MK-24 torpedoes at the Argentine ship, hitting it twice. The *Belgrano* had originally been commissioned in 1939 as the U.S.S. *Phoenix*, having survived the Japanese attack on Pearl Harbor in 1941 almost untouched. After the second world war, it had been sold to Argentina in 1951, and recommissioned under its new name, commemorating the famous Argentine patriot. The torpedoes exploded below the engine room, knocking out all electrical power to the ship; and just below the prow, causing it to list heavily to port. Captain Hector Bonzo immediately gave the order to abandon ship. The *Belgrano* sank at about 5:00 P.M., some forty minutes after being attacked. The second-largest ship in the Argentine Navy was also the largest warship sunk in naval warfare since the end of World War II. Of the 1,042 crewmen, 368 died, some in the engine-room explosion, but more of exposure while waiting to be rescued from gale-force winds, freezing temperatures, and heavy seas. Some were found the next morning frozen to death in their life rafts. The *Belgrano*'s two accompanying destroyers fled the scene immediately after the attack, abandoning their shipmates to their fates for almost a day, and perhaps inflicting more casualties on their country-men than had the British torpedoes. Argentina immediately protested that the *Belgrano* had been thirty-six miles outside of the exclusionary zone, and that "the sub was even more south than the cruiser." Mrs. Thatcher replied: "Had we left it any later, it would have been too late, and then I might have had to come to the Commons with the news that some of our ships had been sunk" (179). She added: "The worry that I live with hourly is that Argentine forces, in attacks both naval and air, will get through to our forces" (180).

Ireland at once sought a meeting of the United Nations Security Council to call for an immediate cessation of hostilities and a negotia-ted settlement under United Nations auspices; the Soviet Union de-nounced the attack as "colonial brigandage." There were muted grumblings among the governments of Europe. But the meeting of the Security Council was delayed. That same day, two armed Argentine tugs, the *Comodoro Somellera* and the *Alferez Sobral*, were attacked by missile-carrying Lynx helicopters as they ventured into the zone, ostensibly searching for the pilots of a downed Argentine Canberra bomber; the *Somellera* was sunk, the *Sobral* severely damaged. On May 4th a British Vulcan bomber again attacked the airstrip at Puerto Argentino, followed by separate attacks by Sea Harriers there and at Goose Green. One Harrier was shot down.

Also on the 4th the British suffered their first major loss, when the destroyer H.M.S. *Sheffield*, serving on radar picket duty on the Argen-tine side of the islands, was struck by an Exocet missile fired by a French-made Super-Etendard jet. The result was disastrous. Two missiles had been fired while the attacking jets were beyond the vessel's radar range; one missed, the other skimmed the surface of the water, at a height of fifteen feet, underneath the ship's radar umbrella. By the time the Exocet was spotted, only twenty seconds remained before it smashed into the superstructure, exploding next to the main control room, and completely disabling the vessel's defense, power, and fire control systems. The fires spread quickly throughout the center of the ship, melting the aluminum superstructure. Captain James Salt was forced to abandon ship after five hours of futile struggle. Twenty crew-men were killed, many others burned. The abandoned hulk continued to burn for another seven days, at which point, after several attempts to tow the damaged hulk back to port, it was deliberately sunk to eliminate a potential navigational hazard.

The *Sheffield* had been the first of the new Type 42 class of British destroyers, launched in 1971, and heralded as the prototype for a new generation of sleek, modern warships. Heavy steel plate had been abandoned in favor of lightweight aluminum. Several of the gun emplacements had been removed, and various types of ship-to-air and ship-to-ship missiles installed, together with the enhanced radar and electronic devices designed to fool the enemy's defenses. Due to budgetary cutbacks, anti-missile missiles had not been included, although they had originally been proposed. The *Sheffield*-class destroyers had been designed essentially to operate in British coastal waters or in the North Sea, where land-based air cover could be provided. Without a blanket of radar planes and jet fighters, it and the rest of the British fleet were highly vulnerable to missile attack. Fortunately for the British, Argentina had only a handful of the Exocets, and France had joined the arms embargo against Patagonia, making resupply extremely difficult. On May 6th two British Sea Harriers collided in stormy weather; no trace of pilots or planes was ever found.

On May 7th Britain widened the total exclusionary zone to an area twelve miles from the Argentine coastline, saying that any Argentine ships or planes caught in that area by the British would be considered hostile, and subject to immediate attack. Eighty members of the British Labour Party signed a petition seeking an immediate cease-fire. The following day, on May 8th, Argentina rejected a peace proposal by President Fernando Belaunde Terry of Peru, which called for a seventy-two hour truce, withdrawal of all military forces from the Falklands, and negotiations under United Nations sponsorship. Britain had already agreed to change its negotiating stance, from its earlier insistence that the islanders' wishes be "paramount," to a somewhat modified version which would "take into account the wishes and aspirations of the inhabitants" (181). They further agreed to conclude negotiations within a year, and to allow an interim administration by the United States, Brazil, Peru, and West Germany. With the Argentine rejection of this proposal, efforts to achieve a negotiated settlement moved to United Nations Secretary-General Javier Perez de Cuellar, previously touted as a possible mediator. Perez de Cuellar had rejected this role several weeks earlier when he had failed to receive the basic support from the combatants that he felt he needed as a prerequisite. Perez de Cuellar's plan was similar to that of his countryman, President Belaunde Terry; it included an immediate cease-fire, a withdrawal of British and Argentine military forces in several stages under United Nations supervision, an end to all economic sanctions, and an interim administration of the islands under United Nations auspices, with United Nations-sponsored talks on the future of the islands and its inhabitants. The issue of sovereignty would be left to a later date. Mrs. Thatcher stated in Parliament: "We welcome the ideas that the Secretary-General has put forward and can accept them as a framework on which more specific proposals could be built" (182).

Francis Pym, British Foreign Secretary, made the following official reply to the Secretary-General's proposals: "In our view Resolution 502 must be implemented without delay; an unconditional ceasefire could not under any circumstances be regarded as a step towards this; and implementation of a ceasefire must be unambiguously linked to the commencement of an Argentine withdrawal, which must be completed within a fixed number of days" (183). Argentina stated: "The first step toward a solution must be an immediate ceasefire." Later, Defense Minister Amadeo Frugoli added: "Argentina has clearly stated that its sovereignty over the islands should be recognized . . . Argentina is open to any diplomatic negotiations as long as they do not affect its honor and legitimate rights" (184). Costa Mendez indicated on May 9th that negotiations must lead eventually to Argentine sovereignty over the Falklands.

During the first week in May, England commandeered the passenger liner *Queen Elizabeth II* for use as a troop transport, ordered four more frigates to the South Atlantic, dispatched another squadron of Sea Harriers to the fleet by air via Ascension Islands, and sent several Nimrod radar planes to the area. Argentina devalued the Argentine peso by 17 percent, and posed a 7 percent war tax on selected goods sold abroad, plus domestic sales of gasoline, cigarettes, and liquor. On May 9th British ships shelled targets near Port Stanley, and attacked and captured an Argentine fishing vessel, the *Narwal*, which Britain claimed had been shadowing the British fleet and providing intelligence to the Argentine Navy; an Argentine naval officer was discovered on board. On May 11th, a British frigate sank an Argentine supply ship, *Islas de Los Estados*, in Falkland Sound. The next day two Argentine Skyhawks were shot down by Sea Wolf missiles while trying to evade British fire. One of the British frigates was holed by a bomb that passed completely through it, causing minimal damage. On May 14th, British troops attacked a radar station and airstrip on Pebble Island, at the northern tip of the Falklands group, destroying eleven small aircraft, including six Pucaras, and suffering only two minor casualties. At about this time, the frigate *Battleaxe* and destroyer *Exeter* joined the British fleet.

Meanwhile, the diplomatic efforts continued, with limited success. On May 13th, the American State Department announced that retired General Vernon Walters had been sent to Buenos Aires to assuage Argentina's anger at America's support of Great Britain. Walters received a cordial welcome by the junta, and was assured that Argentina had no intention of seeking military aid from the Soviet Union. The following day, May 14th, Margaret Thatcher gave a speech in which she noted that a negotiated settlement "may prove unattainable. I hope with all my heart that the negotiations will succeed. I do not want to see one more life lost in the South Atlantic—whether Argentine or British—if it can be avoided" (185). Costa Mendez indicated: "It is

Britain, and not Argentina, which is delaying negotiations." Mrs. Thatcher responded by saying that, if the talks had indeed broken down, Britain would "have to turn to the only other course open to us" (186). The basic stumbling blocks, other than the perennial issue of sovereignty, were the wishes of the islanders, and the structure of the talks themselves. Britain wanted open-ended negotiations; Argentina desired a time limit of six months. Britain feared a second invasion if, at the end of any artificial termination date, Argentina was dissatisfied with the progress of the talks; Argentina feared endless procrastination by the British. Mrs. Thatcher assured the House of Commons that British forces in the South Atlantic would be maintained until the withdrawal of the Argentines, at the same time noting that the sovereignty issue was now "negotiable." Francis Pym stated: "We must never forget who is the aggressor, who invaded whom, who embarked on an unlawful and dangerous course, who first took up arms and thus put lives at risk, who fired the first shot. Argentina knows how to avoid further military conflict. It can begin its withdrawal now" (187). Costa Mendez indicated: "We are not saying Britain must accept at the beginning our sovereignty . . . we are not putting sovereignty as a precondition for talks." President Galtieri added: "We are not going to renounce sovereignty but we can talk to reach the goal. Although not for another 149 years" (188). On May 17th members of the Common Market renewed their economic sanctions against Argentina for another week only, as dissent began to spread among the European ambassadors.

Also on May 17th, Sir Anthony Parsons presented Britain's final position on the Falklands negotiations to the Secretary-General. The British proposals called for: withdrawal of both sides within fourteen days after signing an agreement to a position at least 150 nautical miles from the Falklands; supervision of the withdrawal, and governance of the Falklands, by a United Nations administrator appointed by the Secretary-General, who would rule the islands in consultation with the Executive and Legislative Councils; negotiations on the future of the islands, without prejudice to the rights of either side in the dispute, and exclusion of the South Georgia and South Shetland Islands from this agreement. Argentina replied two days later, objecting to the exclusion of the Dependencies, insisting that all forces withdraw completely to their home bases, and demanding that administration of the Falklands be placed solely in the hands of a United Nations Administrator, advised by equal numbers of Argentine and British councillors. Further, Argentines from the mainland would be allowed to buy property on the islands as if they were citizens there. On May 20th, Margaret Thatcher replied: "It was manifestly impossible for Britain to accept such demands. Argentina began this crisis. Argentina has rejected proposal after proposal. One is bound to ask whether the junta ever intended to seek a peaceful settlement or whether they have sought merely to confuse and prolong the negotiations while remaining in illegal possession of the islands . . . . (Our) proposals have been rejected. They are no longer on the table'' (189). The Labour Party generally supported Mrs. Thatcher, except for a small, breakaway faction of thirty-three members headed by leftist Anthony Wedgwood Benn, who forced a division on the question. Michael Foot, Labour Party Chairman, accused Benn of "stabbing in the back those who are being sent into battle.'' The Argentines immediately stated that their reply had not been intended as a rejection of the British proposals, but to no avail. May 20, 1982 marked the end of the last attempt to find a negotiated solution to the Falklands puzzle.

Prime Minister Thatcher immediately gave orders to begin the British counter-invasion of the Falkland Islands. During the early-morning hours of May 21st, the troop-ferrying liner *Canberra* and the assault ships *Fearless* and *Intrepid* were brought into the northern opening of Falkland Sound, the long strait dividing the two main islands, accompanied by frigates, destroyers, landing craft, helicopters, and a number of other ships. For the past several days Sea Harriers had been pounding the airstrips at Puerto Argentino and Goose Green; British warships had also shelled military targets there. British intelligence had revealed that most of the Argentine soldiers were located at the capital (7,500 men), Goose Green/Darwin (1,500 men), and Fox Bay on West Falkland Island (1,000 men), with scattered outposts of 20-50 troops each elsewhere. The site chosen for the landing was Port San Carlos, a small community of sheep farmers located on San Carlos Bay, at the northwest corner of East Falkland Island, just inside the northern opening to Falkland Sound. The bay provided a sheltered anchorage for the supply ships, with surrounding hills and long, sandy beaches ideal for use by the landing craft. Approximately 1,000 British soldiers were on the beaches by dawn, together with tanks, missile batteries, armored cars, and other military equipment. More troops and supplies were put ashore throughout the day by landing craft and helicopters. The small Argentine garrison at Port San Carlos was quickly scattered after an initial exchange of gunfire; nine Argentine soldiers were captured, most of the rest fleeing into the interior. The British also began conducting small diversionary commando raids on Fox Bay and elsewhere.

The British suffered losses even before the landings began, when one of their Sky King helicopters went down in bad weather while ferrying troops between two ships; twenty-one of the crew and soldiers were lost at sea, nine were rescued. No other casualties were counted until sunrise. At 10:00 A.M. the Argentine Air Force attacked *en masse* with wave after wave of Pucaras, Mirages, Skyhawks, and Daggers. One British frigate, the *Ardent*, went down under a barrage of missiles, with twenty-two dead and thirty wounded. Four other vessels were damaged in the initial attacks, two sailors being killed. The British claimed destruction of nine Mirage fighters, five Skyhawks, two Pucaras, and four Argentine helicopters; Argentina admitted the loss of six aircraft, but claimed to have sunk two British vessels, including a destroyer. Britain admitted the loss of one Sea Harrier. Argentine newspapers reported decisive victories over the British forces (190).

May 22nd was a day of consolidation for both the Argentine and British forces, with no attacks on either side. *Canberra* was converted into a temporary hospital ship, treating British and Argentine soldiers alike. The 5,000 British troops began securing the ten-square-mile beachhead, built landing pads for Harriers and helicopters, and continued unloading more men and materiel from the supply ships. The following day the Argentine Air Force returned, attacking the British forces with as many as forty aircraft simultaneously. One unexploded bomb lodged in the engine room of the British frigate, *Antelope*; after the ship was moved to a new anchorage, a bomb expert attempted to defuse the explosive, but was killed when it blew up in his face. The resulting fire burned all night, and the *Antelope* sank the next morning, without further loss of life. H.M.S. *Argonaut* was crippled when its engine room was damaged by bombs, but remained on station with weapons intact. Britain claimed five Mirage jets and one Skyhawk shot down, with another of each probably destroyed. Two Argentine helicopters were hit by Sea Harriers.

By May 24th the British bridgehead had expanded into the nearby hills, and much of the heavy armor and military vehicles had been dispersed away from the open beaches. Missile emplacements sprouted on each of the hilltops. Argentine jets again attacked in force, damaging two British supply ships. The British claimed two Argentine Skyhawks and six Mirages destroyed, with the loss of one Sea Harrier. The *Canberra* finally was moved out of San Carlos Bay; a field hospital on shore took the place of its medical facilities. The converted liner *Queen Elizabeth II* arrived at the task force with 3,000 troops on board. The Common Market once again deliberated on the problem of sanctions against the Argentines, now that the week's extension of the original penalties was running out; in a resounding diplomatic victory for Britain, the sanctions were extended indefinitely, with Ireland and Italy dissenting.

May 25th was Argentine National Day, *Veinticinco de Mayo*, and, as expected, the Argentine Air Force made its greatest effort of the war, throwing seventy planes, perhaps all those serviceable, at the British fleet. Wave after wave of Argentine fighters bombed and strafed British ships and British soldiers alike. The destroyer *Coventry*, on duty at the north end of Falkland Sound, was hit by several 1,000-pound bombs, sinking within a few hours, with twenty-one sailors dead. Just north of the Falklands, the *Atlantic Conveyor*, loaded with helicopters and other military supplies, was devastated by an Exocet missile, one of two fired by the Argentines that day. Twelve died, including the Captain, Ian North. Some of the ship's cargo was later salvaged. Fortunately for the British, all of the Sea Harriers on board had already been offloaded; also, the British believed the Argentines had expended the last of its air-to-ship Exocets by hitting a target they thought was an aircraft carrier. Another dozen Argentine aircraft were claimed destroyed by the British.

On the same day, Argentina finally persuaded the United Nations to convene a meeting of the Security Council, something for which it had been calling since the British counter-invasion. In his speech, Costa Mendez stated: "My country is at this moment resisting an invasion. It is doing so with all the means at its disposal, and by the determination and the courage and patriotism of its people" (191). He was seconded by Panama, a member of the Security Council, and by other Latin American members of the General Assembly. The Council then adopted Resolution 505 (May 26th) urging the Secretary-General to seek negotiations between the two warring parties, and to work toward a ceasefire. At the Organization of American States, Costa Mendez fared significantly better. In a forty-five minute speech to the group, he said that the United States had "turned its back on the region to assist a European state, also Anglo-Saxon, also an atomic power, also a world power, in the prosecution of its criminal, aggressive, colonialist adventure" (192). American support for Britain, he continued, was "illegal and repugnant. The future of the inter-American relationship is under threat" (193). He was given a standing ovation. In his response, American Secretary of State Alexander Haig pointed out that it had been Argentina who had first used force in the conflict, that it had been Argentina who had rejected Haig's peace initiatives. The Organization of American States subsequently voted 17-0, with four abstentions, to condemn Britain's "unjustified and disproportionate armed attacks" on the Falklands, petitioned the United States to halt all aid to Great Britain, and urged its members to provide Argentina with material assistance in its struggle against English imperialism.

May 26th was relatively quiet, with no Argentine air attacks on British vessels, although British Sea Harriers did raid entrenched enemy positions near Puerto Argentino. British ground troops now numbered over 5,000 men. By Thursday, May 27th, Britain was beginning to expand its beachhead. Woodward ordered an assault on the nearest Argentine garrison, at the little settlement of Darwin, five miles north of a dirt and grass airstrip at Goose Green. Darwin and Goose Green were located on the narrow, five-mile wide isthmus separating Choiseul Sound from Grantham Sound, the two bodies of water that nearly cut East Falkland Island in half; Darwin was also the terminus for the only dirt road stretching from Port Stanley/Puerto Argentino to the western part of the island. Its strategic importance had been recognized very early by the Argentines, who had 1,700 troops dug into trenches on the flanks and tops of several hills. This Argentine base would have to be taken before the British could move on Port Stanley.

Under the command of Lieutenant Colonel Herbert "H" Jones, the Second Battalion of the Parachute Regiment (the "Paras") launched its attack on Darwin at 2:00 A.M. on May 28th. They were supported by two 105 m.m. guns; earlier in the evening, frigates operating from

Falkland Sound had shelled the isthmus. Low cloud cover prevented the Sea Harriers from providing bombing support. Darwin itself fell easily. The Argentine soldiers retreated to Goose Green, five miles further south, into prepared, fortified trenches on the highlands. Six Argentine Pucaras attacked the British forces, shooting down a British helicopter; four of the propeller-driven fighters were themselves destroyed by hand-held Blowpipe missiles and small-arms fire. The British troops were close to defeat, pinned down by several entrenched machine guns, when Jones himself led a final charge that destroyed the emplacements; he was killed in the fighting. Shortly thereafter the clouds lifted, and three Sea Harriers began dropping anti-personnel bombs on the Argentine lines. By nightfall the pace of the action had slackened somewhat, after fourteen hours of battle; Major Christopher Keeble, who had taken command of the Paras on the death of his commanding officer, radioed Goose Green, suggesting that the Argentine commanders there meet with him to discuss surrender terms. After negotiating through the night, the Argentines released 133 civilians that had been held hostage at the recreation center at Goose Green for the past month. At 9:00 A.M. Comodoro Wilson Drozier Podrozo, Commander of the Argentine air squadron at Goose Green, and Lieutenant Colonel Halo Piaggi, Commander of the Argentine ground forces there, formally surrendered their troops. Six hundred British soldiers had captured 1,400 Argentines. The Argentines had lost 250 men killed to seventeen British dead. Also captured were howitzers, anti-aircraft guns, three damaged Pucaras, and small arms and ammunition in great quantity. A Sea Harrier pilot who had been downed the day before while bombing Goose Green emerged from his hiding place shortly after the surrender. During this same period, another force of Marines and Paras was moving toward Puerto Argentino through the northern part of East Falkland Island, taking the small communities of Douglas and Teal Inlet. The 3,500 troops aboard the *Queen Elizabeth II* were finally landed at the original beachhead at Port San Carlos, starting at about this date. The British troops killed in the battle were buried together at Port San Carlos; the many Argentine dead were buried in a common grave near where they fell, at Goose Green. Argentina press reports spoke only of having "lost communication" with their forces at Goose Green.

On May 29th President Galtieri, in a speech made at Army Headquarters to celebrate the 172nd anniversary of the founding of the armed forces, stated: "To the millions of men and women from our homeland and from other American countries who come to offer themselves as volunteers, thank you. I have no more weapons, nor cannons, nor tanks for them. We have no more ships or planes to be manned. May it be God's wish that when this unequal fight against the extra-continental aggressor and those who support him is over, the torch we have hoisted to illuminate the awakening of America and those who have been deprived in the world, may never go out" (194). Argentine air raids on

British positions and ships continued at a reduced pace, a clear indication that the war was taking a terrible toll on both planes and pilots. One Skyhawk was reported shot down by Great Britain on the 24th. British forces began their slow advance in a giant pincers movement aimed at the Argentine defense positions before Puerto Argentino.

The next day Major General Jeremy Moore took command of the British land forces for their final sweep toward Stanley. Bombardment of the Argentine forces and fortifications near that enclave increased both from air and sea. Britain reported that the Argentines had been reduced to rolling bombs out of the rear doors of their C-130 transports in an effort to stop the British forces. The British troops advanced largely on foot by forced marches across the bogs and peat marshes of the interior. Minor Argentine outposts, surprised by the rapid British advance, either surrendered or fled. By May 31st, Britain held 1,600 Argentine prisoners-of-war. Also on that day, British paratroopers took Mount Kent, ten miles west of the capital, giving them a commanding position overlooking the forthcoming battle zone. Giant Chinook helicopters ferried 105 m.m. guns to the top of the hill, with sufficient range to hit every enemy target in the Argentine camp. By Tuesday, June 1st, British forces were probing the outer reaches of the Argentine defense perimeter around Puerto Argentino.

Faced with the prospect of imminent disaster, Argentina immediately sought a meeting of the United Nations Security Council to press for a ceasefire. Mrs. Thatcher responded on June 2nd by saying: "I am asking the invader to return his troops to the mainland. That is not humiliation. I am just trying to repossess islands which are British sovereign territory. That is liberty, justice, and democracy" (195). She added: "To hand something to the Argentines, to an invader and an aggressor and a military dictator, that would not be magnanimity, it would be treachery or betrayal of our own people" (196). Panama and Spain thereupon introduced a resolution in the Security Council calling for an immediate ceasefire. The resolution was amended to include simultaneous implementation of Resolution 502, previously accepted by the Security Council at the time of the Argentine invasion in April. The vote (on June 4th) was 9-2, with four abstentions; the vote failed on vetoes by Great Britain and the United States. Following the vote, the American Ambassador to the United Nations, Jeane Kirkpatrick, made an astonishing speech, saying: "I am told that it is impossible for a government to change a vote once it is cast. But I have been requested by my Government to record the fact that, were it possible to change our vote, we should like to change it from a veto, a no, that is, to an abstention" (197). Secretary of State Haig had originally ordered Kirkpatrick to vote no, but had later changed his mind on the advice of Deputy Secretary of State Walter Stoessel. The embarrassing about-face represented a low point for American diplomacy during the war, and won no friends for the United States either in Britain or in Latin America. An Argentine diplomat charged that "the United States has no foreign policy at all'' (198).

British troops occupied Two Sisters, another hill west of the capital, on June 2nd; Mount Harriet was also seized at about this time. Also on this day, two Sea Harriers were shot down by Argentine fire, but both pilots escaped injury. On the 3rd, Harriers dropped bales of leaflets over Puerto Argentino, some urging the Argentine commander to surrender, others offering safe conduct for any soldiers willing to lay down their weapons. Also on this date, a British Vulcan bomber was forced to land in Rio de Janeiro after missing a rendezvous with a refueling tanker. On June 4th and 5th, freezing fog shrouded the developing battlefield around Puerto Argentino/Port Stanley, slowing military operations on both sides. In Argentina various government officials and military commanders began making press statements that indicated some doubts regarding the outcome of the imminent battle. Rear Admiral Ramon Asara noted: "It is so unfortunate that so many men have died fighting over these islands. I really do not accept that they justify such a cost. Yes, I would say they are not worth fighting for'' (199). An unnamed Latin American diplomat stated: "I suggest what we are witnessing is an effort to somehow win the defeat'' (200). General Lami Dozo said: "Argentina will have to seek a new place in the world once the Malvinas conflict is over." General Menendez, however, maintained his bravado: "We should not only defeat them, but we should do it in such a way that the defeat will be so crushing that they will never again dare to invade our soil'' (201). Although he spoke very bravely, Menendez nonetheless continued to withdraw his outlying troops to the defense perimeter around Puerto Argentino. The Soviet Ambassador to Argentina, in a thirty-minute meeting with General Galtieri, offered his country's "sympathy with the Argentine people's hard fight against British imperialism'' (202). Costa Mendez pointedly embraced Cuban President Fidel Castro at a meeting of the Nonaligned Movement in Havana, the first visit ever made to Cuba by an Argentine Foreign Minister; he later signed a $100 million trade pact with Castro, telling the Cuban president that he was "astonished that the U.S. has given Britain arms and assistance to kill our people'' (203).

By June 6th British troops had encircled the Argentine defense perimeter, and had begun systematically shelling Argentine positions with guns stationed on the adjoining hills. Major General Moore was quoted as saying: "The Argentines are squeezed into a tight corner. They will be a little more squeezed before we're finished'' (204). Argentine Air Force Brigadier General Jose Miret stated Argentina would not "humiliate itself before the United Kingdom arrogance." Costa Mendez told newsmen that "there will be surprises'' in the forthcoming battle. Denis Healey, spokesman on foreign affairs for the British Labour Party, crticized the government for ruling out future negotiations, saying: "Magnanimity in victory is a precondition of statesmanship. Unfortunately, the Prime Minister seems to have ruled that out. She is behaving toward Argentina rather as Prime Minister Begin behaves toward the Arabs. Although that is an understandable line to take and undoubtedly has a lot of popular support, it is possible to doubt whether it is in Britain's long-term interest" (205).

President Ronald Reagan of the United States made an official visit to England on June 7th; Queen Elizabeth II welcomed him with these words: "These past weeks have been testing ones for this country, when once again we have had to stand up for the cause of freedom. The conflict in the Falklands was thrust on us by naked aggression, and we are naturally proud of the way our fighting men are serving their country. But throughout this crisis, we have drawn comfort from the understanding of our position shown by the American people" (206). Reagan responded by saying that the British troops in the Falklands had fought "for a cause, for the belief that armed aggression must not be allowed to succeed, and that the people must participate in the decisions of government under the rule of law" (207).

Southwest of Puerto Argentino, the British discovered that the little settlement of Bluff Cove had been left vacant by the retreating Argentines. Since this settlement represented another point on the Argentine southern perimeter where pressure could be applied, Moore decided to rush troops into the area by sea, using the landing craft *Sir Galahad* and *Sir Tristram*, rather than risk a slower land movement that might be detected and forestalled. The first landings, on the evening of June 6th, were successful, but were detected by Argentine radar. A second landing scheduled for the early morning hours of June 7th was disrupted by the onset of a winter storm with gale-force winds, the disembarkation being delayed until afternoon. By then the storm had cleared, but the ships' positions had already been reported, and the two vessels were attacked at 2:00 P.M. by four Argentine fighter-bombers. *Sir Galahad* was set on fire by two bombs, and *Sir Tristram* was strafed repeatedly. Fifty men died of wounds or burns caused by bombs and exploding ammunition aboard the ships, and by leaking oil burning on the water. Later that day, Mirage jets sank a small landing craft in Choiseul Sound, and damaged the British frigate *Plymouth* in Falkland Sound. The *Plymouth* caught fire after being hit by bombs, but was able to control the flames with the help of helicopters, and remained in service. The British claimed seven Argentine jets destroyed; Argentina admitted two fighters lost. Also on June 7th, British troops captured Mount Low, north of the Argentine forces. The British reported sixty Argentine soldiers killed during the previous five days in small clashes between patrols near Puerto Argentino. An Argentine Canberra bomber was also reported shot down. Four British troops were reported killed when their helicopter crashed. General Moore urged Menendez to "lay down your arms. Let's end the killing" (208). Mrs. Thatcher told the Commons: "If the Argentines tell us that they are prepared to withdraw, we shall enable them to do so with safety, dignity, and dispatch . . . . otherwise, we shall have to take back by force what the Argentines would not give up" (209). President Galtieri said: "We will fight for weeks, months, or years, but we will never give up sovereignty over the islands'' (210).

On June 8th, Brigadier General Menendez was quoted as saying: "My troops have their feet planted on Argentine territory. They are in excellent physical and spiritual shape.'' Costa Mendez told reporters in Buenos Aires that further talks on a ceasefire would require "a true British desire to negotiate . . . Thus far, Britain has been an emissary of ultimatums and we do not accept ultimatums'' (211). A thousand Argentine prisoners-of-war were removed from the war zone on the converted ferry, the *Norland*, which would transport them to neutral Uruguay for repatriation. Comodoro Wilson Drozier Pedrozo, one of the passengers, formally protested over the British treatment of the prisoners, saying that they should not have been left in the war zone, where they were subject to air attack by their own forces, that they should not have been shipped out through San Carlos Bay, and that they should not have been made to pick up loose ammunition (some of which exploded) around the Goose Green battlefield. Britain responded that the prisoners had themselves volunteered to move the shells and mines, and that San Carlos Bay was the only point from which any troops, British or Argentine, could then be embarked.

On June 10th press reports indicated that Peru had sent ten Mirage jets to Argentina to replace aircraft lost over the Falklands. On that same day tens of thousands of Argentines gathered in the square facing the Presidential Palace to celebrate Malvinas Day, commemorating Louis Vernet's appointment as first civilian Argentine Governor of the Malvinas; the crowds urged President Galtieri to continue the fight against Britain, shouting: "Be strong! Don't back down! Long Live Argentina!'' (212). On June 12th British troops seized Mount Longdon, six miles west of the capital, giving the British control of all the hills surrounding the Puerto Argentino area. On June 13th, British Defence Minister Nott announced that the *Glamorgan* had been damaged by a missile fired from the Argentine shore positions, with the loss of nine sailors; the vessel itself remained serviceable. On June 11th, Pope John Paul II made an official visit to Argentina, where he was faced with banners proclaiming: "Holy Father, bless our just war.'' His response was blunt: all wars, he said, are "absurd and always unjust'' (213). By June 13th, the pressure on the Argentine perimeter was becoming unbearable, as the British moved to within two or three miles of Puerto Argentino. Many of the British warships sailed close to shore, where they could shell the Argentine fortifications continuously. Sea Harriers continued dropping anti-personnel bombs on major troop concentrations. The British marines and paratroopers advanced inexorably on the Argentine positions, forcing constant withdrawals. The hills surrounding the capital sprouted with 105 m.m. guns capable of reaching any target within the Argentine enclave. Clearly, Brigadier General Menendez faced only two possible alternatives: surrender, or wholesale slaughter of his troops, much of it at long range. Tumbledown

Mountain and Mount William were occupied by the British on the 13th.

A new, three-pronged offensive began in the early morning hours of June 14th, and soon broke through the Argentine lines, taking the old British marine barracks, Government House, and the capital's major communications center on Wireless Ridge, all on the outskirts of Port Stanley. By noon the British soldiers had moved into Port Stanley itself, fighting a bloody battle against entrenched, lightly-fortified positions. An Argentine Mirage jet was shot down during the action. As their positions crumbled, many of the Argentine troops broke and ran, scattering throughout the capital. The remnants of the original townspeople huddled together in a brick church, the strongest building in town, and in the sturdier houses. Brigadier General Menendez requested a meeting with Major General Moore about noon, to discuss a ceasefire and terms of surrender. Reportedly, Moore wanted unconditional surrender of all Argentine forces on the islands; Menendez sought to limit the surrender terms to the Port Stanley area, and to delete the term "unconditional." Menendez finally agreed to surrender all the Argentine troops on East and West Falkland if the offending word was dropped. A ceasefire was formally reached by both parties at 4:00 P.M. Falklands time on June 14th, effective 8:59 P.M. The shooting part of the Falklands War had finally ended.

The name of the capital was immediately restored to Port Stanley. The Argentine soldiers were rounded up, stripped of their weapons, and herded together into temporary prisoner-of-war camps. Major General Moore sent a message to the British government, stating: "The Falkland Islands once more are under the government desired by their inhabitants—God save the Queen" (214). Michael Foot, Leader of the Opposition, told the House of Commons: "There will be genuine, widespread rejoicing at the prospect of the end of the bloodshed" (215). Mrs. Thatcher was quoted as saying: "The battle of the Falklands was a remarkable military operation, boldly planned, bravely executed, and brilliantly accomplished. We owe an enormous debt to the British forces and to the merchant marines. They have been supported by a people united in defence of our way of life and of our sovereign territory." When questioned about the future of the islands, she added: "Freedom is expensive to defend. We shall have to extend the airstrip [at Port Stanley] . . . We shall have to have Rapier [missiles], we shall have to have submarines, we shall have to have some ships" (216). David Owen, former Labour Foreign Secretary, countered: "A fortress Falklands will not serve the best interests of the Falkland Islanders. To live for years with the constraint of the Argentine navy interfering with shipping and with possible bombing attacks from the air is no recipe for peace. Nor is the isolation of being cut off from the mainland a tolerable long-term solution" (217). In Argentina the head of the Radical Party, Carlos Contin, stated: "The armed forces have triumphed even with a loss in the Malvinas. We have received them in triumph because they have revived the prestige of the nation" (218).

Another Argentine political leader, Raul Alfonsin, was more blunt: "The government should go now, it should halt this usurpation of power" (219). Jorge Mario Eastman, Interior Minister of Colombia, stated: "Argentina's defeat is a triumph for the [view] that international disputes must be resolved through legal procedures and not aggression" (220).

Rex Hunt, the islands' former governor, was appointed Civil Commissioner; he would share power in the future with the islands' military commander, each attending to his own responsibilities, but both participating in meetings of the Island Councils. Lord Shackleton, who had produced the 1976 report on the islands' economic prospects, was asked by the British government to update his findings, and to make some suggestions about developing the islands in the future. The British were astonished to find over 11,000 Argentines still remaining on the islands, making a total of about 13,000 Argentine troops who had participated in land war. Rear Admiral Woodward noted: "They are already suffering from malnutrition, exposure, trench foot, scabies, and diarrhea, brought on by lack of food and pure water, proper clothing, shelter, and sanitation. Even feeding them for a week presents huge problems" (221). The prisoners of war were repatriated to Argentina as quickly as possible, the first ships leaving by the weekend of the 19-20th. About 600 officers and technicians were held as temporary prisoners in response to Argentina's refusal to accept an unconditional surrender, or to acknowledge that the war was "over." The British also confiscated large amounts of war materiel, including land-based Exocet missiles (one of which had damaged the *Glamorgan* during the last few days of fighting), and plentiful stocks of ammunition.

On the evening of the 14th, President Galtieri was scheduled to make a speech from the balcony of La Casa Rosada, the Presidential Palace. A mob gathered on the Plaza de Mayo in front of the mansion, and began to shout anti-government slogans. Finally the crowds had to be dispersed by riot police. Galtieri gave his twelve-minute address to the television cameras. In his speech, the President blamed the Argentine defeat on superior weapons supplied Britain by the United States. If Britain, he said, can "accept that the situation of the islands can never return to what it was before April 2, . . . we will maintain our attitude of negotiating for the return of sovereignty. [But if they] proceed to restore the colonial regime . . . there will be no security or definite peace, and the responsibility for deepening the conflict will fall on Great Britain" (222). Costa Mendez seconded these sentiments by saying: "What has occurred in no way alters Argentine sovereignty over the Malvinas, and does not affect the decision to continue our struggle on all fronts, opportunities, and forms to gain full recognition of Argentine sovereignty over these islands" (223). He added that the surrender of Argentina was due to "the collaboration and support of the United States" in providing Britain with technologically superior armaments. But the Argentine people, clearly shocked by the outcome of a struggle they had been consistently told they were winning, continued to mount massive demonstrations against the military government of Leopoldo Galtieri. On the evening of the 16th, Galtieri met with his top army generals to discuss the continuation of the war. When he discovered that only two of the fourteen officers (including himself) supported his policy of actively pursuing the war, he promptly resigned, at 6:00 A.M. on the morning of June 17th. The remaining generals chose Major General Cristino Nicolaides, a Galtieri *protege*, as the new army chief, and a full member of the junta. Interior Minister Major General Alfredo Oscar Saint Jean automatically succeeded as interim President, until a permanent successor could be picked. Admiral Anaya also offered his resignation to his group of admirals, but they refused to accept it. The English-language *Buenos Aires Herald* noted: "It is time to get down to the serious business of building the kind of strong, stable, democratic nation Argentina could be, and to leave behind forever the embarrassing stigma of the underdeveloped world where power struggles and stagnation are the order of the day" (224).

On June 15th, Mrs. Thatcher said: "We went to recapture the islands, to restore British sovereignty, to restore British administration. I do not intend to negotiate on the sovereignty of the islands in any way except with the people who live there" (225). She further indicated: "As to the United Nations Resolution [502], the withdrawal by the Argentines was not honoured, and our forces had to go there, because they would not withdraw. Indeed, they had to recover and recapture British territory. I cannot agree with the right honourable gentleman [Michael Foot] that these men risked their lives in any way to have a United Nations trusteeship. They risked their lives to defend British sovereign territory, the British way of life, and the right of British people to determine their own future" (226). On the 16th, there were reports that President Ronald Reagan was pressuring Thatcher to accept a compromise settlement of the Falklands question with Argentina— Thatcher firmly resisted all such persuasion. Argentine prisoners of war broke loose from their captors at Port Stanley on the following day, rioting throughout the town, and setting two buildings on fire before they could be contained. The melee apparently started when the troops were being marched to the *Canberra* for transport to Argentina; a rumor spread through the Argentine soldiers that the vessel was leaving without them. Also on Thursday, the 16th, Peter Blaker, British Defence Minister of State, announced that the official count of British military and civilian dead totalled 255 persons, with about 300 wounded. The British estimated Argentine losses at 700-1,000 killed. Publication of a new Gallup poll in England indicated a 17 percent surge in popularity for Mrs. Thatcher and her government.

On June 18th, amid reports that Britain had begun repatriation of the captured Argentine prisoners of war, the Argentine Foreign Ministry acknowledged in a statement made to the United Nations Security Council that there was a "cessation of hostilities," but noted that the cease fire would remain "precarious as long as the British attitude continues in force, evidenced by military occupation, blockade, and aggression" (227). A "total cessation of hostilities," the Ministry continued, would be possible only when Britain withdrew its land and naval forces from the Falklands, and lifted economic sanctions." Also on this day a curfew was imposed on Port Stanley. The British noted that three civilian residents of Stanley had been killed during the final battle there. Britain also announced that the airstrip near Port Stanley was being repaired and extended by 2,000 feet, and that the H.M.S. *Illustrious*, Britain's new aircraft carrier, was being sent to the Falklands together wth four smaller warships, as part of a regular rotation of men and materiel. Francis Pym, British Foreign Secretary, stated in a radio interview that the new Argentine leaders gave "ground for some hope. We were getting no answers of any kind from Galtieri and the junta before. [We hope] a new regime will come to a rapid conclusion and that it will enable normality to return at long last to the region." Pym noted that Britain wanted Argentina to make an unequivocal declaration confirming that all hostilities had ceased; if they would, he said, he foresaw eventual Argentine involvement in the Falklands. "It will take time. But in the end it will be to the interests of the islanders and the benefit of their future that a normal relationship with Argentina be re-established" (228).

The following day, Saturday, June 19, 1982, marked the last military confrontation of the war, as British ships and troops converged on the South Sandwich Islands, where Argentina had maintained a weather and research station, Corbeta Uruguay, since 1977. Although British helicopters fired some machine-gun rounds into the air, no injuries were reported on either side. The eleven-man Argentine garrison and the 10-20 scientists were captured and repatriated. Also on the 19th, the British liner *Canberra* arrived in the Argentine port of Puerto Madryn with 4,200 Argentine prisoners of war; London announced that approximately 11,845 Argentines had been captured by British forces in the Falklands. The Buenos Aires newspaper, *La Prensa*, reported that "the struggle against the British will be centered [in the future] exclusively in the political and diplomatic field. The three armed forces—although not in the totality of their sectors—are convinced that no warlike actions should be undertaken now or in the near future. There will be a formal cessation of hostilities" (229). Another report noted that Galtieri had been forced to resign because he had wanted to continue an active military effort against the Falklands. Civilian politicians in Buenos Aires took advantage of the governmental chaos to call for return to civilian government. Meanwhile, the top-ranking officers in the three branches of the Argentine military service were meeting continually in an effort to find a compromise candidate for president acceptable to all factions. Brigadier General Lami Dozo put forward his own candidacy, and was supported by Admiral Anaya in an attempt to break the long-standing tradition allowing only army officers to become President.   The stalemate could not be broken, however.

The European Economic Community lifted its economic sanctions against Argentina on the 20th, stating they would be reimposed if war was resumed.   The *Sunday Times* reported that Argentina had been holding seven members of the British Secret Air Service since May 19th; the soldiers had apparently been providing intelligence information on Argentine Air Force plane departures to the British fleet.   A Sea King helicopter which crashed in Chile in mid-May was part of the operation, the newspaper said.   Other newspapers in Argentina interviewed returned prisoners of war, and reported accounts of inadequate winter clothing, poor food distribution, and chaotic logistical support.   A British newspaper stated that the British fleet had been saved by faulty Argentine bombs and duds; at least six British warships had been hit by bombs that would have sunk them, if they had exploded.   Another thousand Argentine prisoners were returned home on June 21st. The high-ranking military officers in Argentina finally proved unable to agree on a compromise presidential candidate;   on June 22nd, the Argentine Army took full power, the Air Force and Navy withdrawing from the junta in protest.   Retired Army General Reynaldo Bignone was named new Argentine President, effective July 1st.   In return for promises from the Navy and Air Force not to obstruct the new government, the Army agreed to hold civilian elections for the presidency in 1983.   General Nicolaides was regarded by most observers as the real power in the government.

Margaret Thatcher flew to Washington to confer with President Ronald Reagan on June 23rd.   Secretary of State Alexander Haig, when questioned by reporters, noted: "I think the Prime Minister is very clear that we wouldn't expect anyone to tell us how to deal with our property, and we're not going to presume to tell her how to deal with hers" (230). Thatcher stated: "[Reagan] didn't raise it [the question of sovereignty] at all.   There is no question of sovereignty to discuss. The only question of sovereignty arises in discussions with the people of the islands.   The islands are British now" (231).   Civil Commissioner Rex Hunt returned to the Falklands in triumph on June 25th.   On June 28th, three British journalists imprisoned on spy charges in Argentina at the beginning of the war were released on bail.   The new Argentine government was sworn in July 1st, after last-minute efforts to bring the Air Force and Navy back into the junta collapsed.   The following day, Argentina released a list of its official losses in the war, including 645 dead or missing in action, and over 1,100 wounded or "sick."   The Argentines claimed 9,804 soldiers had participated in the Falklands fighting.   Also on the 2nd, Britain announced that Rear Admiral John Woodward, Commander of the British naval task force, was being replaced by Rear Admiral Derek Roy Reffell, and Major General Jeremy Moore, Commander of the British ground forces, who was already slated for retirement, was being replaced by Major General David

Thorne.

Argentine Admiral Carlos Castro Madero noted on July 3rd that Argentina now had the capability of building an atomic bomb, and might begin constructing a nuclear-powered submarine within one year. Also on this date the Argentine Army established a commission to investigate published reports of logistical problems during the Falklands struggle. Rear Admiral Woodward, on his return to London July 5th, noted that his task would have been much easier with a full-sized aircraft carrier capable of handling Phantoms, Buccaneer jet fighters, and Gannet early-warning radar planes (232). On the same day, while commenting on the fact that Britain still held 600 Argentine prisoners, most of them officers, the new Argentine Foreign Minister, Juan R. Aguirre Lanari, stated that "an end to the hostilities on the part of Argentina in the South Atlantic exists as fact" (233). Margaret Thatcher named on July 6th an official commission to examine the causes of Britain's failure to prevent Argentine capture of the Falklands, to be headed by Lord Franks.

The Common Market agreed on July 7th to provide $200,000 in emergency aid, and other unspecified amounts in long-term financial aid, to help rebuild the Falklands' economy. On July 8th Argentina released its only acknowledged British prisoner of war, who had been shot down near the capital during May. Mrs. Thatcher announced on the same day that the government would bring back to England the bodies of any Britons killed in the Falklands for reburial in England, if the soldier's next of kin requested it. British military officials noted that the thousands of plastic mines strewn haphazardly over the Falklands were hampering efforts to bury the hundreds of Argentine dead, many of whom remained scattered over the battlefields three weeks after the end of the fighting. Ten soldiers, including one Argentine, were wounded and one Briton was killed by mine explosions while trying to clear the mines from the fields surrounding Port Stanley. British officials also noted that many booby traps had been found in civilian buildings in the capital. Also on the 8th, Commissioner Hunt said that the Falklanders should reconsider their determination to leave the islands a British colony. On the 9th, Brigadier General Lami Dozo said Argentina had lost thirty-four fighters and bombers during the war, but that he expected most to be replaced within the month, saying: "The reversal at Puerto Argentino was only an episode, not the finale." General Nicolaides added: "We remain convinced that the Malvinas are an indivisible part of our territory, and we will not stop until we have reclaimed them" (234).

Britain dropped on July 11th its condition that Argentina formally acknowledge the war's end before the final lot of prisoners would be returned, thereby clearing the way for the repatriation of 593 Argentine officers and technicians. They were returned to Argentina on July 14th. Foreign Minister Aguirre Lanari, however, stated: "We cannot accept any type of condition set by Great Britain for formally declaring an end to hostilities" (235). The United States ended trade sanctions against Argentina on the 12th. By July 13th, inflation in Argentina had reached 400 percent as a result of the war and public disenchantment; the peso fell from 15,000 to the dollar to 40,000 to the dollar within a week. On July 17th the British military office admitted to falsifying many of its press releases during the war to encourage Argentine belief that they were facing overwhelming military superiority. As an example, a spokesman cited the fact that, despite reports to the contrary, only twenty Sea Harriers were actually on duty in the South Atlantic at any one time. Britain lifted its blockade of the exclusionary zone around the Falklands on July 22nd, but suggested that Argentine ships and aircraft stay at least 150 miles from the islands "to avoid misunderstandings." Mrs. Thatcher said that the British forces "continue to have authority to take all necessary measures to protect themselves from attack anywhere in the South Atlantic and to defend the Falkland Islands and the Dependencies, in accordance with the inherent right of self-defense recognized in Article 51 of the United Nations Charter" (236). Argentina responded by saying that it rejected "the existence of zones of exclusion or limits of any kind in seas that pertain to Argentine jurisdiction and . . . any incident that results from their establishment will be the sole responsibility of the United Kingdom." General Menendez and four other Argentine generals involved in the Falklands fighting were removed from their posts on July 26th. By July 30th, the black market exchange rate for the Argentine peso against the United States dollar reached 65,000-1. A report in the August 1st edition of London's *Sunday Times* said that many of Port Stanley's residents wanted to shift their capital to Port Louis, the original capital of the islands, to escape the thousands of mines scattered over the countryside around Port Stanley by the Argentines, leaving the 2,500 British military contingent as the sole residents of that town. By the end of August, the airstrip at Stanley had been lengthened to accomodate a squadron of Phantom fighter-bombers.

In January of 1983 the official report of the British bipartisan panel appointed to investigate the antecedents of the war exonerated Mrs. Thatcher's government from any blame, and stated that the invasion could not have been predicted before March 31, 1982. A Ministry of Defence report criticized press censorship, and concluded that Britain needed to retain a strike capacity in its naval and air forces, with adequate radar warning systems. In mid-January, Thatcher visited the Falklands for the first time; Argentine President Bignone called her presence there "a new act of provocation and arrogance" (237). Thatcher noted: "One thing the islanders have made clear is that these islands are British. They are the Queen's loyal subjects and they wish to stay that way." In March there were reports that Britain would allow visits by Argentine citizens to the graves of their relatives at Goose Green. The Island Legislative Council ruled that such visits would only be allowed if the Argentine government formally declared an end to hostilities. In May a group of Argentine civilians set sail on a private boat to visit the islands, but were recalled at the insistence of their government. A group of British relatives of war dead visited the graves at Port San Carlos in April. On April 2nd, ex-President Galtieri was interviewed by the Argentine newspaper *Clarin*; his blunt remarks about military bungling and incompetence resulted in his arrest on April 12th. He was convicted of violating military regulations, and sentenced to forty-five days in prison.

Margaret Thatcher on May 13th dissolved Parliament and called for new British elections, to be held on June 9, 1983. Her Conservative Party platform indicated that British policies on the Falklands would remain the same, that there would be no negotiations with the Argentines regarding British sovereignty over the islands in the foreseeable future. The Labour Party Manifesto, published March 29th, called for the British government "to restore normal links between the Falklands and the Latin American mainland," stating "that the United Nations must be involved in finding a permanent settlement of the problem" (238). Throughout the campaign, Anthony "Tony" Wedgwood Benn and many other Labour leaders criticized Thatcher for her handling of the Falklands War. Several days before the election, Labourite Denis Healey publicly stated that Mrs. Thatcher had used the Falklands issue for personal political gain; the resulting public outcry was so great that Healey was forced to withdraw his statement later in the day. In fact, the Falklands War had consistently had the backing of a large majority of the British population, as demonstrated from many opinion polls taken on the subject in 1982 and 1983. This "Falklands factor," noted by so many political commentators during the 1983 British elections as a decisive factor in the campaign, gave Mrs. Thatcher, along with other issues, a landslide victory on June 9th. Her 144-seat majority in the House of Commons is the largest margin enjoyed by any British political party since 1945. The Labour Party was left in disarray, its leaders and policies discredited; Tony Benn, head of a leftist Labour faction, lost his seat in Parliament for the first time in thirty years. Party Chairman Michael Foot also seemed destined for retirement by year's end. With the British elections of 1983, with the judgments passed by the British people on its elected leaders, the circle was complete, and the Falklands War, barring any future incursions by the Argentines, can finally be said to have come to an end.

IV
Pekoe and Pekoe:
Two Views on the Falklands
Background to the Interviews;
The Official British Position;
The Official Argentine Position

1. Background to the Interviews

We have attempted in this history to avoid advocacy of any kind, to relate the events as they happened and as they were reported in the media. We support neither Britain nor Argentina. Such views as we do express regarding the war, its background, the participants, and the blunders made by both sides, are given in Chapter V, "Reading the Tea Leaves." Feelings on both sides of the Falklands question run high, and we feel it only proper that representatives of both the Argentine and British governments should have the opportunity to state their respective cases, and to comment on their respective actions before, during, and after the events of 1982. We were fortunate to secure the cooperation of the Argentine and British missions to the United Nations, who graciously granted us interviews with ranking members of their staffs, and subsequently took time from their busy schedules to review the transcripts of the interviews, correct and amend them, and return them to us with commendable speed. We were greatly impressed with the professionalism exhibited by both missions.

The interviews were conducted by Dr. Jeffrey M. Elliot in New York during the last week of April, 1983, over a two-day period. They are presented here exactly as transcribed and corrected by the participants. Extraneous verbal niceties have been pared from the interviews with the consent of both counsellors, to make the written versions more readable. The interviews are arranged in the order received by us in their final form; the arrangement should not be considered as indicative of our support for either country's position.

Representing the British side is Marrack I. Goulding, at the time of the interview Counsellor and Head of Chancery for the United Kingdom Mission to the United Nations. Mr. Goulding was born September 2, 1936, in Plymouth, England. He attended St. Paul's School (London) and Magdalen College at Oxford University, where he earned First Class Honors in Classics. He joined the British Diplomatic Service in 1959, and was sent to Lebanon to learn the Arabic language. He has held a number of important diplomatic posts, including: Political Officer and (later) Information Officer at the British Embassy, Kuwait (1961-1964); a member of the Arabian Department at the Foreign Office in London (1964-1968); Head of Chancery at the British Embassy in Tripoli, Libya (1968-1970); Head of Chancery at the British Embassy in Cairo (1970-1972); Private Secretary to the Minister of State at the Foreign and Commonwealth Office in London (1972-1974); a member of the Central Policy Review Staff at the Cabinet Office in London (1975-1977); Counsellor at the British Embassy in Lisbon (1977-1979); and Counsellor and Head of Chancery at the United Kingdom Mission to the United Nations in New York (1979-1983). He was appointed British Ambassador to Angola in May of 1983. Mr. Goulding is married, with three children.

The Argentine view is expressed by Raul Alberto Ricardes, Counsellor for the Argentine Mission to the United Nations. Dr. Ricardes was born March 23, 1945 at Buenos Aires, Argentina. He graduated as a lawyer from the School of Law and Social Sciences at the University of Buenos Aires in 1963, and later received his doctorate in international law from the same school in 1973. He was a Parvin Fellow at the Woodrow Wilson School of Public and International Affairs, Princeton University, from 1974-1975. Ricardes entered the Argentine Foreign Service Institute on March 1, 1972 as Vice-Consul, finished the course there in December, 1973, with the second highest average in his class, being promoted to Third Secretary. He was subsequently promoted to Second Secretary in 1976, First Secretary in 1979, and Counsellor in 1982. Ricardes has served in the Treaties' Section of the Legal Department and in the Latin American Department in the Foreign Office in Buenos Aires; he has also served in the Department of International Cooperation of the Under-Secretariat of International Economic Affairs there. Since 1978 he has been part of the Permanent Mission of Argentina to the United Nations. His special assignments have taken him to Geneva, India, Sri Lanka, Cuba, Nicaragua, and many other countries. In addition to his diplomatic posts, Ricardes has also been a Professor of History at the No. 2 National School "D. F. Sarmiento" in Buenos Aires, a Professor of History and Law at the National School of Buenos Aires, University of Buenos Aires, and an Interim Professor of International Public Law at the School of Law and Social Sciences, University of Buenos Aires.

2.   The Official British Position: An Interview Conducted by
Dr. Jeffrey M. Elliot with M. I. Goulding, Former Counsellor and Head of Chancery, United Kingdom Mission to the United Nations

JE: What in your opinion are the basic issues behind the Falklands conflict?

MG: The first key issue is that, in the Falkland Islands, you have a community—a small community in terms of numbers of people (approximately 1,800 inhabitants). It is, however, a community which exists as a community and has been there for a very long time. Indeed, many of the islanders have been there for six or seven generations. These people regard the Falklands as their home—they were born there, reared there, educated there, worked there, gave birth to their children there. They have very clear views about the future of that territory—about the kind of life they wish to lead. That's the first salient fact.

The second is that the sovereignty of the Falklands has long been subject to dispute. The Argentines believe that the islands belong to them. They believe that the islands were wrongly taken from them in 1833. Discussions related to sovereignty have been going on for many, many years. The dispute had been dormant for a long time, but it was revived by the Argentines in 1965. The last round of discussions took place in February, 1982. We participated in those discussions in good faith in an effort to find a solution to the differences between ourselves and the Argentines. Then, suddenly, for no apparent reason, those discussions were suspended and a military attack was launched against the Falkland Islands. This came out of the blue. Indeed, at the end of the February talks a joint communique was agreed to in which both sides expressed satisfaction with the negotiations process. Then, six weeks later, we suddenly discovered that an Argentine fleet was sailing toward the Falklands. This created a situation which no responsible government could accept. It is intolerable that, because of a dispute over sovereignty, one party—in this case, Argentina—should take the law into its own hands, and break every article of the United Nations Charter, in a naked attempt to occupy the islands by force.

The British Government was extremely reluctant to use force to repossess the islands and went to great lengths to avoid having to do so. We explored, we believe, every possible avenue which could have led to a peaceful settlement of the dispute. We endorsed fully the efforts of Secretary Haig, with whom we cooperated in every way, in order to devise some kind of settlement—perhaps an interim agreement—that would be acceptable to ourselves and the Argentines. Those attempts failed. In addition, we supported the efforts of the Secretary-General of the United Nations, Mr. Perez de Cuellar, to work out an acceptable settlement. On May 17th, we proposed such a settlement—one which would have given the Argentines considerably more than they have today. However, the Argentines rejected our proposal—one which, I might add, was based firmly upon the principles elaborated by the Secretary-General of the United Nations. This left us no choice but to repossess the islands by force—something which, as I say, we were reluctant to do, but which in the end we were obliged to do.

JE: There are those who contend that this was a war that neither country wanted, fought over a place that neither country needed. Why was it so important to recover the islands?

MG: The first word that comes to mind is "principle." We cared little that these were remote islands, with few inhabitants, and that they were of little or no material value to Great Britain. These facts are relatively unimportant. This is a territory for which, and for whose inhabitants, we are responsible. In recent years, we have had many discussions with the islanders about their relationship with Argentina. We knew very clearly—because they told us in no uncertain terms—their views about Argentina. We knew very well that they did not want to be subjected to Argentine rule. No responsible country which finds that its territory, or part of its territory, is occupied by a foreign power, can permit such aggression to go unchallenged. This was particularly true in the case of the Falklands, where the inhabitants were told after the Argentine invasion that they could no longer speak English, that their education would be drastically altered, that no broadcasts would be permitted in English, and that they would have to drive on the right hand side of the road instead of the left. In short, we could not accept a situation in which 1,800 people, or 180 people, or 18 people should be subjected against their wishes to the domination of a foreign power which had no right to be there.

JE: It has been said that, while the Falklands were a matter of national pride to the British, there were other reasons why it wanted to repossess the islands, including their natural resources—i.e., oil, natural gas, krill—and to divert attention from a rather shaky domestic political and economic situation at home.

MG: The latter suggestion I reject with contumely. It's a cheap shot. To suggest, as the question does, that a prime minister would sacrifice 255 lives, as well as undertake the enormous risks associated with an operation of that kind, all in the interest of political expediency, is too ridiculous to merit a response.

The former suggestion is marginally more respectable. But the British Government has, at no time, been motivated by concern for the potential wealth or resources of the islands. Rather, the British Government recognizes that the Argentine claim to the Falklands constitutes a problem for the United Kingdom—constitutes an obstacle to good relations with an important country in South America with whom we desire good relations. It is for this reason that we explored numerous avenues in discussions with the Argentines and the islanders. Sadly, we failed in our efforts. But it was not our fault that we failed. At no stage in those negotiations—going back some fifteen or seventeen years—was there any truth in the charge that Great Britain was clinging to the islands to take advantage of the potential wealth or resources of the region.

Our concern, from the very beginning, has been to resolve the problem between ourselves and Argentina in a way that would be acceptable to the islanders—I stress this point, "in a way that would be acceptable to the islanders," because that is the nub of the problem.

JE: Were you surprised how quickly and fiercely the dispute became a war?

MG: The British Government was surprised, very surprised, that the Argentines should attempt to invade the islands. As I've said, we had been in discussion with the Argentines for a very long time. The Argentines had just put forward proposals for giving a new form to those discussions. We were considering their proposals. We were totally surprised that the Argentine Government, having just advanced those proposals, and having themselves characterized the last round of discussions as being "positive," should launch an unprovoked attack on the islands. So, yes, we were surprised.

JE: Throughout the discussions, did the British Government take the position that the question of sovereignty was negotiable? Did your government approach the negotiations with an open mind on this issue?

MG: Oh yes, it was discussed. The question of sovereignty was included in the discussions, subject to the caveat that the British Government would not be prepared to accept a solution on sovereignty which was not acceptable to the islanders.

One of the ideas which was discussed was an idea called "leaseback." Under leaseback, the United Kingdom would have ceded sovereignty to Argentina in return for a long-term lease of the islands by Argentina to Great Britain, perhaps for a period of 100 years, so that the islands would have remained under British administration. This would have ensured the perpetuation of the British way of life. This was tried out on the Argentines, as well as the islanders. The Argentines did not say yes, but they did not say no. The islanders, however, were quite opposed to the plan. They felt that there would be insufficient safeguards to protect their interests under such an arrangement. Having witnessed what took place in the Falklands last year, one can only have sympathy for the islanders' position.

JE: Why do you think Argentina challenged Great Britain in the Falklands, knowing full well that, should war erupt, it was not a war they were likely to win?

MG: I query the basic premise of that question. I don't think that when the Argentine junta took the decision to invade the islands, they believed that it was a war they could not win. Indeed, I think that their supposed military advantage was one of a series of miscalculations by the Argentine Government. First, they miscalculated the British reaction. I do not know for certain, but from what I've read, my impression is that they did not believe that the British Government would react militarily to the seizure of the islands. Secondly, they miscalculated the international reaction. Again I am speculating, but my impression is that they believed that their seizure of the islands would be hailed by the international community as a "legitimate act of decolonization." Thirdly, they miscalculated what would actually happen on the battlefield. Still speculating, my guess is that they thought that if they actually gained possession of the Falklands—which is 350 miles off their coastline and 8,000 miles off ours—they would enjoy a military advantage. But, as has been shown in past wars, geography and equipment and numbers of troops are not always enough—morale and training are equally important factors. I read, not long ago, that the Pentagon had concluded that it was the superior morale and training of the British forces, not superior equipment or numbers of men, that won the war.

JE: Do you consider United States support of Argentina, as evidenced in that now-famous vote in the United Nations, a betrayal of Great Britain?

MG: There were four important United Nations votes that bear on the Falklands Conflict. First, the initial resolution—502—which was a British draft adopted by the Security Council on April 3rd by a vote of ten in favor, one against, and four abstentions. Secondly, there was Resolution 505 of the Security Council, which was adopted unanimously in May. Thirdly, there was the resolution tabled by Panama and Spain in early June, which was vetoed by the United States and the United Kingdom. Those were the three votes in the Security Council. Then there was the vote in the General Assembly on November 4, 1982. The General Assembly resolution was tabled by the twenty Latin American members—counting Haiti as Latin, for this purpose. The United States voted in favor. The American position was particularly interesting; if you analyze the vote, you will find that the United States voted in favor with the Communist bloc, the radical Third World countries, and Israel, while almost all Western countries and most of the moderate Third World countries abstained or joined with Britain in voting against. That's the way the vote went.

If you ask me to assess United States support for the United Kingdom, I would run to superlatives. The support of America throughout this long and difficult period was superb. This is clearly evidenced by Secretary Haig's efforts and by United States support of the British position in the several rounds in the Security Council. Now, as for the vote you asked me about—the vote in the General Assembly in November—this vote came after the dust had settled, nearly five months after the Argentines had surrendered in the Falklands. There's no point in making any pretense about it; there is a difference of perception between the United States and the United Kingdom about where we should go from here. The American Government is inclined to think that there should be negotiations about sovereignty. We take the firm position that there should not. That difference of view was expressed in the vote in the General Assembly. But it is a perfectly legitimate difference of opinion between two countries which remain close friends and allies. So, I would not make too much of that vote, though I don't deny that we tried very hard to persuade the United States to abstain on that resolution.

JE: How likely is it that British military forces will be withdrawn from the islands, and a solution found to the problem of sovereignty?

MG: The British Government has taken the position that it will not negotiate. It's our view that it's too soon to talk about negotiations at this time. It may be possible sometime in the future, but for the moment it is offensive—and "offensive" is the right word, because it causes offense in the United Kingdom—that the Argentines, the guilty party, the party that broke all the Charter principles relating to the peaceful settlement of disputes, the non-use of force, and self-determination, should come piously to the General Assembly six months after their offense and call for negotiations. That is the height of hypocrisy. The British Government is not ready, nor are the islanders ready, to sit down around a table with the Argentines and talk about sovereignty. We are, however, very ready to talk about normalizing relations. We are ready to talk about restoring diplomatic relations. We are ready to talk about lifting commercial embargoes. But we are not ready to talk about the transfer of sovereignty over the Falklands to the Argentines.

The Argentines, in statement after statement, have made it very clear that they are only interested in one outcome to any negotiation. They see negotiation as being an inexorable process leading to the transfer of sovereignty over the Falklands from the United Kingdom to Argentina and to the imposition of Argentine rule, with all that that implies.

JE: Do you support the British Labour Party's call for negotiations, including negotiations about sovereignty, once the furor over the Falklands has died down?

MG: I'm not sure that the Labour Party has said that they would be prepared to enter into negotiations with the Argentines on an open agenda at the present time. But they have certainly taken the view that the United Kingdom should be ready to enter into negotiations with the Argentines, a position which the British Conservative Government does not now share. I would, therefore, be opposed to such negotiations—at least for the present.

JE: As you look at the Falklands War, and the status of public opinion in Great Britain, would the people of your country tolerate a government which, at the present time, called for negotiations? Would not that position be disastrous politically?

MG: I don't know the answer to that question. That's a question which could only be measured by taking a poll on that specific point. My impression is that there is a general feeling in the United Kingdom, as in other countries, that when you've got a problem, you should talk about it. But the crucial question is what the reaction of Parliament would be. In Great Britain, both of the major political parties have, since 1965, explored various avenues for resolving the issue. But neither has succeeded in finding the basis for a negotiated solution which would be acceptable to Parliament. That is why there can be no question of negotiations of a kind which would lead to the transfer of sovereignty to the Argentines. Parliament would not accept such a solution.

It may well be that, if you took a straw poll in the United Kingdom today, people would say, yes, we ought to have negotiations. If, however, you think ahead to the kind of outcome that might emerge from those negotiations, it is very difficult to envisage Parliament accepting any solution which would be acceptable to the Argentines—unless, of course, there is a complete change of heart on the part of the Argentines. The events of last spring and summer have, I suspect, reinforced that view in Parliament. Clearly, it would be even more difficult now for Parliament to accept any solution that was not wholly agreeable to the islanders.

JE: Is there any evidence to suggest that the Argentines might be preparing now or in the near future to attack the islands a second time?

MG: I know of no "hard evidence" to that effect and, if I did, I probably shouldn't be able to talk to you about it. What we do know, however—and we view it with great concern—is repeated belligerent statements by Argentine spokesmen in which they talk about a second war or about never relaxing the struggle until the Argentine flag is flying proudly over the islands, and so on. There seems to have been no reduction in the fervor with which Argentine civilian and military leaders support the cause of recovering the Falklands, and sometimes they give expression to that support in rather worrying and bellicose terms. We are, therefore, having to maintain a substantial garrison in the Falklands to ensure that if the Argentines are foolish enough to make another military attempt to seize possession of the islands, we can resist that attempt with the necessary force.

JE: How long can the United Kingdom bear the economic burden of the Falklands? Does Great Britain have the resources necessary to rebuild the islands and provide for their continued welfare?

MG: Unfortunately, I do not have detailed figures in hand. It is a substantial cost, but a perfectly bearable one. It's an exaggeration to suggest that the British budget will become unbalanced because of the cost of maintaining the present garrison in the Falklands.

Regardless of the costs, however, we get back to the question of principle. The principle is an important one, and it is worth defending. We cannot and will not abandon principle for the sake of dollars or pounds. To do so would be to impeach our honor and credibility. We cannot allow that to happen.

JE: Britain's victory over Argentina in the Falklands, while cheered by the British people, did not touch off dancing in the streets, but was instead greeted with more of a feeling of gratitude than a sense of celebration. Why?

MG: Really, it was a mixture of all those things. It certainly precipitated feelings of joy, cheering, and excitement. When a ship came home, there was considerable excitement—a localized thing, such as a parade in London or whatever. Overall, the attitude of the British people was, I think, one of satisfaction with regret—satisfaction that a job that had to be done had been well done, but regret that the job had

had to be done at all. There was not, however—and this has been misrepresented in Britain, too—an outburst of national chauvinism. Instead, there was tremendous grief that 255 British people had lost their lives, as well as grief for the hundreds of Argentines who died in the conflict. So the reaction, certainly now, a year later, is quite a sober one.

JE: With what you've said about the Argentine invasion, I wonder why your government would even consider the thought of negotiations in the near future. How could such negotiations be justified in the face of what you describe as Argentine aggression?

MG: Let me preface my answer by saying that Argentina is an important country in South America—a country which historically has had very close ties with the United Kingdom. After all, there are large numbers of people of British descent in Argentina. It is a nation with which we would like to have good and close relations.

Before the conflict, we believed it was possible to negotiate a solution which, while it would not satisfy the Argentines completely, would remove a major irritant to our relations with them. We tried out several possible solutions, as I've said, but with no success.

Since the conflict, our attitude toward the negotiations has changed fundamentally. As your question implies, the Argentines have demonstrated by their actions on the 2nd of April that they were not negotiating in good faith. They have demonstrated that when they talk about the interests of the islanders, they are simply using empty words, for they showed absolutely no respect toward the interests of the islanders while occupying their territory. This has changed our attitude toward them.

And, of course, Argentine actions have likewise changed the attitudes of the islanders, who now view them with anger and suspicion. I must repeat: the islanders are central to any future settlement of the dispute. I am not saying that negotiations are ruled out forever. But negotiations about sovereignty are certainly out for now. We are very ready to talk to the Argentines about ways of normalizing our relations and putting this problem to one side, if you like. But until there is a fundamental change of heart in Argentina, we will remain exceedingly reserved about any negotiation about sovereignty.

JE: Is there a danger that the British might conclude too much from their success in the Falklands—the danger that they may hark back to the days of Empire?

MG: My short answer to the question is no. We are a country which prides itself on realism and pragmatism. The United Kingdom has had to adjust its views, in particular, its view of its role in the world. That adjustment is continuous. But I don't believe, myself, that in any influential circles in the United Kingdom there are any illusions about Britain's power in the world. We are a powerful country. However, we are not going to be misled by our victory in the Falklands campaign into trying to recreate the British Empire or any nonsense like that.

JE: What steps is your government currently taking to fortify the islands against future Argentine aggression? What contingency plans do you have in the event of an Argentine attack?

MG: I cannot talk in detail about that. I can, however, make some general comments. Prior to the Argentine invasion in April, we had eighty men stationed in the Falklands. Today, we have considerably more than that. Moreover, we have fighter aircraft there now, which we didn't have before. We also have ships stationed there, which we didn't have at the time of the invasion. We are confident that we have taken sufficient precautions to ensure that a future Argentine invasion would be strongly and effectively opposed.

JE: The British Government, according to the Argentines, is trying to whitewash the guilt of its "unlawful occupation" by invoking the right of self-determination of the inhabitants of the islands, knowing full well that this is a specious issue—that the islanders have no legitimate right to self-determination. How would you respond to this charge?

MG: It is a very familiar argument. The Argentines have argued, and continue to argue, that the principle of self-determination, one of the most important principles enshrined in the United Nations Charter, can be set aside in the case of the Falklands. They justify their argument by saying that the Falklands were illegally seized from Argentina in 1833.

Well, you can crawl forever over the history of what happened between 1780 and 1833. Indeed, a number of other nations—Spain, France, Argentina, the United States—could base a claim to sovereignty over the Falklands on those events. We base our claim on the fact that, since 1833, there has been a settled British population in those islands who regard them as their home, and who have been there for six or seven generations. If you were to accept the Argentine argument that everything that has happened since 1833 should be ignored, you are, in effect, saying that the frontiers of the world should be redrawn as they were in 1833, or any date that might be arbitrarily chosen. This violates the very principle of self-determination that has been the basis of both the League of Nations and the United Nations—namely, that self-determination applies to the settled inhabitants of a territory at the time, and that they alone should decide their fate.

The Argentines wouldn't accept for a moment that the future of Argentina should be determined by the descendants of those who were there in 1833. There has been an enormous immigration into Argentina since that time. Nobody is saying that those people or their descendants should be disenfranchised. Throughout the continent of South America, indeed North America too, if you are going to freeze the political picture at some distant point in the past, you are going to produce grotesque results. If that argument is pursued, who are the indigenous inhabitants of Argentina today? After all, as I've said, Argentina is a country of immigrants. The great majority of Argentines and their ancestors have been in Argentina for a much shorter period of time than the Falklanders have been in the Falklands.

JE: Throughout this conflict, the Falkland Islands Company Ltd., has come in for considerable criticism. Indeed, the Argentines charge that the company controls most of the land and possesses a virtual monopoly on goods and services in the islands. Is the presence of the Falkland Islands Company an impediment to peace?

MG: I would respond to that contention by saying first, and generally, that there's been a great deal of misrepresentation concerning the role of the Falkland Islands Company. The Argentines, early in this conflict, seized upon the Company, calling it "exploitative," and attempted to capitalize on that allegation in their propaganda. I would refer to the comments made by representatives—elected representatives—of the Falklanders, who visited the United Nations to express their views on the subject. For them, the Falkland Islands Company is an integral part of the life of the islands.

To repeat, the Falklands are populated by 1,800 people. Their main occupation is sheep-farming for wool. Wool is a commodity whose price goes up and down in the world market. It is only with a financial, if you like, institution of the size of the Falkland Islands Company that the individual sheep farmer has protection against the ups and downs of the market. The Company can afford to buy the wool at a reasonable price, from the viewpoint of the farmer, and hold it until the market improves before selling it. The individual sheep farmer in the Falklands can't do that. The Falkland Islands Company may look a bit old-fashioned to some, but it performs a very important economic function in the Falklands by protecting the islanders against fluctuations in the world wool market.

JE: What role did Prince Andrew play in the war? Was he merely a flag-waver or did he engage in actual combat? Why was he sent to the islands?

MG: Prince Andrew was not sent as a flag-waver. He is a serving member of the British Armed Forces, and, as it so happened, the ship he was in during those very rushed days in early April was included in the task force. There was no question of withdrawing an officer from his ship simply because he happened to be a member of the British Royal Family. So, Prince Andrew went with his ship, and he engaged in combat duties like the other young officers.

JE: Has the Falkland Islands Government been restructured since the war? Have any fundamental changes been made in the governmental system and its relationship with the British Crown?

MG: No, not really. There have been no elections since the war. The last election took place in December of 1981. There have, however, been some changes made in the government. Before the war, there was a governor of the islands. The functions of the governor are now shared between a civil commissioner and a military commissioner. This was brought about because of the introduction of comparatively large numbers of troops into the islands. The armed forces now outnumber the civilian population in the Falklands. So, it's sensible to have a military commissioner to deal with military-related matters and a civil commissioner to deal with the rest.

JE: Are all major policy decisions made jointly by the two commissioners?

MG: Well, both commissioners are essentially executors of government policy. That policy is formed by the British Government collectively in London. In addition, the civil commissioner has responsibilities similar to those the governor of the islands used to have, in relation to the formulation and execution of policy at the local level. But at the macro level, the policy is made by the British Government in London, and executed by the civil and military commissioners.

JE: Clearly, the war was extremely costly, both in terms of lives and money. Do you see any positive things coming out of the conflict?

MG: Almost none, I would say. The conflict has been a wholly disagreeable experience—something we would fervently have wished never to happen. There is the positive satisfaction for Britain of having done well a job that had to be done. But the consequences for the islanders were entirely negative. They've had their way of life disrupted, brutally disrupted. They were very badly treated by the occupying forces. They've had their islands peppered with mines—plastic mines—which will take years to clear. They've had a large portion of their livestock killed and eaten by the occupying forces. They now find, because of the continuing threat from Argentina, a garrison stationed in their islands which exceeds them in number. They've had a lot of publicity and attention focused on them, which they don't especially like. Their way of life unhappily has been disrupted for a long time to come.

As far as the United Kingdom is concerned, we've lost 255 men. We lost a number of ships. And the taxpayers incurred a lot of expense. All of this was necessary to defend a principle, but none of it was welcome. So, I think it's very difficult to identify positive results from the conflict. I wish it had not happened. I wish the Argentines hadn't been so foolish as to invade the islands.

JE: When Argentine forces arrived in the Falklands in April of 1982, they had orders, they maintain, to avoid bloodshed at all costs. Moreover, they offered immediate compensation for what little damage had been done there, and made special provisions to avoid friction and misunderstanding. Does this explanation square with the facts?

MG: No, not at all. I know Mr. Cheek, who is a member of the elected Falkland Islands Legislative Council. I respect absolutely his honesty and integrity. If you gave me time, I could produce all sorts of details which would substantiate what Mr. Cheek told the United Nations about Argentine aggression and mistreatment. In sum, I would point to several major abuses, to wit: People were herded into uncomfortable living quarters. People were held, in groups of fifty or so, in a community hall for thirty-eight days. People were driven from their homes and kept in confinement on other islands. There was whole-sale and indiscriminate raiding of livestock. There was expropriation of private buildings for occupation by the Argentine forces. There were instances of rough treatment of islanders by individual Argentine officers. And anti-personnel mines were scattered indiscriminately and without record. The list goes on and on. It was a very rough occupation.

JE: After Argentina surrendered to the British in the Falklands, General Galtieri was forced to step down as president. Since then, a great deal of finger pointing has ensued in Argentina. Indeed, in the spring of 1983 Galtieri was arrested for trying to shift the blame for the Argentine defeat from himself to his subordinates. Are you surprised by the public reactions to the Argentine defeat? Does it give you cause for concern?

MG: Well, as I've already said, we are concerned—very concerned—about recent developments in Argentina. We feel that Argentina continues to pose a threat to the Falklands. That is why we must maintain a large garrison there.

I have not, however, been surprised by the reaction. We know that the Argentines harbor bitter resentment over the outcome of the war. It seems to be universally held in Argentina that the Falklands belong to them. It's something that Argentine children absorb from the moment they take their first suck at their mother's breast. It is dinned into them at school. And Argentina's leaders exploit it to full advantage.

The failure of the attempted seizure of the islands last April has clearly been a major shock, a trauma, to the body politic of that country. Therefore, it came as no surprise that General Galtieri should try to shift the blame, and that there should be a strong counter-reaction in the armed forces. There is no illusion on the part of the British Government about the passion with which the people of Argentina believe that the Falklands belong to them. Equally, I would like to think that there is no illusion in Argentina about the determination with which the British Government holds to the view that one cannot simply write off the interests of the 1,800 inhabitants who regard those islands as their home and have done so for many generations.

JE: Did Prime Minister Thatcher talk directly to General Galtieri prior to the outbreak of war? Did she attempt to dissuade him from taking the actions that he did?

MG: I don't think a conversation of that kind took place. General Galtieri had not been in power for very long at the time of the Argentine seizure of the islands. The discussions—the continuing discussions we had had with the Argentine Government—had been taking place at the ministerial level, rather than at the head of government level. When it looked, in the last days of March of last year, as though the Argentines were planning to do something foolish, we made several approaches to them. However, I am pretty sure they were all made by, or in the name of, Lord Carrington rather than Mrs. Thatcher. Those exchanges came to an end when the then Foreign Minister, Dr. Costa Mendez, said that the diplomatic channel was closed.

JE: Could your government have anticipated the response of the Argentines in seizing the islands, on the basis of what they knew of General Galtieri and the political climate in Argentina?

MG: The answer is no. We knew that General Galtieri was particularly attached to a desire to "recover" the Falklands for Argentina. But we were, if you like, misled by the way in which his people had taken part in that round of negotiations in February, and were therefore taken by surprise when the attack was launched at the beginning of April.

JE: Earlier in this interview I asked you why the Falklands were so important to the British. I wonder why you think the islands were so important to the Argentines, to the point that they would risk war, international condemnation, and the loss of life and materiel.

MG: I don't know. That's a short answer to your question. It's a puzzling phenomenon. I don't know Argentina myself. I can only speculate that successive Argentine Governments have found it convenient to build up the Falklands controversy as an external issue on which they could concentrate popular feeling. It's a familiar phenomenon in these regimes which aren't terribly democratic or parliamentary. I suppose it was thought by the rulers of Argentina to be convenient to have an external issue on which they could whip up public enthusiasm, perhaps to distract the public from other more serious problems. That's really the only explanation that comes to mind.

It seems, however, that almost every Argentine believes that the Falklands belong to Argentina, and that it is a sacred national cause to "recover" those islands. One has to recognize that, and accept it as a fact of life. Likewise, I hope they would recognize that it is a fact of life that we are not prepared to accept imposition of an alien and unwanted regime on 1,800 people who treasure their own way of life in territory which they regard as belonging to them and which they have inhabited for six or seven generations.

JE: Asked about the Argentine invasion, the Panamanian representative to the United Nations argued that invading the island was the only way Argentina could dramatize for the world a claim it had been making continuously for 150 years. Can you understand their frustration over the negotiations process and their ultimate decision to invade the islands?

MG: The argument is rather like the argument about the chap who likes the look of the car next door, and so attempts to persuade the owner to part with it on his terms. When he fails, the chap pinches the car, claiming that he had exhausted all other avenues. The fact that you want something doesn't necessarily mean that you have a right to it.

I would make the same point to the Argentines if we were negotiating the issue today. Indeed, we told them—over and over—that if they wanted to obtain sovereignty over the islands, they would have to convince the inhabitants that that was in their interest. The Argentines said, in response to that, "Look at all those Welsh people in Patagonia. They're quite happy living under Argentine rule. Why can't the Falklanders be happy living under the Argentine flag?" We said then that it was up to the Argentines to persuade the islanders that such was the case. The Argentines had opportunities to do this. In this regard, the Communications Agreement of 1971 is much talked about. It's an agreement which caused some heartburning to some people in Britain who felt that it would permit the Argentines to put a foot in the door. Under the agreement, the Argentines were to provide sea communications, air communications, etc. There was another agreement under which they would supply oil products to the islands, and so on. Those agreements gave them opportunities to establish direct contact with the islanders. It gave the two sides an opportunity to learn more about each other. It is, I think, quite possible, that if the Argentines had allowed more time, perhaps a generation or two, they might have succeeded in winning over the islanders' confidence. After all, a generation or two isn't that long in matters of this kind. Had they been patient and continued to establish rapport with the islanders, they might have persuaded them to take a different view about their long-term relationships with Argentina and Britain. They could have gradually built a closer relationship with the islanders. But you don't woo a lady by raping her, which is what they did. Their decision to invade the Falklands has put off for a very long time indeed any chance they had of convincing the islanders that it was logical—geographically, politically, economically—to move towards a close relationship with Argentina.

JE: No single episode in the war so upset world opinion as the seemingly heartless British sinking of the Argentine cruiser, *General Belgrano*, in which a total of 321 Argentine sailors were killed. In retrospect, was this action a mistake? If you had it to do over again, would you have taken the same action?

MG: I think it would be presumptuous of me to express a view on that. At the time, we were in a state of war with Argentina. Ships were being sunk, planes were being shot down, and people were being killed. The judgment of the commanders on the spot was that the *Belgrano* presented a threat to the task force. It is not for me to say that they should have suppressed that judgment because there were public relations disadvantages associated with sinking the *Belgrano*. In that sort of situation, you really do have to leave it to the commanders on the spot.

Moreover, I would say that your question somewhat exaggerates the public relations damage that we suffered as a result of the sinking of the *Belgrano*. It was terrible that so many Argentines were killed. But people were killed on our side, too. There was a war going on. And in war people die. That's why war is so ugly. I do not think, however, that here at the United Nations we suffered greatly because of the sinking of the *Belgrano*. There is talk here about how the President of Peru's initiative was sabotaged; it is said that it was about to succeed, but that it was literally torpedoed by the sinking of the *Belgrano*. From having been involved in those negotiations, I do not believe that that was the case. There were much bigger factors which decided the fate of the President of Peru's initiative, or Secretary Haig's plan, or the Secretary-General's ideas.

JE: Speaking of former Secretary of State Alexander Haig, how would you assess his contribution to the peace process? Did he make a significant contribution?

MG: He made an enormous contribution. He worked extremely hard. He explored every possible avenue. He succeeded in retaining the trust of both sides, which is no mean feat in that sort of situation. He did everything that could possibly be done to achieve a negotiated settlement. It was not his fault that he failed. Nor was it our fault. The fault must be placed directly upon the guilty party—the Argentines.

JE: The Argentine Government contends that, from the very beginning of the negotiations, they repeatedly offered to grant guarantees and protections to the islanders under the auspices of the United Nations—that they wanted very much to preserve the lifestyle of the inhabitants of the Falklands, as well as their customs and traditions, with the primary goal of respecting their interests. Does this claim square with your understanding of what took place?

MG: All the evidence suggests that those are just empty words. After the Argentines proclaimed, on April 2nd, that they had restored Argentine sovereignty over the Falklands, what did they proceed to do? They changed the curriculum in the schools. The official language was changed from English to Spanish. Broadcasts in English were stopped and shortwave radios were confiscated. And, again, it's a small thing, but it had a certain presentational importance—the islanders had to drive on the right hand side of the road, instead of on the left. It doesn't matter very much, given the small number of cars in the Falklands. But it's a symbol, if you like, of the attitude of the invading forces—the occupying forces. And they were hell bent on assimilating the islanders as quickly as they could into the Argentine cultural system.

JE: Do Argentine citizens have the legal right to purchase property in the Falklands, and do they enjoy all other civil rights regarding the disposition of property?

MG: There are, as your question suggests, restrictions on the freedom of Argentines to purchase real estate in the Falklands. There are many countries which restrict the right of "foreigners" to acquire real estate. In the Falklands, there was a special reason for doing so. The Argentines made no secret over the years of their desire to obtain sovereignty over the islands. If Argentine citizens enjoyed unrestricted freedom to buy real estate in the Falklands, the Argentines could, over a period of years, transform the population of the islands into an

113

Argentine population. The islanders do not want that. It was the Island Council—the elected representatives of the people—which adopted legislation limiting the "right" of Argentines, or indeed, any other foreigners, to acquire real estate in the islands.

JE: According to the Argentine Government, the so-called representatives of the British settlers in the Falklands do not represent the opinions or aspirations of the inhabitants. They are, they claim, "puppets" of the United Kingdom. Is there any truth to this charge?

MG: I would say that that line of argument illustrates how little the Argentines understand the problem. In no sense can the Island Council be described as a "puppet" of the British Government.

Indeed, British governments have, over the years, presented a number of ideas to the Island Council. Some of these they have strongly opposed. As a result, we have decided not to pursue further those particular ideas. So it's quite wrong to think of the Island Council as an instrument of the British Government.

I want to reiterate my answer to your very first question. The islanders are a population in their own right, who have lived in that part of the world for a very long time and who regard it as their home. They don't have any other home. Their home is not in the United Kingdom. They belong to the Falklands. And that's the territory in which they want to go on living.

Neither the Island Council nor the Falklanders are puppets of the British Government. If the Argentines had been able to persuade the islanders—and that was the challenge the Argentines faced—that they could continue to enjoy their present way of life under the Argentine flag rather than the British flag, then the possibility might have existed that they would have chosen Argentine rule. That possibility still exists in theory, though in practice, as I have said, the events of last April have made it highly improbable. The important point is that the British Government will continue to respect the islanders' right of self-determination. It is up to them to choose.

JE: The Falklands War, insists the Argentine Government, is a classic example of a large nation which sought to cling to its colonial possessions and maintain its privileges through the use of domination and force. What truth is there, if any, in this charge?

MG: I would invite the Argentines who say that to go back to their dictionaries to see what the word "colonialism" actually means. Colonialism means the imposition by one country of its rule over some other country, by implication against the wishes of the population. If you look at the history of decolonization, the people who were under colonial rule have decided that they wanted to rule themselves. Initially, the colonial powers, including, I confess, the United Kingdom, were reluctant to agree to that, and pressure had to be exerted by the colonial peoples to persuade the colonial powers to grant them their independence. It started, in our case, with India in 1947, and the process accelerated in the 1950s and '60s. In every case, we granted independence in response to the wishes of the people of that territory. Now, there are a number of territories, remnants, if you like, of the British Empire, where the people have chosen not to become independent. Basing ourselves foursquare on the principle of self-determination, we have respected that wish.

It's not just a case of territories whose inhabitants have white faces, as the Argentines are quick to suggest. For example, you have the Turks and Caicos Islands, an island territory in the Caribbean of some 6,000 people, all of whose faces are black. The British Government discussed with their elected leaders the possibility of independence and put forward a package of proposals, including a substantial amount of aid from Great Britain. But the people of the Turks and Caicos Islands chose not to become independent. They held an election and decided to remain a United Kingdom Crown Colony. I don't hear anyone complaining about that being an unacceptable example of British colonialism. The United Nations Committee of 24 visited the islands, observed the election and, if you like, gave the result the United Nations seal of approval.

The Falkland Islands are another case in point. This is not a case of foreign settlers occupying a territory against the wishes of the inhabitants. It is in no way similar to Southern Rhodesia, where the white settlers occupied a territory in which they were outnumbered twenty or thirty to one by the local inhabitants. It's a territory in which the inhabitants themselves wish to maintain the status quo, and under the principle of self-determination that is their right. The Argentines cannot pick and choose, and say, okay, you can have self-determination in one territory but not in another.

The Falklands have been a non-self-governing territory, to use United Nations parlance, ever since the United Nations was founded. We have reported every year to the United Nations on our administration of the islands, as we've reported on our administration of the other non-self-governing territories which remain under British rule. Under Article 73 of the United Nations Charter, which sets out very clearly the ground rules for the administration of non-self-governing territories, it is stated quite specifically that the interests of the inhabitants should be paramount. So, I come back to the point that the Argentines cannot pick and choose, and say we should have self-determination here but not there. We believe that our administration of the Falklands is entirely consistent with that chapter of the United Nations Charter which lays down the ground rules for countries charged with the administration of non-self-governing territories.

JE: As a longtime diplomat, does what has happened in the Falklands make you less optimistic about the value of diplomacy? Are there limitations to the power of diplomacy? If so, what?

MG: No, not at all. I regret enormously that shots had to be fired. I regret enormously the foolishness of the Argentines in seizing the islands. I regret enormously the stupidity of Argentina in not accepting the proposals for a negotiated interim settlement which we put forward, and which, from Argentina's point of view, were quite generous. If they had accepted those proposals, the Argentine flag would be flying over the Falklands today, alongside the Union Jack and United Nations flag.

JE: Can your government accept now, or in the future, joint administration of the Falklands? Would this be an acceptable solution to the problem?

MG: I won't say "never," because that's not a word you're supposed to use in politics. But I really can't see it. The British Government responded positively to the Secretary-General's ideas—a year or so ago—for a kind of interim United Nations administration. This was a last ditch effort to avoid an armed conflict, in which Britons and Argentines would be killed. The Argentines wouldn't accept it. And so we had to use force to repossess the islands. That really changed everything. Would the islanders now accept joint administration? Why should they? And why should they allow the Argentines back into the islands, when Argentine troops behaved so badly last April, May, and June, when they're still trying to rebuild their livestock from the depredations of the Argentine armed forces, and when their kids still can't go out and play because there are mines all over the islands?

So, joint administration might have been a possibility in May and, indeed, we put forward a proposal similar to, but not identical with, joint administration, when we responded positively to the Secretary-General's suggestion of a United Nations administration on an interim basis. But the proposal lapsed when the Argentines rejected it and obliged us to use force to recover the islands.

JE: Finally, historians are fond of looking for lessons in conflicts of this kind. Is there anything that can or should be learned from the events in the Falklands?

MG: That question requires a lot of thought. Off the cuff, I would mention two lessons. First, you should always plan for the worst. When you're dealing with certain kinds of regimes, you should never assume that reason is going to prevail. You should always, in your planning, allow for the foolish and irrational act.

Secondly, and this is of course a United Nations point of view, I believe that the conflict illustrated very clearly the continuing relevance of the principles laid down in the United Nations Charter and the desperate need for member states to carry out their obligations under the Charter if disaster and bloodshed are to be avoided. If Argentina had respected those principles—self-determination, peaceful settlement of disputes, non-use of force, respect for the decisions of the Security Council—many hundreds of lives and many billions of dollars would have been saved, on both sides.

3. The Official Argentine Position: An Interview Conducted by Dr. Jeffrey M. Elliot with Dr. Raul Ricardes, Counsellor, Argentine Mission to the United Nations

JE: From your perspective, what lies at the heart of the Malvinas controversy?   What is the key issue or issues behind the conflict?

RR: The controversy, as the public sees it, dates back only to April of last year, with the outbreak of war in the Malvinas. That phase of the dispute with Britain is now just a prologue. We must emphasize the new face of the conflict and put the issue into proper perspective.

For Argentina and, for that matter, the entire world community, this is an important issue—one which must be resolved in the interests of justice and fairness. The nature of the question was clearly defined by the British Government in 1946, when they included the Malvinas on their list of non-self-governing territories. This simple act reveals the essence of the problem—at least in part—and suggests the reasons for the conflict which ensued.

In the international arena, the nature of the dispute between Argentina and the United Kingdom was clearly defined by the United Nations in 1964. In that year, the Committee on Decolonization thoroughly considered the situation. The result was United Nations Resolution 2065. This measure called for the decolonization of the Malvinas.

Let me draw the issue more sharply. This is a dispute involving sovereignty between two nations: Argentina and Great Britain. The only way this issue can ultimately be resolved is to find a solution to the problem of sovereignty. That is the essence of the problem. In finding such a solution, many factors must be considered, chief of which is the interests of the inhabitants. My government has long been concerned about the welfare of those who reside in the Malvinas. Indeed, we have made it very clear—to the Falklanders, to the British, to the United Nations—that we will take positive steps to ensure the welfare of those who inhabit the Malvinas. And our commitment goes well beyond words. We are prepared to guarantee the individual rights and privileges of the islanders. These guarantees would be mandated by Argentine law, as well as by special statutes which could be negotiated between both governments, and guaranteed by an international organization, such as the United Nations.

I am optimistic about the future. From my perspective, I hope it will be possible, in the not too distant future, to resume negotiations with the United Kingdom. My government is prepared to begin such talks. And we are prepared to abide by whatever agreements are mutually agreed to. It is vital, I think, that these negotiations reflect the spirit and intent of past United Nations initiatives, and that our actions demonstrate our commitment to justice, equity, and peace.

JE: It has been said by some commentators that the Argentine Government believed, from the very beginning of the Malvinas war, that the British would not respond militarily, that they would voluntarily surrender the islands without a fight. Is this true?

RR: Any answer I could give would be speculative. As you know, there is no document which suggests that this was indeed the case. Here at the United Nations, we have been working as diplomats to achieve a viable diplomatic solution to this dispute. Others can speculate about this or that. No good would be served by rehashing the details.

I think that, instead of going back in time, we must look to the future. We must put our heads together and attempt to work out an acceptable solution. When we look to the past and, in particular, the conflict itself, I don't think we are creating the conditions necessary for future negotiations. After a conflict—any conflict—there are negotiations. The framework for these negotiations was established by the United Nations General Assembly almost twenty years ago. The decision taken by my government to recover the islands was one which I am not in a position to define. I cannot tell you all of the factors which figured in that decision. The fact is, however, the Malvinas belong by historical right to Argentina. The British Government has no legal right to them. They were taken by force by the British in 1833. At the time they were taken, they were of strategic importance. And they are equally important today, though for somewhat different reasons. As you know, in those times there was no communication between the Atlantic and Pacific Oceans, other than through the Magellan Strait. The way to control the area was by controlling the Malvinas.

If you look at a map of the nineteenth century, you will see very clearly that the policy of the British Empire then was to control the principal links between the seas and oceans. This strategy was not limited to the Malvinas. One need only look at Cape Town, or Malta, or Gibraltar, or Cyprus. These were all part of a strategy adopted by the British Government, which viewed the Malvinas as strategically important, in order to control Latin America. This fact cannot be ignored. It is central to the entire dispute. The British would prefer to ignore this fact. But it will not go away. It is a fact.

JE: As you see it, what should now be done to heal the wounds inflicted by this conflict, to work out a mutually acceptable agreement between the two sides?

RR: As you know, after a conflict, there are two paths which can be pursued: the emotional one and the rational one. Ever since the end of the war, we have followed the emotional path. We must now, before it is too late, begin to walk the rational path. That is the only path that offers any real hope for a permanent solution to this problem. No other path will lead to real negotiations, and, certainly, no other path will result in an acceptable resolution of the dispute.

What we must do now, I think, is to build upon the actions taken by the United Nations—specifically, the General Assembly—and attempt to work out a solution which is compatible with the Charter of the United Nations. Our best hope is direct negotiations between the two parties involved. Moreover, I think that we in the United Nations can play an important role in resolving this conflict. The Secretary-General, Mr. Perez de Cuellar, has demonstrated great leadership and resolve in this area. Hopefully, he will be able to help us find a way out of the darkness which surrounds the present situation.

JE: Has the British Government shown an interest, since the end of the war, in returning to the negotiating table and working out an acceptable solution?

RR: No, it hasn't. It has shown no interest whatsoever in resuming negotiations. As the newspapers suggest, the British Government views the Malvinas conflict as a political tool, one which the Conservative Government has attempted to exploit to full advantage. For political reasons, they believe it would be unwise to resume negotiations concerning the Malvinas. This is, I think, a grave mistake. We should not play politics with peace. It is too precious to endanger for political reasons. There is no capital to be gained, in the long run, by exacerbating this situation. It will only make it more difficult to solve the problem. The time has come for negotiations. We must demonstrate a firm commitment to that process. Politics as usual is unacceptable. The future of the Latin American region demands much more. My government believes that peace is possible. But it will take effort. We are not afraid of that process. We welcome it. We want to build a lasting peace, one which is anchored in the time-honored principles of the United Nations.

JE: What overtures has your government made, if any, to reestablish dialogue with Great Britain on this matter? How have your efforts been received?

RR: My government has said publicly many times, as well as in notes we have sent to the Secretary-General, that we are ready to reestablish negotiations according to the principles enunciated by the General Assembly. I don't think that the policy of "Fortress Malvinas," which seems to be the attitude of the British Government at the present time, is helping the situation. It is only making future negotiations more difficult. The only way to reach some sort of solution of a permanent nature is to reopen negotiations. Short of that, we cannot solve this problem. We must not be afraid to talk. Clearly, it is better to talk than to fight. And the problem will not go away by pretending it doesn't exist. It does. And we must face it squarely. My government is prepared to do just that. Hopefully, the British will recognize that it is in their interest to join us in that effort.

JE: Why should the British Government, given Argentina's invasion of the Malvinas, reopen negotiations? Even if the British Government were inclined to talk, would the British people tolerate a government which made concessions to a nation which launched a military attack on territories it regards as its own?

RR: Yes, I think so. I wouldn't, however, like to get into a lengthy discussion of the internal political situation in the United Kingdom. We do not like to meddle in the internal affairs of another nation. But

I think that reopening negotiations is something which the British Government, be it this government or another, now or in the future, will have to take into consideration. No nation, however large or powerful, can ignore international law. Great Britain belongs to the United Nations. As a member, it is pledged to support the actions of that body. The United Nations has said, on several occasions, that the present situation is unacceptable. A solution must be found to the problem of sovereignty. We must put an end, once and for all, to the legacy of colonialism which exists in the Malvinas. Colonialism is incompatible with the principles of the United Nations. It does violence to the very ideals upon which that organization was founded. The world community will not turn its collective back on subjugated peoples. And it will not permit any nation, whoever it may be, to exercise such control over a people. Sooner or later, Britain will have to face this fact. The days of colonialism are gone. These are new times, and they demand a new ethic. Subjugation is unacceptable to freedom-loving people. We cannot permit such behavior to go unchecked. It threatens the very foundations of world peace and international law.

JE: In Argentina, the military defeat, instead of uniting the country, seems to have polarized it. How deep and widespread is citizen discontent? What steps is your government taking to defuse the issue and reassure the nation?

RR: I can tell you with certainty that all major Argentine political parties, regardless of their ideological orientations, accept two basic facts. First, the Malvinas War was fought over sovereignty. And all political parties support Argentine sovereignty over the islands. To solve that dispute, we must pursue the path of negotiations. So, all political parties are squarely behind the position adopted by my government and endorsed by the last session of the General Assembly. Second, our interest in, and commitment to, the Malvinas is not rooted in political advantage, but in international law. The Malvinas are a national cause. This is a national cause for our government, our parties, and our people. This position will not change, regardless of who is in power. So, the next constitutional government will consider the question of the Malvinas as a national priority. And the resolution of the Malvinas controversy must be solved through mechanisms established by the United Nations.

JE: After the Argentine defeat in the Malvinas, General Galtieri was pressured to step down as president. Not long ago, he was arrested for public statements in which he attempted to blame the military for Argentina's defeat. Is Galtieri responsible for what happened, or is he simply a convenient scapegoat?

RR: After a conflict, particularly one which ended as unhappily as the Malvinas, there can be a real shock to society. We are now living in the wake of that shock. This war has jolted the body politic of Argentina. It has touched a deep chord in our people, and it has produced strong emotions.

Despite the events of recent days—which are inevitable and understandable—there is basic agreement among the various political parties which will assume power at the beginning of next year, that we must reach some sort of national consensus regarding Argentina's role in the world community. One of the most significant issues in this regard is the Malvinas. We are a developing country, we are a Latin American country, we are part of the Third World bloc of countries. As such, we must look to other nations in similar positions with similar goals and aspirations. In the Malvinas war we enjoyed the unqualified support of the Latin American Continent. That is because these nations understand only too well the real issues which precipitated the conflict.

Our primary objective is to put an end to colonialism, particularly in the Malvinas. The objective of the Latin American countries, as former colonial territories themselves, is to oppose any colonial presence on the continent. No issue is more sacred to us than our freedom. And we will not rest until that freedom is secured. The Malvinas involve the freedom of Latin America. It is that simple. The Malvinas symbolize the colonial struggle that has plagued our continent for hundreds of years. We cannot rest peacefully knowing that colonialism is alive in our midst. It is a cancer which must be rooted out.

JE: With the Malvinas War now history, what lessons will emerge from this conflict? What has the war taught your country, both about itself and the rest of the world?

RR: When the war ended, we were forced to examine the whole chain of events which had ensued. This resulted in a reevaluation of the position of our country in the world community. And, as I stated earlier, Argentina will continue to view itself as a developing country. As such, we will undertake those initiatives which speak most profoundly to our special interests and concerns.

The Malvinas War has strengthened our ties with other Latin American nations, and has reestablished our commitment to other developing countries. We must forge new alliances and look for new bases of cooperation. In this regard, we must seek new means of technical, scientific, and economic cooperation with those nations which share our values and goals.

I think the decision taken by the European Economic Community during the Malvinas Conflict was no doubt an illegal one. No nation should be able to impose sanctions against another, except in the framework of a mandating Security Council resolution. The United Nations Charter states quite clearly that it is the Security Council, and only the Security Council, which should have the power to impose such sanctions. The European Economic Community instituted sanctions because Argentina was determined to rid the region of the vestiges of colonialism. I don't understand why the European Economic Community has not imposed similar sanctions against other countries who have clearly violated the territorial integrity of other nations. Despite clear violations by these nations—serious violations threatening world law and order—the European Economic Community has chosen to ignore the matter. Instead, they chose, for whatever reasons, to single out Argentina for selective punishment. This is both discriminatory and unfair. It reveals a clear double standard. And it confuses principles of justice and equity.

JE: Following the adoption of United Nations Resolution 1, the United States Government applied coercive measures against the Argentine Republic and gave its support, including material support, to the United Kingdom. Did the American actions surprise your government? Had you counted on receiving its support? How have American actions affected relations between the two countries?

RR: I don't think there will be a significant change in American-Argentine relations. Keep in mind, the United States voted in favor of Resolution 37/9. This was a very significant action by the American Government, as it reaffirmed that government's commitment to international law. Moreover, it signified support for the resumption of negotiations, and the need for working out a long-term solution to this problem. So, the United States during the General Assembly did not side with the United Kingdom against Argentina. It endorsed the very principles for which we fought and continue to fight so hard today.

JE: Will United States support of Britain in the Malvinas force Argentina to turn more toward the Soviet Union in the future?

RR: As the question suggests, there has been considerable speculation to that effect. Such thinking, however, fails to take into account the nature of Argentine foreign policy. We've had very good trade relations with the Soviet Union; these began to develop around 1974 or 1975. And they continued to improve during the period 1976-1981. So, no, there has been no real change in our relations with the Soviets. Trade relations with the Soviet Union are important to our economy. Trade relations with the Soviet Union are important to our economy.

What the Soviet Union said, through its government, is that the colonial situation in the Malvinas must end, that the issue of sovereignty must be resolved. And it voted in favor of those resolutions which supported our view as to what should be done to resolve the problem.

JE: It has been said that, at a minimum, United States backing of Britain in the Malvinas will cost it the support of Argentina, in opposing Fidel Castro's mischief-making in South America. To what extent is this true?

RR: As you know, we received clear and open support from the Latin American Continent during the Malvinas Conflict. Cuba was one of those nations which endorsed our position. And, like the Soviet Union, we have normal relations with the Cuban Government. But this has very little to do with ideology *per se*. The fact that we received support from Cuba does not mean that both our countries share ideological identity . . . We have good relations with the Soviet Union and Cuba, as we have good relations with the United States and France. Our goal is good relations with all countries. This does not necessarily presume ideological agreement.

JE: In the Malvinas Conflict, Argentina received almost universal support from its Latin American neighbors. However, several countries, such as Mexico, deplored your government's use of violence to gain the islands, and only Peru offered military aid. Why, if your position was just, did you not receive wider and deeper support from the rest of Latin America?

RR: I don't think that the Mexican Government was hostile to our position—quite the contrary. Don't forget that last year, when twenty Latin American countries asked for inclusion of a special agenda item to be considered in the plenary sessions on the Malvinas situation, the document was signed by the President of Mexico. I think this symbolizes the extent of the support our position enjoyed in the Latin American bloc.

In your question, you make a distinction between the issue of sovereignty and our alleged use of force. I can assure you that, on this issue—namely, the future of the Malvinas—we have received and will continue to receive the unqualified support of the Latin American Continent. This is especially true now that the war is over. This brings us back again to the issue of sovereignty, which is the bottom line in this dispute.

JE: As you look at the situation today, do you have any real hope that the issue will be resolved? Are you optimistic about the chances for a negotiated settlement?

RR: Here, you're asking for a personal opinion. And I will give you my personal opinion. I am a lawyer, so I believe in law. I am a diplomat, so I believe in diplomacy. I was born in Argentina, and I have studied not only the history of my country, but world history in general. And I believe that, as one English historian has stated, all conflicts between states must be put in historical perspective. In this sense, I think that the Argentine flag will one day fly over the Malvinas. This is inevitable. It is only a question of when.

In the end, we will prevail—not through force or threat of force—but through reason and law. Peaceful negotiation is our strongest weapon, as right is clearly on our side. The days ahead will require reason and understanding, patience and determination. These are the very essentials of diplomacy. And because I believe in diplomacy, I believe we will be successful in the end. There is no alternative. Force or violence will not result in a permanent solution. If anything, they will forestall such a solution.

JE: Does Argentina have plans to rearm and again attempt to recover the islands by force?

RR: No, we have no such plans, now or in the future.

JE: Given the present situation, why would your government preclude a military invasion in the future? Might you not be successful?

RR: The Argentina people believe in democracy. And we believe in peace. Regardless of the differences which divide us, all major segments of the body politic believe that this dispute can best be resolved through peaceful means, and carried out through diplomatic channels. As you know, national elections will be held in Argentina on October 30th, and there will be a new government sworn in on January 30, 1984. Whichever party wins, they will support the resumption of diplomatic negotiations. The vast majority of Argentines—government officials, army officers, and lay citizens—support this point of view.

JE: How would you assess the costs of the war? How extensive were your losses in terms of life, money, materiel, and pride?

RR: For a nation such as Argentina, which has experienced one crisis after another, there comes a time when that nation must take stock of itself and of its place in the world. The Malvinas War underscored the need for genuine constitutional reorganization, for greater political, economic, and social stability.

JE: Will Argentina, as a result of the Malvinas War, have trouble in securing international loans in the future? Without futher credit, won't the economy collapse, causing certain chaos?

RR: No, I don't think so. I don't think the war has had a profound effect on the economy. The economic situation in my country was not good in 1981. The economic plans which were implemented during the preceding six years were not as successful as most would have wished. The economy was in trouble prior to the war. Perhaps the war contributed to the problem, but it did not cause it.

JE: Among the 13,000 or so troops camped upon the Malvinas for the seventy-four days of the occupation, perhaps 90 percent are said to have lacked intensive combat training. Was this a major contributing factor to the defeat your country suffered? If so, what military lessons have you learned from this experience?

RR: Now that the war is over, it will be necessary for the armed forces to make a thorough evaluation of their professional skills and readiness. Actually, that is something which is taking place at the present time. Once that analysis is completed, programs and policies will be implemented to correct some of the failings suggested by your question.

JE: It has been said that pride, patriotism, politics, and economics motivated the Argentine invasion. To what extent is this true? Which motive was the strongest?

RR: I think you left out the most important motive—namely, principle. We sometimes forget that there are principles worth fighting for, worth dying for. Our actions in the Malvinas were motivated by principle. As I stated, what we have in the case of the Malvinas is a foreign occupation—one which took place over 150 years ago. These islands were taken by force, by the British, in 1833. They have no legitimate right to the islands. The Malvinas belong to Argentina. And it is our aim to recover our territory.

The United Nations Charter makes it crystal clear that no nation, however large or powerful, has the right to threaten the territorial integrity of another. This is a fact of international law, one which is accepted by the entire world community. We believe that all nations are bound by this stricture—and that includes the United Kingdom. Justice demands that we recover our territory. No nation could do less. We cannot permit Great Britain, because of its power, to run roughshod over the territorial rights of Argentina. To do so would be to encourage international lawlessness. And that we cannot allow.

JE: Does your government support now, or will it in the future, joint administration of the Malvinas? Will you accept a compromise of this kind, or will you insist upon complete sovereignty?

RR: That is something I cannot answer at the present time. What I can tell you now, in broad terms, is that we are ready to open negotiations, and to explore various options for resolving this dispute. But I cannot tell you what will be the position of the next constitutional government. We will have to wait and see.

JE: Throughout this interview, you have expressed great faith in the negotiations process. What makes you think, given the fact that negotiations have been taking place for more than eighteen years, that they will prove any more successful in the future than they have been in the past?

RR: I think that the process of decolonization is at an end. And the Malvinas problem is part of the problem of decolonization. We are living in a new age—an age in which science, technology, communications, etc., have linked the world community in new and closer ways. The days of empire are gone forever. The world will not accept colonialism or its manifestations. And so, I am optimistic—optimistic because I can sense the direction in which the world is headed. The tide is irresistible. It is only a matter of time until the Malvinas problem will be settled. And when it is, it will be settled upon terms favorable to Argentina. In the end, right will prevail.

JE: During this conflict, the Argentine Government repeatedly challenged the position of the Falkland Islands Company, Ltd. and its hold on the area. Why has your government been so critical of the Company and its influence?

RR: As I said, we respect and will continue to respect the customs and traditions of those who inhabit the Malvinas. We will protect their rights, as we would hope they would respect ours. We are a nation of immigrants, a nation of diverse peoples from diverse places. Indeed, there are many nationalities currently residing in Argentina. Each is free to pursue its own economic interests. In fact, there are large numbers of Britons presently residing in Argentina. These individuals live and work with no problems. They respect the legal framework of Argentine society, and they operate within the economic guidelines in which all citizens operate. At the same time, they have been protected and supported by all Argentine governments in their efforts. We have no objections to such activities or to any other lawful activity they want to develop in our country.

In the case of the Falkland Islands Company, we believe that it wields too much influence in the islands, so much so that they maintain a virtual stranglehold on the economic life of the territory. We would like to see an economy which respects the basic economic and social rights of the people. On the other hand, the Company has significantly distorted the nature and extent of our involvement in the Malvinas, giving the outside world a very biased picture of our interests and concerns. Also, the Falkland Islands Company, which in fact has a monopolistic control of the economy in the islands, has always pressured the British Government to defend its own best interests.

JE: If Argentina were to attain sovereignty over the Malvinas tomorrow, how would life be different?

RR: As you know, our government is organized along the lines of a national federation, quite similar to that of the United States. I think that my government would be ready to accept that, within the limits of the confederation, the inhabitants of the Malvinas would have absolute guarantees of their rights, their language, their religion, and all of those things which presently unite them. We have no desire to destroy their culture, their traditions, their way of life. That would be wrong. And we will not resort to such practices. They will have the right to live and work much as they presently do.

JE: The Argentine Government has said, on numerous occasions, that it wishes to protect the interests and rights of the islanders, but the question arises as to how these statements square with your country's behavior while occupying the islands. For example, Mr. Cheek, an elected member of the Legislative Council, has stated that during the occupation, Argentina ignored the democratically elected leaders of the island; imposed restrictions on free speech; placed limitations on movement and communication; interfered with the daily work practices of the islanders; shot, beat, confined, and harassed the local inhabitants; smashed, soiled, and looted private property; and showed a basic contempt for the rights and opinions of the inhabitants. How can you reconcile such statements with what you've just said?

RR: Unfortunately, Mr. Cheek has never had anything good to say about Argentina, and I think that he has been quite partial and emotional. Despite his allegations, there is not a single documented case of the kind which you suggest. At no time have we violated the personal integrity of the islanders or encroached upon their basic freedoms. The only charge which has a ring of truth—and it is grossly exaggerated—is that, during the occupation, some livestock were accidentally killed. In this case, compensation was paid to those islanders who were affected. But that is the only example of such misconduct, if you could call it that, with any evidence to support it, and we must also remember that there was a state of war.

JE: The Falklanders contend that, like any other peoples, they have the right to determine their own future. If they wish to retain their ties with Great Britain, don't they have that right?

RR: This goes back, once again, to the issue of sovereignty. Do the 1,800 inhabitants of the Malvinas have the right to self-determination? No. Keep in mind, the territory we are talking about was seized illegally by the United Kingdom, and the lawful inhabitants of the islands—the Argentines—were sent away and replaced by British subjects. So, really, these people are arguing for self-determination for the British in our territory. Self-determination just doesn't apply in this case. That is why we cannot recognize such a right. To do so would be to legitimize the presence of the United Kingdom.

JE: What do you think explains the fact that, by and large, the major media in the United States endorsed the British position in the Malvinas War? Did the reactions of the American media surprise you?

RR: No, they didn't surprise me. The media in the United States have, for quite some time, presented a very distorted picture of Argentina and its people. As you know, the relationship between Argentina and the United States was not particularly good during the Carter administration. I must say, quite candidly, that the media paid very little attention to the rights of the Argentines in this conflict, choosing instead to focus almost exclusively on the occupation itself. The position of the Argentine Government was, in most cases, either distorted or not presented at all. When it was presented, the media did so through Argentine officials. This created an impression of partiality. The American public thus concluded that they were hearing a partisan view of the conflict. Had those same views been expressed by television anchormen, they would have evoked a greater feeling of objectivity.

JE: There are many who believe that, despite the claims of the Argentine Government, the sovereignty issue was quite peripheral to the war in the Malvinas. In reality, they argue, the war was a convenient way for the Argentine Government to divert attention from a deteriorating political and economic situation at home. The Malvinas, they contend, were used to unite the people and distract them from the more compelling problems which plagued Argentine society. How would you respond to such charges?

RR: Unfortunately, in conflicts of this kind, people harbor a great many misconceptions. The sovereignty issue was *the* issue which motivated our actions in the Malvinas. Otherwise, it would have been difficult, if not impossible to marshall the support necessary to prosecute the war. After all, our people are not stupid. They will not march off blindly into war. The war must be justifiable. And the people of my country are not so naive or gullible that they will believe anything they are told by their leaders. They are not willing to spill their lives and fortunes for the sake of political expediency. No, the sovereignty issue was the main force behind the war. No other issue figured into our considerations.

JE: What impact did the political and economic sanctions voted by the United States and other nations have on Argentine society? How did these measures affect the war effort? Are their effects still being felt?

RR: These days, I think, the situation is changing, and the links between the European Economic Community and Argentina are slowly being reestablished. I think the possibility is good that we will once again have normal relations with these nations, despite what has happened over the past year or so. It is not in our interests, nor theirs, to break off relations. Such relations are to our mutual benefit.

JE: If you were to address your country in the aftermath of the Malvinas war, and you had an opportunity to speak to them about the war and its meaning, what would you say?

RR: I would tell them what I told you earlier—namely, that in any conflict of this kind, we must pursue two paths: patience and imagination. I think we must demonstrate new resolve in exploring the diplomatic avenues open to us, and I think we must look for new and different ways of resolving this situation. That is the challenge before us.

JE: Finally, if you had a similar opportunity to address the American public, what would you tell them about the war?

RR: I would tell the American public that we, as Argentines, regard the support they gave us during the last session of the General Assembly as an act of justice, and that it is our hope that the United States will continue to maintain a fair position in the future. I hope and trust that our support in America is strong and solid, as we regard our relations with your country as important, and bound for mutually convenient improvement.

We understand that the United States has close links, historic links, with the United Kingdom. But at the same time, I think the American people should remember that they too were once part of a colonial empire, that they too had to fight a war of independence, that they too needed the support of other nations in that struggle. Today, we are in a similar position. This is a war of independence. We are fighting to reclaim territory that is ours by right. No one can doubt that right is on our side. And while we understand America's close ties with Great Britain, we would hope that Americans would understand that we are only doing what they did several hundred years earlier. The spirit of America lives in the minds and hearts of the Argentine people, who want no more and no less than the Americans wanted in their own revolution.

V
Reading the Tea Leaves
Claims and Blames;
To the Last Dregs;
Prognostications

1. Claims and Blames

In chronicling a war like the Falklands Conflict, one is left with a series of unanswered and perhaps unanswerable questions regarding rights, responsibilities, claims, and blames. Who really owns or should own the Falklands? Why did two apparently civilized nations go to war over a group of 2,000 worthless islands in the South Atlantic? Could the fighting have been prevented? Why did Argentina lose and Britain win? Could the outcome have been changed? How do military experts assess the strategy and weaponry used in the war, and how will these affect planning for future conflicts in other parts of the world? Finally, will there be another war or series of wars in the Falklands, or can a negotiated settlement finally be reached? We will examine these questions in order.

In looking at the historic claims made by Argentina and Britain for sovereignty over the Falklands/Malvinas, one is struck by the obvious sincerity of both sides, and by the absolute impossibility of reaching a fair and impartial decision based upon existing evidence. Some assessments can be made, however. If we regard the first sighting of the islands as a basis for sovereignty, Spain would seem to have the stronger case, based upon Francisco Camargo's apparent description of the Falklands in 1540. It should be emphasized, however, that none of the early supposed sightings are certain; determining the actual discoverer of the Falklands with any degree of assurance may be impossible at this late date, due to lack of supporting documentation. If we regard actual occupation of the islands as a basis for claiming sovereignty, the Spanish again have the stronger case, based upon succession to the French colony of 1764, which France sold to Spain three years later; the French colony existed a year before the British settled Port Egmont. However, both the British and the Spanish withdrew their colonies, thereby leaving themselves open to charges of abandonment, and perhaps negating their original claims. If we regard proximity to the

Argentine mainland as a basis for sovereignty, Argentina would seem to have little case, since the Falklands lie beyond the 200-mile territorial limit claimed by Argentina and generally recognized by most countries around the world. If we regard Argentine succession to Spanish claims as a basis for sovereignty, Argentina has at best a dubious case, since 1) Spain abandoned its colony on the Falklands; 2) although Spain administered the Falklands through Buenos Aires, such arrangements are and were common for the sake of expediency, and by no means necessarily indicated that the Falklands were considered part of the South American mainland—the Falklands always had their own governor; and 3) Argentina did not succeed to any part of the Spanish Empire except southeastern South America, which may or may not have included the Falklands. The Argentine claims to sovereignty over the Falklands Dependencies, on grounds that they are governed from Port Stanley, seem spurious, for reasons stated above. Britain has controlled and occupied these islands from their respective discoveries.

Argentina did occupy the Falklands itself in 1820, and maintained a tenuous colony until the British displaced them. It is upon this fact that Argentina's strongest claim is based. But even this claim includes its share of deficiencies, the chief being that Argentina never actually controlled more than a small section of the Falklands, that part near Puerto Soledad, during its twelve years of occupancy. The sealers and whalers who used the islands as a way station did not acknowledge Argentine sovereignty or control, and generally refused to pay taxes for their catches. Argentina's half-hearted attempts to impose its authority over these transients failed. Further, the Argentine colony never consisted of more than fifty or a hundred settlers, and these few colonists made few attempts to farm, raise livestock, or otherwise conduct themselves as permanent residents. Still, there is no doubt that the acting Argentine governor was forcibly ousted from the islands by the British, and that this displacement was protested by the government of Argentina as a breach of its sovereignty. The grounds cited by the British for imposing control are dubious at best. In fact, the Argentine assertion that the British were seeking to control the seas near Cape Horn is probably correct.

Such changes of sovereignty among colonial possessions of the great naval powers of the day were common to the end of the nineteenth century, generally resulting from major or minor wars between one or another countries, or personal adventurism by officers largely working autonomously, thousands of miles and months sailing time away from their home bases. Naval captains and even high-ranking army officers were a law unto themselves—witness, for example, the unauthorized British incursion into Argentina in 1806. During the age of imperialism the great powers were suitably imperialistic, ignoring the niceties when they wished. So it was in the Falklands.

Given the justice of the Argentine protest over what was probably an illegal seizure of the islands by Great Britain, what justice is there in the British position? In fact, irrespective of the circumstances surrounding British occupation of the islands in 1833, the British have physically governed the islands longer than all of the previous owners combined. Further, neither Argentina nor Spain had made any attempts to develop the islands, beyond Vernet's grandiose schemes, and no private individuals owned any expanse of land under Spanish or Argentine rule except for Vernet and his grantees. Under British government, perhaps 2,000 permanent settlers have developed the land, half of which was privately owned, the rest being owned by the Falkland Islands Company. Moreover, it is clear from recent events that the Falkland Islanders are at least partially self-governing, having thwarted various proposals made by both sides to end the struggle through negotiations. The fact that most of the islanders are descended from five or six generations of a continuously resident population is not, as the Argentines have claimed, irrelevant to the issue. The Argentine refusal to consider the islanders' wishes when addressing the question of sovereignty was and is foolishly shortsighted, since it makes the issue one of human rather than legal rights, thereby diminishing the stature of their case in the eyes of the democratically governed world. It was inevitable under such circumstances that the United States would at least passively support Great Britain; Argentina's failure to predict this is another sign of its collective blindness to world realities.

The justice in both countries' positions on the Falklands question *demands* justice from both countries if the problem is ever to be settled; it demands the understanding of both sides equally, and not the petulant outbursts of nationalism, jingoism, or warmongering that have been so evident these past few years. Justice also demands equal consideration of the rights of the resident population of the islands, who know nothing of claims and counterclaims, but only the fact that their tranquil lives have been horribly disrupted by a horrible war. The statesmanship and maturity that might provided an honorable settlement to all parties seems sadly lacking in the history of the Falklands conflict, particularly at the governmental level. In fact, the real causes of this war have more to do with governmental blunders than with historical or actual claims of sovereignty, as we shall see.

2. To the Last Dregs

War, by its very definition, requires at least two sovereign entities as participants; a war may be started by one country acting alone, but needs an enemy or enemies to continue. It takes two to fight. The outbreak of war in the Falklands puzzled many outside observers, and sent others running to their gazetteers and atlases. While scarcely idyllic, these islands were sufficiently isolated from the world's cares that they were seemingly immune to any but the most modest of disruptions, such as those occasioned by the Saturday-night drunk. The world had mildly been aware of the disagreement between Britain and Argentina on the islands' sovereignty, but such disagreements are common in this world, and are usually handled on a more civilized basis. Why here? Why now? The answers lie in the shortsightedness of both governments involved.

While Britain agreed to negotiate with the Argentines over the Falklands question in 1965, it did so halfheartedly, without any sense of urgency or purpose. Indeed, one is struck while studying the recent history of the Falklands by Britain's seeming inability to decide just what it wanted to do with the islands. At times the British government appeared ready to cede the Falklands to Argentina, in whole or in part, irrespective of the inhabitants' wishes; on other occasions, Britain said it would respect the desires of the natives without actually taking steps to defend them should the worst come to pass. Of course, the Falkland Islands occupied only a small part of Britain's attention during a period filled with perilous crises. Still, the basic policy followed by the Foreign and Commonwealth Office during the decades of negotiations seemed to be a fervent desire that the issue would just get up and walk away. The professionals of the British Foreign Service consistently underestimated the persistence of their Argentine counterparts, consistently misjudged the long-term effects of delay on the Argentine populace and government, and consistently downplayed threats of action by the Argentine military if negotiations remained stalemated. From the Argentine point of view, seventeen years of negotiations, with little more to show than a minor trade and travel agreement, were more than sufficient to address the key issues, particularly the sovereignty question. There were signs from the very beginning of the negotiations that Argentina was willing to compromise on some middle ground, if the end results would allow them to at least show the Argentine flag in the islands. One cannot condone the Argentine military solution, but the invasion is at least understandable, given the fact that virtually nothing had been achieved for thousands of hours of work on both sides.

Whether from lack of attention, or more probably from lack of consideration, Britain never seemed to take Argentina seriously, or to understand its peculiar viewpoint on matters related to national honor. It is, of course, easy to make judgments retrospectively; yet one fact stands out quite clearly: Britain made a series of minor diplomatic oversights that blended together into one horrendous blunder, including: its inability to educate its public, either in the Falklands or in Britain itself, on the dangers and options involved; its lack of decision, either to stand by the Falklands and provide a sufficient military presence to defend them, or to abandon the islands, all at once or over a period of time, by forcing the issue and transplanting those islanders unwilling to live under an Argentine administration; its failure to predict the consequences of its actions, such as withdrawing the armed icebreaker *Endurance* during a period of mounting tensions; its faulty diplomatic and military intelligence, which provided the government with only two days' advance notice of the Argentine invasion; and, finally, a certain condescension in its dealings with the Argentine government, which contributed mightily to the failings mentioned above. Alone, these might have been minor bumps on the road to good relations between two sovereign countries. Cumulatively, they helped bring on a war neither government really wanted. In the end, Britain had helped maneuver itself into a position in which Margaret Thatcher had no option, in her opinion, but to strike back. Her responsibility for putting herself into that corner, for causing the deaths of over one thousand men and women, is surely equal to that of Galtieri's.

As for Leopoldo Galtieri, the man who would have written himself into the history books by recapturing the Falklands for Argentina, the man who boasted that he would see 40,000 of his countrymen dead before giving up the struggle for the Malvinas, it is perhaps fortunate that his incompetence so greatly exceeded his overbearing ego that he managed within four months of assuming office to trap himself into a situation where only a military miracle could save his country, his cause, even his own position. By his own admission, in an interview published after his fall in the Argentine magazine, *Clarin*, Galtieri miscalculated at every turn, judging that the United States would remain neutral; that Britain would do nothing but protest to the United Nations; that in the unlikely event of military action, Britain would receive no help from other nations, and did not have in any case the military capability to retake the Falklands; that Argentina could defend its beachhead on the Falklands with ill-trained conscripts; that Brigadier General Menendez, having deployed his soldiers so poorly that even Galtieri noticed their misplacement on his visit to the Falklands, was still the man to lead the Argentines to victory; that after the Argentine surrender, Galtieri could still continue fighting a shooting war, while remaining leader of his country. Here was a man with his head firmly planted in the ground. How ironic that Leopoldo Galtieri, the man who would have made the Malvinas Argentine territory once again, has instead probably doomed any such possibility for at least another generation, if not longer. Had he waited another year, Britain might not have had the military capability to retake the islands; had he waited five years, he probably could have had a condominium leaseback handed to him by the British government. Men with guns in their hands have no patience.

With both sides failing to take the other seriously, a confrontation was almost inevitable sooner or later. The crisis was precipitated by a conjunction of unfavorable events following the February, 1982 negotiating session between Britain and Argentina. Although Britain somehow believed that relations were back to normal following these discussions, Argentina clearly came away from the talks with a feeling of *deja vu*, and a sense that nothing would ever come from the negotiations. At that point Galtieri, undoubtedly pressured by Anaya and the General's own subordinates, decided to increase the stakes and put pressure on the British. The first sign of this new policy was the release in Buenos Aires of the text of the proposed agreement. Simultaneously,

Galtieri ordered preparation of a military option, in the event discussions reached an impasse within the next few months. Galtieri was not only impelled by his own sense of destiny and by the higher ranking officers in the Argentine military, but by a declining economy that threatened an end to the junta system itself. He gambled—and he lost. As the month of March progressed, both sides began to lose control of the situation, essentially just reacting to events and to each other's responses to those events. Surely President Galtieri felt himself by the end of March in as much of a corner as Margaret Thatcher did; the riots of March 30th and 31st forced his hand. To save himself more than his country, he ordered the invasion to proceed, thereby raising the stakes one step higher.

Once the Argentine forces were committed, neither side could back down, since doing so would mean the end of whichever government broke ranks first. Furthermore, one of the two governments was almost certain to fall in any event, depending on the war's outcome. By this time, any real possibility of a negotiated settlement had long since passed. Barring the unlikely event of a battlefield stalemate, the war would continue until one or the other side emerged victorious, thereby vindicating the judgment of the political leader in queston, and dooming the fate of the loser. This is in fact exactly what happened.

Why did Britain win? The British victory was composed of equal measures of professionalism and luck, both essential factors in the prosecution of a war. On paper, Argentina appeared to have a decided edge, in men, materiel, planes, position, and supply lines. The Argentine advantage, however, was eroded away by the British forces as the war developed, the experience of the British military being a decisive factor. Britain also used the press much more efficiently than Argentina, giving the impression of evenhandedness, truthfulness, even humbleness in advancing its claims, when in reality the military manipulated the few reporters assigned to the fleet by feeding them exaggerated but believable reports about the large numbers of British troops, ships, and planes being sent to the South Atlantic. While the Argentine press releases were discredited almost from the first day of the campaign, Britain's official government press office was regarded by most westerners as the only news source that was even partially veracious. In other words, Britain won the psychological war, and by doing so, gave an enormous boost to its military position. As the war progressed, even Argentina began believing British claims. This was, of course, precisely what Britain intended.

The sinking of the Argentine ship *General Belgrano* not only removed from the seas Argentina's most powerful warship, but also effectively marked the end of the naval war in the Falklands; thereafter, Argentina kept its ships within sighting distance of the mainland. Argentina seemed to have a large advantage in air power at the beginning of the conflict, but never was able to use its large numbers of fighter-bombers to establish control of the air space over the Falklands. Instead, twenty

British Sea Harriers flying round the clock effectively knocked the Argentine Air Force out of the sky in the first two weeks of the shooting war. The slower Harriers showed an uncanny ability to outmaneuver the faster but clumsier Skyhawks and Mirages, shooting down the Argentine planes in an astonishing ratio of about fifteen British kills to every one for Argentina. The Argentine Air Force demonstrated immense bravery and tenacity in attacking the British fleet, which was bottled up in Falkland Sound with no room to maneuver. But its best efforts were thwarted by a high number of dud bombs, including six that actually hit British ships, by the myriad of antiaircraft missiles thrown at the attacking Argentine jets, and by the short amount of combat time (2-10 minutes) that each Argentine plane actually had over the target areas. Essentially, each Argentine aircraft had to line up over the combat zone, quickly dump its bombs and missiles, perhaps turn around once for a strafing run, and then head back to home base, or run the risk of running out of fuel. This left the Argentine craft at an enormous disadvantage in pursuing the Sea Harriers, in picking better targets, in avoiding missiles. In the end, Argentina lost perhaps one-half to two-thirds of its serviceable combat planes, depending on which claims one chooses to believe; more importantly, the Argentines lost a large percentage of its trained fighter pilots, a resource that will be far more difficult to replace than the aircraft themselves.

On land Argentina fared little better. Brigadier General Menendez, who had spoken out against the original Argentine invasion, was simply the wrong man to be defending the Argentine beachhead. He consistently showed himself incapable of making the simplest military judgments. His strategy, his placement of troops, his supply lines, his responses to British actions, all demonstrated woeful military incompetence. Paradoxically, President Galtieri recognized Menendez's deficiencies on his only visit to the islands, but refused to replace him, on the grounds his removal might demoralize the Argentine populace and soldiery. The British forces were allowed to land at San Carlos Bay virtually unopposed. Argentine troops at Goose Green were reinforced by Menendez, but provided with no further support when they most needed it. Once Goose Green fell, Menendez seemed to pursue a persistent policy of retreat, falling back from entrenched positions at the least sign of pressure from the advancing British. As a result, he soon found himself besieged at Puerto Argentino/Port Stanley, encircled by land and cut off by sea, with no air support whatsoever. At the end, his soldiers broke and ran before the final British attack. Contributing to the Argentine defeat on land was the dichotomy between the Argentine enlisted men and their elitist officers, many of whom never moved from their relatively plush surroundings in Port Stanley, while the men in the trenches were struggling to find something hot to eat and something warm to wear. A number of the intermediate officers abandoned their units under British military pressure, leaving them in charge of their sergeants or corporals. The vast gap between the privileged officer class and the poorly trained conscripts that comprised much of the Argentine army resulted in a demoralization of the forces in the field, and a tendency for them to crumble before the relentless British onslaughts. Contributing to this was Argentina's poor supply chain; while goods and war materiel piled up in Port Stanley, the soldier in the field received less and less in food, clothes, and weaponry as the war progressed. He felt abandoned by his own people, and consequently did not fight as well as he could have fought, had he been properly maintained and directed. The fault for the military debacle must lie directly with the heads of the Argentine armed services.

Leaving aside political considerations, could Argentina have won the military struggle? There is no certain answer to this question, but most observers seem to feel that Argentina could at least have made a better showing in the Falklands than it did. Argentina's three surviving submarines were never a factor in the struggle; one was apparently unserviceable, but the remaining two could and should have been deployed near the British fleet. The lone Argentine aircraft carrier could have been deployed near enough to the Falklands to increase Argentine air cover there tremendously. The sinking of a British aircraft carrier would have halved British air power, as well as demoralized the entire British expeditionary force—this should have been the first priority of the Argentine Navy. The Argentine Air Force probably did as well as possible with the mixture of old and new equipment available to it; if more Exocet missiles had been purchased, if newer aircraft had been obtained, perhaps the outcome might have been different. The Argentine Army made a very poor showing indeed; with better officers, better supply lines, with more aggressive tactics, Argentina could have at least fought the British to a standstill, and perhaps driven them off the beaches at Port San Carlos. But they did not, a fact over which military historians will be pondering for decades to come.

3. Prognostications

The Falklands War marked the first use in combat of the Exocet air-to-ship missile (also available in land-to-ship and ship-to-ship versions), and the first combat test of the Sea Harrier fighter-bomber, both of which demonstrated astonishing capabilities. Of the five or six air-to-ship Exocets fired, two hit their targets, destroying the British vessels in question, and raising serious questions about the future viability of the surface fleet as now constituted. One land-to-ship Exocet was also fired, severely damaging a British warship. The presence of these missiles and others of their ilk provoked a continuing debate among naval experts that reached no evident conclusion. Some of these savants declared that the days of the surface navy had nearly passed; others, particularly high-ranking officers from those countries with large navies, expressed the opposite view, saying that the reasons behind the severe British losses had more to do with Britain's lack of radar and air cover than with any defect in naval strategy.

There can be no doubt that British losses would have been less if it had had one or more aircraft carriers capable of launching modern naval fighters, as well as downward-peering radar planes that could have picked up low-flying aircraft. Without this radar umbrella, Britain was effectively blind, relying completely on destroyers located west of the Falklands for radar cover—these ships were unable to "see" Argentine craft flying fifteen or twenty feet over the waves. Often, the British ships operating in Falkland Sound had no more than ten or twenty seconds notice of incoming Argentine fighter-bombers. Such tactics would not have worked against a modern American battle group composed of one or more centrally located carriers, with surrounding destroyers, light cruisers, nuclear submarines, and other vessels—the Argentine planes would have been detected and met at long range. The Exocet has made the small navy obsolete; almost any country in the world can now afford to blast its neighbor's naval forces right out of the water. The larger question of anti-ship missiles has not been answered, however, and probably cannot without actual combat experience. There are far more sophisticated missiles in the Soviet and American arsenals. Their capabilities are known, their ultimate effectiveness still a mystery.

The military experts remained relatively unimpressed with the Sea Harriers as well. Many of them seemed to feel that the Harriers were successful only because they were facing technologically obsolete aircraft, and that they would not have fared as well against modern Soviet or American planes. Others believed that the Harriers deserved their kudos, that this relatively unknown aircraft proved its wings by its reliability, its maneuverability, and its flexibility. None of the major powers expressed much interest in moving toward VTOL aircraft, however. Armchair generals everywhere praised the British landing and subsequent march on Port Stanley as a classic example of the best in military tactics, stressing aggressive attacks, forced marches to surprise the enemy, unrelenting military pressure, psychological warfare, initiative, strong leadership at both the officer and N.C.O. level, good morale, firm supply lines, and excellent motivation. In almost every clash, the attacking British forces faced a larger number of defenders in entrenched positions, a situation which normally would heavily favor the defenders. In every case the British won.

The British may have won the battle, but they have not yet won the war. The basic issues and grievances remain as before, only deepened and made bitter by the hardships inflicted on all sides. The Argentines have experienced a devastating military and moral defeat. The British have suffered hundreds of casualties, loss of an appreciable percentage of the Royal Navy, and are faced with spending billions of pounds in the foreseeable future to maintain a large military garrison and fleet for the health and safety of 1,800 semi-British citizens. The Falklanders have been wrenched by a horribly devastating war that has left their green hills strewn with thousands of undetectable plastic mines. And we are all faced with the possibility at some near or distant future of a new war or series of smaller conflicts that could lead to war. Is there any way out?

There is always a point of compromise if both sides really want to compromise. Realistically, however, neither Britain, Argentina, nor the Falklanders have demonstrated the flexibility, maturity, and sincerity necessary to find a negotiated settlement to the Falklands issue, and we believe that such a solution is unlikely to be achieved in the near future. Britain has for the first time shown some interest in developing the islands financially, and would be hard pressed after such development and the events of the war to then withdraw. Yet Britain will also experience increasing political pressures at home as the cost of maintaining a long-term military base on the Falklands begins to mount. Further, the Labour Party has already indicated a desire to find a negotiated settlement to the problem, and may or may not be willing to support a continuing military presence in the Falklands or anywhere else. Some observers believe that, had Labour been in power at the time of the Argentine invasion of the islands, Britain would have done nothing more than protest the occupation to the United Nations.

Argentina must put its own house in order before it can again have any illusions of repossessing the Malvinas; in particular, the military must forever be confined to barracks, basic democratic freedoms must be restored, and the Argentine economy put back in order. The wishes of the Falklanders must be taken into account, and their way of life preserved; the Argentines cannot reasonably expect the islanders to exchange their rural, democratic way of life, however blighted by the war, for the chaos of modern Argentine society. Argentina must make their country an attractive option for the Falklanders. The Kelpers themselves must take more of an interest in the world at large and in their prospective future, and seek a form of government more in tune with modern-day realities. If they want independence or some in-between status as a self-governing protectorate, they should make such an end possible; if they desire closer union with Britain, they should seek representation there. Clearly, however, the days of the colony as previously constituted have come to an end.

A negotiated settlement of the Falklands question is the only rational long-term solution to the conflict between Britain and Argentina. Such an agreement could be based upon a division of the islands, with West Falkland Island going to Argentina, and Argentina paying the costs for relocating the settlers there; joint administration by Britain, Argentina, and possibly other powers or the United Nations; or a transfer of sovereignty to Argentina, with a leaseback arrangement to Great Britain for an extended period of time, possibly ninety-nine years. Few other options seem viable. Without such an agreement, this stupid, senseless, silly war could once again become a shooting and killing war, on a greater or lesser scale. Argentina now boasts that it can produce an atomic bomb within five or ten years. Perhaps its ultimate solution to the puzzle of national hysteria is making the islands permanently uninhabitable, on the grounds that, if Argentina can't have the Falklands, neither will anyone else. What price victory?

Appendix A
Governors of the Falkland Islands

French Governor at Port Louis:

1764-1767   G. de Bougainville Nerville

British Military Administrators at Port Egmont:

1765-1768   Capt. John McBride
1768-1769   Capt. Rayner
1769-1770   Capt. Hunt
1770-1770   Capt. George Farmer
1771-1772   Capt. Burr
1773-1774   Lt. S. W. Clayton

Spanish Governors at Puerto Soledad (according to Arce and Cawkell):

1767-1773   Felipe Ruiz Puente
1773-1774   Domingo Chauri
1774-1777   Francisco Gil Lemos
1777-1779   Ramon de Carassa
1779-1781   Salvador Medina
1781-1783   Jacinto Altolaguirre
1783-1784   Fulgencio Montemayor
1784-1786   Augustin Figueroa
1786-1787   Pedro de Mesa y Casto
1787-1788   Ramon Clairac
1788-1789   Pedro de Mesa y Casto
1789-1790   Ramon Clairac
1790-1791   Juan Jose de Elizalde
1791-1792   Pedro Pablo Sanguinetto
1792-1793   Juan Jose de Elizalde
1793-1794   Pedro Pablo Sanguinetto
1794-1795   Jose Aldana Ortega
1795-1796   Pedro Pablo Sanguinetto

1796-1797	Jose Aldana Ortega
1797-1798	Luis de Medina Torres
1798-1799	Francisco Javier de Viana
1799-1800	Luis de Medina Torres
1800-1801	Francisco Javier de Viana
1801-1802	Ramon Fernandez Villegas
1802-1803	Bernardo Bonavia
1803-1804	Antonio Leal de Ibarra
1804-1805	Bernardo Bonavia
1805-1806	Antonio Leal de Ibarra
1806-1809	Bernardo Bonavia
1809-1810	Gerardo Bondas

Spanish Governors at Puerto Soledad (according to Boysen and Goebel):

1767-1773	Felipe Ruiz Puente
1774-1777	Franciso Gil
1777-1781	Ramon Caraza
1781-1784	Augustin Figueroa
1784-1790	Ramon Clairac
1790-1793	Juan Jose Elizade
1793-1799	Pedro Pablo Sanguineto
1799-1805	Ramon Villegas
1805-1811	Juan Crisostomo Martinez

Argentine Governors at Puerto Soledad:

1820-1821	Col. David Jewitt
1821-1822	Guillermo Mason
1823-1828	Pablo Aregusti
1829-1831	Louis Vernet
1832-1832	Juan Esteban or Jose Francisco Mestivier
1832-1833	Capt. Jose Maria Pinedo (Acting Governor)
1833-1833	Juan Simon (never served)

British Military Administrators at Port Louis:

1833-1833	William Dickson (interim)
1834-1838	Lt. Henry Smith
1838-1839	Lt. Robert Lowcay
1839-1842	Lt. John Tyssen

British Lieutenant-Governor at Port Louis (Anson):

| 1842-1843 | Lt. Richard Clement Moody |

British Governors of the Falkland Islands at Port Stanley:

1843-1848	Lt. Richard Clement Moody
1848-1855	George Rennie
1855-1862	Capt. Thomas Edward Laws Moore
1862-1867	Capt. James Mackenzie
1867-1870	William Cleaver Francis Robinson
1870-1876	Col. George A. K. D'Arcy
1876-1880	T. F. Callaghan
1880-1891	Thomas Kerr
1891-1897	Sir Roger Tucker Goldsworthy
1898-1904	Sir William Grey-Wilson
1904-1915	Sir William Lamond Allardyce
1915-1919	Sir W. Douglas Young
1920-1926	Sir John Middleton
1927-1931	Sir Arnold Wienholt Hodson
1931-1934	Sir James O'Grady
1935-1941	Sir Herbert Henniker-Heaton
1941-1946	Sir Alan Wolsey Cardinall
1946-1954	Sir Miles Clifford
1954-1957	Sir Oswald Raynor Arthur
1957-1964	Sir Edwin Porter Arrowsmith
1964-1970	Sir Cosmo Dugal Patrick Thomas Haskard
1971-1975	Sir Ernest Gordon Lewis
1975-1977	Sir Neville Arthur Irwin French
1977-1980	Sir James Roland Walter Parker
1980-1982	Sir Rex Masterman Hunt

Argentine Military Governors at Puerto Argentino:

1982-1982	Gen. Oswaldo Jorge Garcia (interim)
1982-1982	Brig. Gen. Mario Benjamin Menendez

British Civil Commissioner at Port Stanley:

1982-Date	Sir Rex Masterman Hunt

Appendix B
The Military Forces
and Their Losses

BRITISH FORCES

Army—about 9,500 troops. Navy—2 light aircraft carriers, 5 destroyers, 12 frigates, 2 assault ships, 2 landing ships, 3 sea-going tugs, 1 hospital ship, 3 transports, 1 freighter, 4 submarines, many others. Air Forces (including Navy planes)—28 Sea Harriers, 10 R.A.F. Harrier GR3s, 4 Vulcan bombers based at Ascension, 16 Victor tankers based at Ascension, several Nimrod surveillance craft, 140 helicopters.

BRITISH LOSSES

Total Casualties—255 dead, about 350 wounded. Navy—5 vessels sunk: *Sheffield* and *Coventry* (destroyers), *Antelope* and *Ardent* (frigates), *Atlantic Conveyor* (container ship); 2 ships severely damaged: *Sir Galahad* and *Sir Tristram* (landing ships); 10 ships damaged, including 2 destroyers and 6 frigates. Air Forces—8 Sea Harriers lost (5 by accidents), 3 Harrier GR3s lost, 11 helicopters lost (5 Sea Kings, 2 Wessexes, 4 Gazelle Scouts); 4 pilots dead.

ARGENTINE FORCES

Army—Argentina claimed 9,804 soldiers on the islands, Britain claimed about 13,000. Navy—1 aircraft carrier, 1 heavy cruiser, 9 destroyers, 4 submarines, many smaller vessels. Air Force—223 fighter-bombers of various types, not all serviceable.

ARGENTINE LOSSES

Total Casualties—712 dead and missing, approximately 1,200 wounded. The Navy lost 321 dead, the Air Force claimed 55 dead. Navy—5 vessels sunk: *General Belgrano* (heavy cruiser), *Santa Fe* (submarine), *Narwal* (trawler), *Sobral* (patrol boat), *Isla de los Estados* (freighter); damaged vessels: 1 frigate, 2 patrol boats, 2 freighters. Air Force—Argentina claimed 19 jets and 1 helicopter lost, Britain claimed 74 fighters lost (28 Skyhawks, 22 Mirage III/Daggers, 13 Pucaras, 4 Mentor trainers, 2 Canberra bombers, 1 Aer Macchi, 3 light craft, 1 C-130 Hercules, plus 11 probable kills, and 12 planes destroyed on the ground). Argentina captured 1 British pilot, Britain took 11,845 Argentine prisoners.

Appendix C
Selected Documents

UNITED NATIONS GENERAL ASSEMBLY RESOLUTION 1514 (XV)

Declaration on the granting of independence to colonial countries and peoples.

The General Assembly, mindful of the determination proclaimed by the peoples of the world in the Charter of the United Nations to reaffirm faith in fundamental human rights, in the dignity and worth of the human person, in the equal rights of men and women and of nations large and small and to promote social progress and better standards of life in larger freedom, conscious of the need for the creation of conditions of stability and well-being and peaceful and friendly relations based on respect for the principles of equal rights and self-determination of all peoples, and of universal respect for, and observance of, human rights and fundamental freedoms for all without distinction as to race, sex, language or religion, recognizing the passionate yearning for freedom in all dependent peoples and the decisive role of such peoples in the attainment of their independence, aware of the increasing conflicts resulting from the denial of or impediments in the way of the freedom of such peoples, which constitute a serious threat to world peace, considering the important role of the United Nations in assisting the movement for independence in Trust and Non-Self-Governing Territories, recognizing that the peoples of the world ardently desire the end of colonialism in all its manifestations, convinced that the continued existence of colonialism prevents the development of international economic cooperation, impedes the social, cultural and economic development of dependent peoples and militates against the United Nations ideal of universal peace, affirming that peoples may, for their own ends, freely dispose of their natural wealth and resources without prejudice to any obligations arising out of international economic cooperation, based upon the principle of mutual benefit, and international law, believing that the process of liberation is irresistible and irreversible and that, in order to avoid serious crises, an end must be put to colonialism and all practices of segregation and discrimination associated therewith, welcoming the emergence in recent years of a large

number of dependent territories into freedom and independence, and recognizing the increasingly powerful trends towards freedom in such territories which have not yet attained independence, convinced that all peoples have an inalienable right to complete freedom, the exercise of their sovereignty and the integrity of their national territory, solemnly proclaims the necessity of bringing to a speedy and unconditional end colonialism in all its forms and manifestations; and to this end declares that: 1) The subjection of peoples to alien subjugation, domination and exploitation constitutes a denial of fundamental human rights, is contrary to the Charter of the United Nations, and is an impediment to the promotion of world peace and co-operation; 2) All peoples have the right to self-determination; by virtue of that right they freely determine their political status and freely pursue their economic, social and cultural development; 3) Inadequacy of political, economic, social or educational preparedness should never serve as a pretext for delaying independence; 4) All armed action or repressive measures of all kinds directed against dependent peoples shall cease in order to enable them to exercise peacefully and freely their right to complete independence, and the integrity of their national territory shall be respected; 5) Immediate steps shall be taken, in Trust and Non-Self-Governing Territories or all other territories which have not yet attained independence, to transfer all powers to the peoples of those territories, without any conditions or reservations, in accordance with their freely expressed will and desire, without any distinction as to race, creed or colour, in order to enable them to enjoy complete independence and freedom; 6) Any attempt aimed at the partial or total disruption of the national unity and the territorial integrity of a country is incompatible with the purposes and principles of the Charter of the United Nations; 7) All States shall observe faithfully and strictly the provisions of the Charter of the United Nations, the Universal Declaration of Human Rights and the present Declaration on the basis of equality, non-interference in the internal affairs of all States, and respect for the sovereign rights of all peoples and their territorial integrity.   947th plenary meeting,
14 December 1960.

GENERAL ASSEMBLY RESOLUTION 2065 (XX)
Question of the Falkland Islands (Malvinas)

The General Assembly, having examined the question of the Falkland Islands (Malvinas), taking into account the chapters of the reports of the Special Committee on the Situation with regard to the Implementation of the Declaration on the Granting of Independence to Colonial Countries and Peoples relating to the Falkland Islands (Malvinas), and in particular the conclusions and recommendations adopted by the Committee with reference to that Territory, considering that its resolution 1514 (XV) of 14 December 1960 was prompted by the cherished aim of bringing an end everywhere to colonialism in all its forms, one of which covers the case of the Falkland Islands (Malvinas), noting the existence of a dispute between the Governments of Argentina and the United Kingdom of Great Britain and Northern Ireland concerning sovereignty over the said Islands: 1) Invites the Governments of Argentina and the United Kingdom of Great Britain and Northern Ireland to proceed without delay with the negotiations recommended by the Special Committee on the Situation with regard to the Implementation of the Declaration on the Granting of Independence to Colonial Countries and Peoples with a view to finding a peaceful solution to the problem, bearing in mind the provisions and objectives of the Charter of the United Nations and of General Assembly resolution 1514 (XV) and the interests of the population of the Falkland Islands (Malvinas); 2) Requests the two Governments to report to the Special Committee and to the General Assembly at its twenty-first session on the results of the negotiations.

1398th plenary meeting, 16 December 1965.

GENERAL ASSEMBLY RESOLUTION 3160 (XXVIII)
Question of the Falkland Islands (Malvinas)

The General Assembly, having considered the question of the Falkland Islands (Malvinas), recalling its resolution 1514 (XV) of 14 December 1960 containing the Declaration on the Granting of Independence to Colonial Countries and Peoples, recalling also its resolution 2065 (XX) of 16 December 1965, in which it invited the Governments of Argentina and the United Kingdom of Great Britain and Northern Ireland to proceed without delay with the negotiations recommended by the Special Committee on the Situation with regard to the Implementation of the Declaration on the Granting of Independence to Colonial Countries and Peoples with a view to finding a peaceful solution to the problem of the Falkland Islands (Malvinas), bearing in mind the provisions and objectives of the Charter of the United Nations and of resolution 1514 (XV) and the interests of the population of the Falkland Islands (Malvinas), gravely concerned at the fact that eight years have elapsed since the adoption of resolution 2065 (XX) without any substantial progress having been made in the negotiations, mindful that resolution 2065 (XX) indicates that the way to put an end to this colonial situation is the peaceful solution of the conflict of sovereignty between the Governments of Argentina and the United Kingdom with regard to the aforementioned islands, expressing its gratitude for the continuous efforts made by the Government of Argentina, in accordance with the relevant decisions of the General Assembly, to facilitate the process of decolonization and to promote the well-being of the population of the islands; 1) Approves the chapters of the report of the Special Committee on the Situation with regard to the Implementation of the Declaration on the Granting of Independence to Colonial Countries and Peoples relating to the Falkland Islands (Malvinas) and, in particular, the resolution adopted by the Special Committee on 21 August 1973 concerning the Territory; 2) Declares the need to accelerate the negotiations between the Governments of Argentina and the United Kingdom of Great Britain and Northern Ireland called for in General Assembly resolution 2065 (XX) in order to arrive at a peaceful solution of the conflict of sovereignty between them concerning the Falkland Islands (Malvinas); 3) Urges the Governments of Argentina and the United Kingdom, therefore, to proceed without delay with the negotiations, in accordance with the provisions of the relevant resolutions of the General Assembly, in order to put an end to the colonial situation; 4) Requests both Governments to report to the Secretary-General and to the General Assembly as soon as possible, and not later than at its twenty-ninth session, on the results of the recommended negotiations.

2202nd plenary meeting
14 December 1973

GENERAL ASSEMBLY RESOLUTION 31/49
Question of the Falkland Islands (Malvinas)

The General Assembly, having considered the question of the Falkland Islands (Malvinas), recalling its resolutions 1514 (XV) of 14 December 1960, 2065 (XX) of 16 December 1965 and 3160 (XXVIII) of 14 December 1973, bearing in mind the paragraphs related to this question contained in the Political Declaration adopted by the Conference of Ministers for Foreign Affairs of Non-Aligned Countries, held at Lima from 25 to 30 August 1975, and in the Political Declaration adopted by the Fifth Conference of Heads of State or Government of Non-Aligned Countries, held at Colombo from 16 to 19 August 1976, having regard to the chapter of the report of the Special Committee on the Situation with regard to the Implementation of the Declaration on the Granting of Independence to Colonial Countries and Peoples relating to the Falkland Islands (Malvinas) and, in particular, the conclusions and recommendations of the Special Committee concerning the Territory: 1) Approves the chapter of the report of the Special Committee on the Situation with regard to the Implementation of the Declaration on the Granting of Independence to Colonial Countries and Peoples relating to the Falkland Islands (Malvinas) and, in particular, the conclusions and recommendations of the Special Committee concerning the Territory; 2) Expresses its gratitude for the continuous efforts made by the Government of Argentina, in accordance with the relevant decisions of the General Assembly, to facilitate the process of decolonization and to promote the well-being of the population of the islands; 3) Requests the Governments of Argentina and the United Kingdom of Great Britain and Northern Ireland to expedite the negotiations concerning the dispute over sovereignty, as requested in General Assembly resolutions 2065 (XX) and 3160 (XXVIII); 4) Calls upon the two parties to refrain from taking decisions that would imply introducing unilateral modifications in the situation while the islands are going through the process recommended in the above-mentioned resolutions; 5) Requests both Governments to report to the Secretary-General and to the General Assembly as soon as possible on the results of the negotiations.

85th plenary meeting, 1 December 1976

SECURITY COUNCIL RESOLUTION 502 OF 3 APRIL 1982

The Security Council, recalling the statement made by the President of the Security Council at the 2345th meeting of the Security Council on 1 April 1982 (S/14944) calling on the Governments of Argentina and the United Kingdom of Great Britain and Northern Ireland to refrain from the use or threat of force in the region of the Falkland Islands (Islas Malvinas), deeply disturbed at reports of an invasion on 2 April 1982 by armed forces of Argentina, determining that there exists a breach of the peace in the region of the Falkland Islands (Islas Malvinas): 1) Demands an immediate cessation of hostilities; 2) Demands an immediate withdrawal of all Argentine forces from the Falkland Islands (Islas Malvinas); 3) Calls on the Governments of Argentina and the United Kingdom to seek a diplomatic solution to their differences and to respect fully the purposes and principles of the Charter of the United Nations.

ORGANIZATION OF AMERICAN STATES RESOLUTION 359

April 13, 1982: The situation obtaining between the Republic of Argentina and the United Kingdom of Great Britain and Northern Ireland in relation to the Malvinas (Falkland) Islands. Whereas: The dispute between the Republic of Argentina and the United Kingdom of Great Britain and Northern Ireland in relation to the Malvinas (Falkland) Islands is endangering the peace of the hemisphere, and the fundamental principles and purposes established in the Charter of the Organization of American States include those of strengthening the peace and security of the continent, preventing possible causes of difficulties and ensuring the peaceful settlement of disputes, the Permanent Council of the Organization of American States, resolves: 1) To express its profound concern over the serious situation that the Republic of Argentina and the United Kingdom of Great Britain and Northern Ireland now face; 2) To express its fervent hope that a rapid, peaceful solution can be found to the disagreement between the two nations within the context of the rules of international law; 3) To offer its friendly cooperation in the peace efforts already under way, in the hope of contributing in this way to a peaceful settlement of the dispute that will avert once and for all the danger of war between countries that deserve the respect of the international community.

ORGANIZATION OF AMERICAN STATES RESOLUTION 360

April 21, 1982: Whereas: In its note dated April 19, 1982, the Government of Argentina requested convocation of the Organ of Consultation, pursuant to Article 6 of the Inter-American Treaty of Reciprocal Assistance, to consider the measures that it would be advisable to take for the maintenance of the peace and security of the hemisphere, and the Permanent Council of the Organization of American States has heard the statement by the Permanent Representative of Argentina denouncing a grave situation that threatens the peace and security of the hemisphere and that affects the sovereignty and territorial integrity of his country, and describing the measures that the Argentine Government has adopted in exercise of the right of legitimate self-defense, the Permanent Council of the Organization of American States resolves: 1) To convene the Organ of Consultation under the provisions of the Inter-American Treaty of Reciprocal Assistance, and in accordance with Article 70 of the Rules of Procedure of this Permanent Council, to consider the grave situation that has arisen in the South Atlantic; 2) To decide that the Organ of Consultation shall meet at the headquarters of the General Secretariat of the Organization on April 26, 1982, at 10 A.M.; 3) To constitute itself and to act provisionally as Organ of Consultation, pursuant to Article 12 of the Inter-American Treaty of Reciprocal Assistance.

MEMORANDUM OF AGREEMENT PROPOSED BY THE UNITED STATES GOVERNMENT ON APRIL 27, 1982

Preamble: On the basis of United Nations Security Council Resolution 502, and the will of the Argentine Republic and of the United Kingdom to resolve the controversy which has arisen between them, renouncing the use of force, both Governments agree on the following steps, which form an integrated whole: 1) Effective on the signature of this Agreement by both Governments, there shall be an immediate cessation of hostilities; 2) Beginning at 0000 hours local time of the day, after the day on which this Agreement is signed, and pending a definitive settlement, the Republic of Argentina and the United Kingdom shall not introduce or deploy forces into the zones (hereinafter "zones"), defined by circles of 150 nautical miles' radius from the following coordinate points [described]; Within 24 hours of the date of this Agreement, the United Kingdom will suspend enforcement of its "zone of exclusion" and Argentina will suspend operations in the same area; Within 24 hours of the date of this Agreement, Argentina and the United Kingdom will commence the withdrawal of their forces in accordance with the following details: Within seven days from the date of this Agreement, Argentina and the United Kingdom shall each have withdrawn one-half of their military and security forces present in the zones on the date of this Agreement, including related equipment and armaments. Within the same time period, the United Kingdom naval task force will stand off at a distance equivalent to seven days' sailing time . . . from any of the coordinate points, and Argentine forces that have been withdrawn shall be placed in a condition such that they could not be reinserted with their equipment and armament in less than seven days; Within fifteen days from the date of this Agreement, Argentina shall remove all of its remaining forces from the zones and redeploy them to their usual operating areas or normal duties. Within the same period, the United Kingdom shall likewise remove all of its remaining forces from the zones and shall redeploy such forces and the naval task force and submarines to their usual operating areas or normal duties; In accordance with its letter of acceptance of even date, the United States shall verify compliance with the provisions of this paragraph, and the two Governments agree to cooperate fully with the United States in facilitating this verification; 3) From the date of this Agreement, the two Governments will initiate the necessary procedures to terminate simultaneously, and without delay, the economic and financial measures adopted in connection with the current controversy, including restrictions to travel, transportation, communications, and transfers of funds between the two countries. The United Kingdom at the same time shall request the European Community and third countries that have adopted similar measures to terminate them; 4) The United Kingdom and Argentina shall each appoint and the United States has indicated its agreement to appoint, a representative to constitute a Special Interim Authority (hereinafter "the Authority") which shall verify compliance with the obligations in this Agreement (with the exception of paragraph 2), and undertake such other responsibilities as are assigned to it under this Agreement or the separate Protocol regarding the Authority signed this date. Each representative may be supported by a staff of not more than ten persons on the islands; 5) Pending a definitive settlement, all decisions, laws and regulations hereafter adopted by the local administration on the islands shall be submitted to and expeditiously ratified by the Authority, except in the event that the Authority deems such decisions, laws or regulations to be inconsistent with the purposes and provisions of this agreement or its implementation. The traditional local administration shall continue, except that the Executive and Legislative Councils shall be enlarged to include: A) two representatives appointed by the Argentine Government to serve in the Executive Council; and B) representatives in each Council of the Argentine population whose period of residence on the islands is equal to that required of others entitled to representation, in proportion to their population, subject to there being at least one such representative in each Council. Such representatives of the resident Argentine population shall be nominated by the Authority. The flags of each of the constituent members of the Authority shall be flown at its headquarters. Pending a definitive settlement, neither Government shall take any action that would be inconsistent with the purpose and provisions of this Agreement or its implementation; 6) Pending a definitive settlement, travel, transportation, movement of persons and, as may be related thereto, residence and ownership and disposition of property, communications & commerce between the mainland & the islands shall, on a non-discriminatory basis, be promoted and facilitated. The Authority shall propose to the two Governments for adoption appropriate measures on such matters. Such proposals shall simultaneously be transmitted to the Executive and Legislative Councils for their views. The two Governments undertake to respond promptly to such proposals. The Authority shall monitor the implementation of all such proposals adopted. The provisions of [this paragraph] shall in no way prejudice the rights and guarantees which have heretofore been enjoyed by the inhabitants on the islands, in particular rights relating to freedom of opinion, religion, expression, teaching, movement, property, employment, family, customs, and cultural ties with countries of origin; 7) December 31, 1982 will conclude the interim period during which the two Governments shall complete negotiations on removal of the islands from the list of Non-Self-Governing Territories under Chapter XI of the United Nations Charter and on mutually agreed conditions for their definitive status, including due regard for the rights of the inhabitants and for the principles of territorial integrity, in accordance with the purposes and principles of the United Nations Charter, and in light of the relevant Resolutions of the United Nations General Assembly. The negotiations hereabove referred to shall begin within fifteen days of the signature of the present Agreement; 8) In order to assist them in bringing their negotiations to a mutually satisfactory settlement by the date stipulated in the preceding paragraph, the Authority shall, after consultation with the Executive Council, make specific proposals and recommendations as early as practicable to the two Governments, including proposals and recommendations on: The manner of taking into account the wishes and interests of the islanders, insofar as islands with a settled population are concerned, based on the results of a sounding of the opinion of the inhabitants, with respect to such issues relating to the negotiations, and conducted in such manner, as the Authority may determine; Issues relating to the development of the resources of the islands, including opportunities for joint cooperation and the role of the Falkland Islands Company; and Such other matters as the two Governments may request, including possible arrangements for compensation of islanders, or matters on which the Authority may wish to comment in light of its experience in discharging its responsibilities under this Agreement; The Governments have agreed on the procedure in [this paragraph] without prejudice to their respective positions on the legal weight to be accorded such opinion in reaching a definitive settlement; 9) Should the Governments nonetheless be unable to conclude the negotiations by December 31, 1982, the United States has indicated that, on the request of both Governments, it would be prepared at such time to seek to resolve the dispute within six months of the date of the request by making specific proposals for a settlement and by directly conducting negotiations between the Governments on the basis of procedures that it shall formulate. The two Governments agree to respond within one month to any formal proposals or recommendations submitted to them by the United States; 10) This Agreement shall enter into force on the date of signature.

RESOLUTION 1, 20TH MEETING, CONSULTATION OF MINISTERS OF FOREIGN AFFAIRS, ORGANIZATION OF AMERICAN STATES

April 28, 1982: Considering: The principles of inter-American solidarity and cooperation and the need to find a peaceful solution to any situation that endangers the peace of the Americas; That a dangerous confrontation has arisen between the United Kingdom of Great Britain and Northern Ireland and the Argentine Republic, which was aggravated today by the events that have arisen from the presence of the British navy in the South Atlantic, within the security region referred to in Article 4 of the Rio Treaty; That the primary purpose of the Inter-American Treaty of Reciprocal Assistance is the maintenance of the peace and security of the hemisphere, which, in the case that has arisen, requires ensuring the peaceful settlement of the dispute; That to facilitate peaceful settlement of the dispute, it is urgent that hostilities cease, since they disturb the peace of the hemisphere and may reach unforeseeable proportions; That it is an unchanging principle of the inter-American system that peace be preserved and that all the American states unanimously reject the intervention of extra-continental or continental armed forces in any of the nations of the hemisphere; That Argentina's rights of sovereignty over the Malvinas (Falkland) Islands, as stated in some important resolutions passed by various international forums, including the Declaration of Inter-American Juridical Committee on January 16, 1976, which states: "That the Republic of Argentina has an undeniable right of sovereignty over the Malvinas Islands," must be borne in mind; and That the peace efforts being made with the consent of the parties must be emphasized, and that inter-American solidarity contributes to that objective, and having seen: Resolution 502 (1982) of the United Nations Security Council, all of whose terms must be fulfilled; Resolution 359 of April 13, 1982, adopted by the Permanent Council of the Organization of American States, and the Declaration adopted unanimously by the Ministers of Foreign Affairs at the opening session of the Twentieth Meeting of Consultation (Doc. 14/82), and in conformity with the Inter-American Treaty of Reciprocal Assistance, resolves: 1) To urge the Government of the United Kingdom of Great Britain and Northern Ireland immediately to cease the hostilities it is carrying on within the security region defined by Article 4 of the Inter-American Treaty of Reciprocal Assistance, and also to refrain from any act that may affect inter-American peace and security; 2) To urge the Government of the Republic of Argentina likewise to refrain from taking any action that may exacerbate the situation; 3) To urge those governments immediately to call a truce that will make it possible to resume and proceed normally with the negotiation aimed at a peaceful settlement of the conflict, taking into account the rights of sovereignty of the Republic of Argentina over the Malvinas (Falkland) Islands and the interests of the islanders; 4) To express the willingness of the Organ of Consultation to lend support, through whatever means it considers advisable, to the new initiatives being advanced at the regional or world level, with the consent of the Parties, which are directed toward the just and peaceful settlement of the problem; 5) To take note of the information received about the important negotiations of the Secretary of State of the United States of America and to express its wishes that they will be an effective contribution to the peaceful settlement of the conflict; 6) To deplore the adoption by members of the European Economic Community and other states of coercive measures of an economic and political nature, which are prejudicial to the Argentine nation and to urge them to lift those measures, indicating that they constitute a serious precedent, inasmuch as they are not covered by Resolution 502 (1982) of the United Nations Security Council and are incompatible with the Charters of the United Nations and of the Organization of American States and the General Agreement on Tariffs and Trade; 7) To instruct the President of the Twentieth Meeting of Consultation to take immediate steps to transmit the appeal contained in operative paragraphs 1, 2 and 3 of this resolution to the governments of the United Kingdom of Great Britain and Northern Ireland and of the Republic of Argentina, and also to inform them, on behalf of the foreign ministers of the Americas, that he is fully confident that this appeal will be received for the sake of peace in the region and in the world; 8) To instruct the President of the Twentieth Meeting of Consultation immediately to present this resolution formally to the Chairman of the United Nations Security Council, so that he may bring it to the attention of the members of the Council; 9) To keep the Twentieth Meeting of Consultation open, especially to oversee faithful compliance with this resolution, and to take such additional measures as are deemed necessary to restore and preserve peace and settle the conflict by peaceful means.

DECLARATION OF THE LATIN AMERICAN GROUP AT THE UNITED NATIONS ON 5 MAY 1982

The Latin American Group at the United Nations held a meeting on 4 May 1982 at the request of the Permanent Representative of Argentina [who] informed the Group on all armed actions that have taken place in the region of the Malvinas Islands between Argentina and the United Kingdom since 25 April 1982 and have seriously affected peace and security in the region and in the world. In these circumstances, the Latin American Group at the United Nations, in a spirit of assistance in the search for a peaceful solution, declares: 1) Its regret at the increasing loss of life which has occurred in the region of the Malvinas Islands; 2) Its urgent call for a cessation of all hostile acts in the region of the Malvinas Islands; 3) That it urges the Governments of the Republic of Argentina and of the United Kingdom to initiate negotiations, with a view to achieving a just, peaceful, practical and lasting solution in accordance with the principles and purposes of the Charter of the United Nations, resolution 502 (1982) of the Security Council in all its parts and the pertinent resolutions of the United Nations General Assembly.

PERU-UNITED STATES PROPOSAL, MAY 5, 1982

Draft Interim Agreement on the Falkland/Malvinas Islands: 1) An immediate ceasefire, concurrent with: 2) Mutual withdrawal and non-reintroduction of forces, according to a schedule to be established by the Contact Group; 3) The immediate introduction of a Contact Group composed of Brazil, Peru, The Federal Republic of Germany and the United States into the Falkland Islands, on a temporary basis pending agreement on a definitive settlement. The Contact Group will assume responsibility for: A) Verification of the withdrawal; B) Ensuring that no actions are taken in the Islands, by the local administration, which would contravene this interim agreement; and C) Ensuring that all other provisions of the agreement are respected; 4) Britain and Argentina acknowledge the existence of differing and conflicting views regarding the status of the Falkland Islands; 5) The two Governments acknowledge that the aspirations and interests of the Islanders will be included in the definitive settlement of the status of the Islands; 6) The Contact Group will have responsibility for ensuring that the two Governments reach a definitive agreement prior to April 30, 1983.

PROPOSED INTERIM AGREEMENT: DRAFT PRESENTED BY THE BRITISH GOVERNMENT TO THE UNITED NATIONS SECRETARY-GENERAL ON 17 MAY 1982

The Government of the Republic of Argentina and the Government of the United Kingdom of Great Britain and Northern Ireland, responding to Security Council Resolution 502 (1982) adopted on 3 April 1982 under Article 40 of the Charter of the United Nations, having entered into negotiations through the good offices of the Secretary-General of the United Nations for an Interim Agreement concerning the Falkland Islands (Islas Malvinas), hereinafter referred to as 'the Islands', having in mind the obligations with regard to non-self-governing territories set out in Article 73 of the Charter of the United Nations . . . have agreed on the following: Article 1: 1) No provision of this Interim Agreement shall in any way prejudice the rights, claims and positions of either Party in the ultimate peaceful settlement of their dispute over the Islands; 2) No acts or activities taking place whilst this Interim Agreement is in force shall constitute a basis for asserting, supporting or denying a claim to territorial sovereignty over the Islands or create any rights of sovereignty over them; Article 2: 2) With effect from a specified time, 24 hours after signature of this Agreement (hereinafter referred to as Time 'T'), each Party undertakes to cease and thereafter to refrain from all firing and other hostile actions; 2) Argentina undertakes: a) to commence withdrawal of its armed forces from the islands with effect from Time 'T'; b) to withdraw half of its armed forces to at least 150 nautical miles away from any point in the islands by Time 'T' plus 7 days; and c) to complete its withdrawal to at least 150 nautical miles away by Time 'T' plus 14 days; 3) The United Kingdom undertakes: a) to commence withdrawal of its armed forces from the Islands with effect from Time 'T'; b) to withdraw half of its armed forces to at least 150 nautical miles away from any point in the Islands by Time 'T' plus 7 days; and c) to complete its withdrawal to at least 150 nautical miles away by Time 'T' plus 14 days; Article 3: With effect from Time 'T', each Party undertakes to lift the exclusion zones, warnings and similar measures which have been imposed; Article 4: On the completion of the steps for withdrawal specified in Article 2, each Party undertakes to refrain from reintroducing any armed forces into the Islands or within 150 nautical miles thereof; Article 5: Each Party undertakes to lift with effect from Time 'T' the economic measures it has taken against the other and to seek the lifting of similar measures taken by third parties; Article 6: 1) Immediately after the signature of the present Agreement, Argentina and the United Kingdom shall jointly sponsor a draft Resolution in the United Nations under the terms of which the Security Council would take note of the present Agreement, acknowledge the role conferred upon the Secretary-General of the United Nations therein, and authorize him to carry out the tasks entrusted to him therein; 2) Immediately after the adoption of the Resolution referred to in paragraph 1) of this Article, a United Nations Administrator, being a person acceptable to Argentina and the United Kingdom, shall be appointed by the Secretary-General and will be the officer administering the government of the Islands; 3) The United Nations Administrator shall have the authority under the direction of the Secretary-General to ensure the continuing administration of the government of the Islands. He shall discharge his functions in consultation with the representative institutions in the Islands which have been developed in accordance with the terms of Article 73 of the Charter of the United Nations, with the exception that one representative from the Argentine population normally resident on the Islands shall be appointed by the Administrator to each of the two institutions. The Adminstrator shall exercise his powers in accordance with the terms of this Agreement and in conformity with the laws and practices traditionally obtaining in the Islands; 4) The United Nations Administrator shall verify the withdrawal of all armed forces from the Islands, and shall devise an effective method of ensuring their non-reintroduction; 5) The United Nations Administrator shall have such staff as may be agreed by Argentina and the United Kingdom to be necessary for the performance of his functions under this Agreement; 6) Each Party may have no more than three observers in the Islands; Article 7: Except as may be otherwise agreed between them, the Parties shall, during the currency of this Agreement, reactivate the Exchange of Notes of 5 August 1971, together with the Joint Statement on Communications between the Islands and the Argentine mainland referred to therein. The Parties shall accordingly take appropriate steps to establish a special consultative committee to carry out the functions entrusted to the Special Consultative Committee referred to in the Joint Statement; Article 8: The Parties undertake to enter into negotiations in good faith under the auspices of the Secretary-General of the United Nations for the peaceful settlement of their dispute and to seek, with a sense of urgency, the completion of these negotiations by 31 December 1982. These negotiations shall be initiated without prejudice to the rights, claims or positions of the Parties and without prejudgment of the outcome; Article 9: This Interim Agreement shall enter into force on Signature and shall remain in force until a definitive Agreement about the future of the Islands has been reached and implemented by the Parties. The Secretary-General will immediately communicate its text to the Security Council and register it in accordance with Article 102 of the Charter of the United Nations.

ARGENTINE DIPLOMATIC NOTE TO DEPARTMENT OF STATE
May 26, 1982

The Embassy of the Argentine Republic presents its compliments to the Department of State and has the honor to inform, with regard to the proposal of the United Nations Secretary General referred to the conflict over the Islas Malvinas and its dependencies, the position of the Government of the Argentine Republic was clearly stated in the Proposed Agreement submitted in the course of the negotiations held at the United Nations, which text reads as follows: "The Government of the Argentine Republic and the Government of the United Kingdom of Great Britain and Northern Ireland, hereinafter referred to as "the Parties", in response to the provisions of Security Council Resolution 502 (1982) of April 3, 1982, and taking into account the Charter of the United Nations, Resolution 1514 (XV), 2065 and other Resolutions of the General Assembly on the question of the Malvinas (Falkland) Islands, have accepted, in accordance with Article 40 of the Charter of the United Nations, the assistance of the Secretary General of the United Nations and have engaged in negotiations and arrived at the following provisional agreement relating to the Malvinas, South Georgia and South Sandwich Islands, hereinafter referred to as "The Islands" for the purposes of this agreement: I: 1) The geographical scope of the area within which the withdrawal of troops is to be carried out shall comprise the Malvinas, South Georgia and South Sandwich Islands; 2) The withdrawal of the forces of both parties shall be gradual and simultaneous. Within a maximum period of thirty days, all armed forces shall be in their normal bases and areas of operation; II: With effect from the signature of this agreement, each party shall cease to apply the economic measures which it has adopted against the other and the United Kingdom shall call for the same action by those countries or groups of countries which, at its request, adopted similar measures; III: 1) Supervision of the withdrawal of the forces of both countries shall be carried out by specialized personnel of the United Nations, whose composition shall be agreed with the parties; 2) The Interim Administration of the Islands while the negotiations for final settlement of the dispute are in progress shall conform to the following provisions: A) The Administration shall be exclusively the responsibility of the United Nations with an appropriate presence of observers of the parties; B) The said Administration shall perform all functions (executive, legislative, judicial and security) through officials of different nationality from that of the parties; C) Notwithstanding the provisions of 2(A) and (B), and in order not to cause unnecessary changes in the way of life of the population during the period of the interim Administration by the United Nations, local judicial functions may be exercised in accordance with the legislation in force on April 1, 1982 to the full extent compatible with this agreement. Similarly, the United Nations interim Administration may appoint as advisers persons who are members of the population of British origin and Argentines resident in the Islands, in equal numbers; D) The flag of the parties shall fly together with that of the United Nations; E) During the period of interim Administration, communications shall be kept open, without discriminatory restrictions of any kind for the parties, including freedom of movement and equality of access with respect to residence, work and property; F) Freedom of communication shall also include the maintenance of freedom of transit for the state airline (Lade) and for merchant ships and scientific vessels, in addition, telephone, telegraph and telex communications, Argentine television transmissions and the state petroleum (YPF) and gas services shall continue to operate freely; IV: The customs, traditions and way of life of the inhabitants of the Islands, and their social and cultural links with their countries of origin, shall be respected and safeguarded; V: 1) The parties undertake to enter immediately into negotiations in good faith under the auspices of the Secretary-General of the United Nations for the peaceful and final settlement of the dispute and, with a sense of urgency, to complete these negotiations by December 31, 1982, with a single option to extend until June 30, 1983, in order to comply with the Charter of the United Nations, Resolutions 1514 (XV), 2065 (XX) and other relevant resolutions of the General Assembly on the question of the Malvinas Islands. These negotiations shall be initiated without prejudice to the rights and claims or positions of the two parties and in recognition of the fact that they have divergent positions on the question of the Malvinas, South Georgia and South Sandwich Islands; 2) The negotiations shall be held in New York; 3) The Secretary-General of the United Nations may be assisted in the negotiations by a contract group composed of representatives of four States members of the United Nations. To that end, each party shall nominate two States and shall have the right by a single vote of one of the States nominated by the other; 4) The Secretary-General of the United Nations shall keep the Security Council assiduously informed of the progress of the negotiations; VI: If the period specified in point V(1) above expires without the attainment of a final agreement, the Secretary-General shall draw up a report addressed to the General Assembly of the United Nations, in order that the latter may determine, as appropriate and with greater urgency, the lines to which the said final agreement should conform in order to achieve a speedy settlement of the question.''

The Argentine Government, in the light of the position stated in the aforementioned proposed agreement, which reflects the reasonableness which has continuously inspired its negotiating behavior, deeply regrets that the peace efforts carried out by the United Nations Secretary-General, in which pursuance and final success the Argentine Republic trusted, have been frustrated as a result of the unilateral decision of the British Government announced on May 20th.

The real possibilities of reaching a peaceful settlement to the conflict and of avoiding, with the responsibility that the situation demanded, further bloodshed and an imminent breaking of peace and security in the hemisphere, finally proved to be disregarded by the intransigence and stubbornness with which the Government of the United Kingdom has tried to make the use of force prevail over reason and peace.

The Government of the Argentine Republic, therefore, formally holds the Government of the United Kingdom of Great Britain and Northern Ireland responsible for the serious consequences which in the future may stem from its denial to exhaust the available means towards a peaceful settlement, and expressly reserves its rights to a legitimate defense recognized by the United Nations Charter.

The Embassy of the Argentine Republic avails itself of this opportunity to renew to the Department of State the assurances of its highest consideration.

UNITED NATIONS SECURITY COUNCIL RESOLUTION 505 OF 26 MAY 1982

The Security Council, reaffirming its Resolution 502 (1982) of 3 April 1982: noting with the deepest concern that the situation in the region of the Falkland Islands (Islas Malvinas) has seriously deteriorated: having heard the statement made by the Secretary-General to the Security Council at its . . . meeting on 21 May 1982, as well as the statements in the debate of the representatives of Argentina and of the United Kingdom of Great Britain and Northern Ireland: concerned to achieve as a matter of the greatest urgency a cessation of hostilities and an end to the present conflict between the armed forces of Argentina and of the United Kingdom of Great Britain and Northern Ireland: 1) expresses appreciation to the Secretary-General for the efforts which he has already made to bring about an agreement between the parties to ensure the implementation of Security Council Resolution 502 (1982), and thereby to restore peace in the region; 2) requests the Secretary-General, on the basis of the present resolution, to undertake a renewed mission of good offices bearing in mind Security Council Resolution 502 (1982) and the approach outlined in his statement of 21 May 1982; 3) urges the parties to the conflict to co-operate fully with the Secretary-General in his mission with a view to ending the present hostilities in and around the Falkland Islands (Islas Malvinas); 4) requests the Secretary-General to enter into contact immediately with the parties with a view to negotiating mutually acceptable terms for a ceasefire, including, if necessary, arrangements for the dispatch of United Nations observers to monitor compliance with the terms of the ceasefire; 5) requests the Secretary-General to submit an interim report to the Security Council as soon as possible and in any case not later than seven days after the adoption of this resolution.

RESOLUTION 2 OF THE GENERAL COMMITTEE, ORGANIZATION OF AMERICAN STATES, ADOPTED 29 MAY 1982

Whereas: Resolution 1 of the Twentieth Meeting of Consultation of American Ministers of Foreign Affairs, adopted on April 28, 1982 decided to "keep the Twentieth Meeting of Consultation open, especially to oversee faithful compliance with this resoluton, and to take such additional measures as are deemed necessary to restore and preserve peace and settle the conflict by peaceful means"; that resolution urged the Government of the United Kingdom "immediately to cease the hostilities it is carrying on within the security region defined by Article 4 of the Inter-American Treaty of Reciprocal Assistance, and also to refrain from any act that may affect Inter-American peace and security", and urged the Government of the Republic of Argentina to "refrain from taking any action that may exacerbate the situation" the same resolution urged the Governments of the United Kingdom and the Argentine Republic "immediately to call a truce that will make it possible to resume and proceed normally with the negotiation aimed at a peaceful settlement of the conflict, taking into account the rights of sovereignty of the Republic of Argentina over the Malvinas Islands and the interests of the islanders"; while the Government of the Argentine Republic informed the Organ of Consultation of its full adherence to Resolution 1 and acted consistently therewith, the British forces proceeded to carry out serious and repeated armed attacks against the Argentine Republic in the zone of the Malvinas Islands, within the security region defined by Article 4 of the Inter-American Treaty of Reciprocal Assistance, which means that the United Kingdom has ignored the appeal made to it by the Twentieth Meeting of Consultation; Following the adoption of Resolution 1, the Government of the United States of America decided to apply coercive measures against the Argentine Republic and is giving its support, including material support, to the United Kingdom, which contravenes the spirit and the letter of Resolution 1; As a culmination of its repeated armed attacks, beginning on May 21, 1982, the British forces launched a broad-scale military attack against the Argentine Republic in the area of the Malvinas Islands which affects the peace and security of the hemisphere; The deplorable situation raised by the application of political and economic coercive measures that are not based on present international law and are harmful to the Argentine people, carried out by the European Economic Community—with the exception of Ireland and Italy—and by other industrialized States, is continuing, and the purpose of the Inter-American Treaty of Reciprocal Assistance is "to assure peace, through adequate means, to provide for effective reciprocal assistance to meet armed attacks against any American State, and in order to deal with threats of aggression against any of them"; The Twentieth Meeting of Consultation of Ministers of Foreign Affairs, resolves: 1) To condemn most vigorously the unjustified and disproportionate armed attack perpetuated by the United Kingdom, and its decision, which affects the security of the entire American hemisphere, of arbitrarily declaring an extensive area of up to twelve miles from the American coasts as a zone of hostilities, which is aggravated by the circumstance that when these actions were taken all possibilities of negotiation seeking a peaceful settlement of the conflict had not been exhausted; 2) To reiterate its firm demand upon the United Kingdom that it cease immediately its acts of war against the Argentine Republic and order the immediate withdrawal of all its armed forces detailed there and the return of its task force to its usual stations; 3) To deplore the fact that the attitude of the United Kingdom has helped to frustrate the negotiations for a peaceful settlement that were conducted by Mr. Javier Perez de Cuellar, the Secretary-General of the United Nations. 4) To express its conviction that it is essential to reach with the greatest urgency a peaceful and honourable settlement of the conflict, under the auspices of the United Nations, and in that connection, to recognize the praiseworthy efforts and good offices of Mr. Javier Perez de Cuellar, the Secretary-General of the United Nations, and to lend its full support to the task entrusted to him by the Security Council; 5) To urge the Government of the United States of America to order the immediate lifting of the coercive measures applied against the Argentine Republic and to refrain from providing material assistance to the United Kingdom, in observance of the principle of hemispheric solidarity recognized in the Inter-American Treaty of Reciprocal Assistance; 6) To urge the members of the European Economic Community, and the other States that have taken them, to lift immediately the coercive economic or political measures taken against the Argentine Republic; 7) To request the States parties of the Rio Treaty to give the Argentine Republic the support that each judges appropriate to assist it in this serious situation, and to refrain from any act that might jeopardize that objective. If necessary, such support may be adopted with adequate co-ordination; 8) To reaffirm the basic constitutional principles of the Charter of the Organization of American States and of the Inter-American Treaty of Reciprocal Assistance, in particular, those that refer to peaceful settlement of disputes; 9) To keep the Organ of Consultation available to assist the parties in conflict with their peace-making efforts in any way it may support the mission entrusted to the United Nations Secretary-General by the Security Council, and to instruct the President of the Meeting of Consultation to keep in continuous contact with the Secretary-General of the United Nations; 10) To keep the Twentieth Meeting of Consultation open to see to it that the provisions of this resolution are faithfully and immediately carried out and to take, if necessary, any additional measures that may be agreed upon to preserve inter-American solidarity and co-operation.

FALKLANDS SURRENDER DOCUMENT, 14 JUNE 1982

I, the undersigned, commander of all the Argentine land, sea and air forces in the Falkland Islands, M.B.M. (Mario Benjamin Menendez), surrender to Major General J. J. Moore CB, OBE, MC, as representative of Her Britannic Majesty's Government.

Under the terms of this surrender, all Argentine personnel in the Falkland Islands are to muster at assembly points which will be nominated by General Moore, and hand over their arms, ammunition, and all other weapons and war-like equipment as directed by General Moore, or appropriate British officers acting on his behalf.

Following the surrender, all personnel of the Argentian forces will be treated with honor in accordance with the conditions set out in the Geneva Convention of 1949.

They will obey any directions concerning movement, and in connection with accomodation.

This surrender is to be effective from 2359 hours (7:59 EDT, 8:59 P.M. Falklands time) and includes those Argentine forces presently deployed in and around Port Stanley, those others on East Falkland, West Falkland, and all the outlying islands.

GENERAL ASSEMBLY RESOLUTION 37/9
Question of the Falkland Islands (Malvinas)

The General Assembly, having considered the question of the Falkland Islands (Malvinas), aware that the maintenance of colonial situations is incompatible with the United Nations ideal of universal peace, recalling its resolutions 1514 (XV) of 14 December 1960, 2065 (XX) of 16 December 1965, 3160 (XXVIII) of 14 December 1973 and 31/49 of 1 December

1976, recalling also Security Council resolutions 502 (1982) of 3 April 1982 and 505 (1982) of 26 May 1982, taking into account the existence of a *de facto* cessation of hostilities in the South Atlantic and the expressed intention of the parties not to renew them, reaffirming the need for the parties to take due account of the interests of the population of the Falkland Islands (Malvinas) in accordance with the provisions of General Assembly resolutions 2065 (XX) and 3160 (XXVIII), reaffirming also the principles of the Charter of the United Nations on the non-use of force or the threat of force in international relations and the peaceful settlement of international disputes: 1) Requests the Governments of Argentina and the United Kingdom of Great Britain and Northern Ireland to resume negotiations in order to find as soon as possible a peaceful solution to the sovereignty dispute relating to the question of The Falkland Islands (Malvinas); 2) Requests the Secretary-General, on the basis of the present resolution, to undertake a renewed mission of good offices in order to assist the parties in complying with the request made in paragraph 1 above and to take the necessary measures to that end; 3) Requests the Secretary-General to submit a report to the General Assembly at its thirty-eighth session on the progress made in the implementation of the present resolution; 4) Decides to include in the provisional agenda of its thirty-eighth session the item entitled "Question of the Falkland Islands (Malvinas)".

55th plenary meeting, 4 November 1982

Notes

1. Arce, 14-16; Cawkell, 1-3; Goebel, 3-11.
2. Goebel, 3-4.
3. Cawkell, 2.
4. Goebel (quoting from Santa Cruz's *El Islario General de Todos las Islas del mundo*), 14.
5. Arce, 18.
6. Ibid., 23.
7. Goebel, 17-29.
8. Arce, 19-23.
9. Goebel, 35.
10. Goebel, 35-43; Arce, 30-31; Cawkell, 7-9.
11. Goebel, 45.
12. Ibid., 135-137.
13. Cawkell, 11.
14. Ibid., 11.
15. Ibid., 12.
16. Goebel, 226-239; Cawkell, 15-22; Arce, 55-57.
17. Cawkell, 22; Goebel, 230.
18. Goebel, 232.
19. Cawkell, 27-28.
20. Arce, 65.
21. Goebel, 271-72.
22. Ibid., 274.
23. Ibid., 275.
24. Goebel, 270-77; Cawkell, 29-32; Arce, 69-70.
25. Goebel, 343.
26. Ibid., 359.
27. Ibid., 370.
28. Ibid., 371-410.
29. Goebel, 410; Cawkell, 35; Arce, 79-80.
30. *British America*, 520.
31. Cawkell, 37.
32. Goebel, 428.
33. Ibid., 431.
34. Graham-Yooll, 150-51.
35. Ibid., 441.
36. Ferns, 229.
37. Graham-Yooll, 152-53.
38. Ferns, 230-231; Graham-Yooll, 153.
39. Ferns, 227.
40. Ibid., 230.
41. Goebel, 454.
42. Arce, 98-99.
43. Cawkell, 43.
44. Ibid., 43.
45. Goebel, 456-57.
46. Ibid., 457.
47. Cawkell, 44-50.
48. Goebel, 458-59.
49. Arce, 101-102.
50. Ibid., 102.
51. Cawkell, 51-55.
52. Ibid., 53-55.
53. Ibid., 55.
54. Ibid., 120.
55. Ibid., 62-63.
56. Cawkell, 103-107.
57. Arce, 103-108.
58. Arce, 109.
59. Ibid., 110.
60. Calvert, 7.
61. *Antarctica Cases*, 10-13.
62. Arce, 111.
63. Ibid., 112.
64. Ibid., 112.
65. *Antarctica Cases*, 26.
66. Arce, 115-116.
67. Calvert, 24
68. Calvert, 18; *New Columbia*

Encyclopedia, 143.
69. Dobson, 20.
70. *New Columbia Encyclopedia*, 144; Calvert, 25.
71. Calvert, 28-30.
72. Calvert, 37; Franks, 4; Goebel (Metford's *Introduction*), ix.
73. Franks, 5; Calvert, 38; *Keesing's Contemporary Archives*, 21693; Goebel (Metford), x.
74. Ibid., x.
75. *Keesing*, 21693.
76. Ibid., 22730.
77. Ibid., 22730.
78. Ibid., 22730.
79. Ibid., 22730.
80. Franks, 6.
81. *Keesing*, 22392.
82. Ibid., 23292.
83. Ibid., 23293.
84. Ibid., 23293.
85. Ibid., 23293.
86. Ibid., 24968; Franks, 7.
87. *Keesing*, 24968.
88. Ibid., 28405.
89. *Keesing*, 28405; Franks, 8.
90. Franks, 8-9.
91. Ibid., 9.
92. *Keesing*, 28405.
93. Franks, 9.
94. Ibid., 13.
95. *Keesing*, 28406.
96. Franks, 14.
97. *Keesing*, 28407.
98. Franks, 18.
99. Ibid., 18-19.
100. Ibid., 20.
101. Ibid., 20.
102. Ibid., 21.
103. Ibid., 21.
104. *Keesing*, 30319.
105. Ibid., 30319.
106. Franks, 22-23.
107. Ibid., 23.
108. Ibid., 24-25.
109. Ibid., 25.
110. Ibid., 26.
111. Ibid., 27-28.
112. Ibid., 28.
113. Ibid., 29.
114. Ibid., 29.
115. Ibid., 30.
116. Ibid., 32.
117. Ibid., 32.
118. Calvert, 54-55.
119. Dobson, 36-37.
120. Franks, 34.
121. Ibid., 35.
122. Ibid., 36.
123. Ibid., 37.
124. Ibid., 37.
125. Ibid., 38.
126. Ibid., 38.
127. Ibid., 38.
128. Ibid., 39-40.
129. Calvert, 57-58; Franks, 40.
130. Franks, 41.
131. Calvert, 56.
132. Franks, 41.
133. Ibid., 42.
134. Ibid., 43.
135. Ibid., 44.
136. Ibid., 45-46.
137. Ibid., 47.
138. Ibid., 48-49.
139. Ibid., 50-51.
140. Ibid., 54-55.
141. Ibid., 55.
142. Ibid., 56.
143. Ibid., 56-57.
144. Ibid., 60.
145. Calvert, 50; Franks, 62-63.
146. Franks, 65-66.
147. Ibid., 67.
148. Ibid., 69-70.
149. Ibid., 70-71.
150. Calvert, 57.
151. Dobson, 40-47.
152. Calvert, 76-77; Dobson, 55.
153. Dobson, 56.
154. Calvert, 77; Dobson, 56.
155. Dobson, 57.
156. Calvert, 80.
157. Dobson, 61-67.
158. Calvert, 67, 69.
159. Ibid., 84.
160. *Business Week*, 19 April 1982, 27.
161. *Time*, 19 April 1982, 32.
162. Dobson, 80.
163. Calvert, 94-95.
164. Ibid., 98.

165. Calvert, 100; *Time* 26 April 1982, 27.
166. *Time*, 26 April 1982, 26.
167. Ibid., 3 May 1982, 27.
168. Calvert, 100-101; Dobson, 132-135; *Time*, 3 May 1982, 26.
169. Calvert, 102.
170. Ibid., 104.
171. Ibid., 106.
172. Ibid., 107-108.
173. *Time*, 10 May 1982, 26; *U.S. News and World Report*, 10 May 1982, 27.
174. Calvert, 108.
175. *Time*, 10 May 1982, 20.
176. Ibid., 20.
177. *Newsweek*, 10 May 1982, 28-32.
178. Calvert, 112.
179. *Newsweek*, 17 May 1982, 28.
180. *Time*, 17 May 1982, 16.
181. *Newsweek*, 17 May 1982, 29.
182. Calvert, 118.
183. Ibid., 119.
184. *Time*, 17 May 1982, 27.
185. Ibid., 24 May 1982, 43.
186. *Newsweek*, 24 May 1982, 39.
187. Calvert, 122-123.
188. Dobson, 146.
189. Calvert, 128-129; Dobson, 148.
190. *Time*, 31 May 1982, 24-34; *Newsweek*, 31 May 1982, 20-26.
191. Calvert, 134.
192. *Newsweek*, 7 June 1982, 22-23.
193. *Time*, 7 June 1982, 38.
194. Dobson, 191.
195. Ibid., 197.
196. Calvert, 137; *Time* 14 June 1982, 34.
197. *Time*, 14 June 1983, 35.
198. *Newsweek*, 14 June 1982, 51.
199. Dobson, 208.
200. *Newsweek*, 14 June 1982, 49.
201. Ibid., 49.
202. *Time*, 14 June 1982, 35.
203. Ibid., 35.
204. *San Bernardino Sun*, 7 June 1982, sec. A, 1.
205. Ibid., 8.
206. Calvert, 139.
207. Ibid., 139.
208. *Los Angeles Times*, 8 June 1982, sec. I, 1.
209. *Time*, 21 June 83, 40-41.
210. Ibid., 41.
211. *Los Angeles Times*, 9 June 1982, sec. I, 11.
212. Ibid., 11 June 1982, sec. I, 20.
213. *Newsweek*, 21 June 1982, 47.
214. *San Bernardino Sun*, 15 June 1982, sec. A, 1.
215. Ibid., 1
216. *San Bernardino Sun*, 15 June 1982, sec. A, 1; *Britain and the Falkland Crisis*, 93.
217. *San Bernardino Sun*, 15 June 1982, sec. A, 1-3.
218. Ibid., 5.
219. Ibid., 5.
220. *Time*, 28 June 1982, 27.
221. Ibid., 25.
222. *Los Angeles Times*, 16 June 1982, sec. I, 1.
223. Ibid., 10.
224. *Time*, 28 June 1982, 26.
225. *San Bernardino Sun*, 16 June 1982, sec. A, 1.
226. Calvert, 143.
227. *San Bernardino Sun*, 19 June 1982, sec. A, 1.
228. Ibid., 4.
229. Ibid., 20 June 1982, sec. A, 8.
230. *Los Angeles Times*, 24 June 1982, sec. I, 6.
231. Ibid., 6.
232. *San Bernardino Sun*, 6 July 1982, sec. A, 8.
233. *Los Angeles Times*, 6 July 1982, sec. I, 1.
234. *San Bernardino Sun*, 10 July 1982, sec. A, 4.
235. Ibid., 13 July 1982, sec. A, 1.
236. Ibid., 23 July 1982, sec. A, 1.
237. *Newsweek*, 24 January 1983, 36.
238. *Los Angeles Times*, 30 March 1983, sec. I, 4.

Bibliography

Antarctica Cases. (United Kingdom v. Argentina; United Kingdom v. Chile): orders of March 16th, 1956; removal from the list. Pleadings, Oral Arguments, Documents. Hague: International Court of Justice, 1956.

Arce, Jose. *The Malvinas (Our Snatched Little Isles).* Madrid: n.p., 1951.

Basilico, Ernesto. *La Armada del Obispo de Plasencia y el Descubrimento de las Malvinas.* Buenos Aires: Centro Naval Instituto de Publicaciones Navales, 1967.

Binyon, Michael. "A Soviet Opportunity?" *World Press Review* (July 1982): 39-40. (Reprinted from *The Times*).

Bishop, Patrick, and John Witherow. *The Winter War: The Falklands.* London: Quartet Books, 1982.

Britain and the Falkland Crisis: A Documentary Record. New York: British Information Services, 1982.

British America. Vol. III in the British Empire Series. London: Kegan Paul, Trench, Trubner, 1900.

Calvert, Peter. *The Falklands Crisis: The Rights and the Wrongs.* New York: St. Martin's Press, 1982.

Cawkell, M. B. R., D. H. Maling, and E. M. Cawkell. *The Falkland Islands.* London: Macmillan, 1960.

Cichero, Felix Esteban. *Las Malvinas: Grieta en el Mapa Argentino.* Buenos Aires: Editorial Stilcograf, 1968.

Coleccion de Documentos Relativos a la Historia de las Islas Malvinas. Vol. I no. 28 in Documentos Para la Historia Argentina, no. 25. Buenos Aires: Univ. de Buenos Aires Departamento Editorial, 1957.

Corominas, Enrique V. *Como Defendi Malvinas.* Buenos Aires: Ano del Libertador General San Martin, 1950.

Crawley, Eduardo. "Latin America Matures." *World Press Review* (July 1982): 40-41. (Reprinted from *South*.)

Crozier, Brian. "The Case for Tidying Up." *National Review* (9 July 1982): 818.

——————————. "Of Order and Chaos." *National Review* (11 June 1982): 682.

Cura, Maria Renee, and Juan Antonio Bustinza. *Islas Malvinas y*

Antartida Argentina. Buenos Aires: Editorial Kapelusz, 1970.

Dobson, Christopher, John Miller, and Ronald Payne. *The Falklands Conflict*. London: Hodder and Stoughton, 1982.

Dunnigan, James F. *How To Make War: A Comprehensive Guide to Modern Warfare*. Updated edition. New York: Quill, 1983.

El Episodio Ocurrido en Puerto de la Soledad de Malvinas el 26 de Agosto de 1833: Testimonios Documentales. Vol. III in Serie Documental. Buenos Aires: Academia Nacional de la Historia, 1967.

Fairlie, Henry. "What the Falklands Teaches Us." *New Republic* (12 July 1982): 8-12.

"The Falkland Islands," *Department of State Bulletin* 82 (2063) (June 1982): 81-89.

"The Falkland Islands," *Department of State Bulletin* 82 (2064) (July 1982): 86-91.

Ferns, H. S. *Britain and Argentina in the Nineteenth Century*. Oxford: At the Clarendon Press, 1960.

Fitte, Ernesto J. *La Agresion Norte Americana a las Islas Malvinas: Cronica Documental*. Buenos Aires: Emece Editores, 1966.

——————. *La Disputa con Gran Bretana por las Islas del Atlantico Sur*. Buenos Aires: Emece Editores, 1968.

Franks, Lord, ed. *Falkland Islands Review; Report of a Committee of Privy Counsellors*. London: Her Majesty's Stationery Office, 1983.

Freedman, Lawrence. "The War of the Falklands Islands, 1982." *Foreign Affairs* 61 (1) (Fall 1982): 196-210.

Gelb, Norman. "The Falklands Factor." *New Leader* (12-26 July 1982): 5-6.

——————. "The Fallout from the Falklands." *New Leader* (31 May 1982): 3-4.

Gellner, John. "The Military Lessons." *World Press Review* (July 1982): 38-39. (Reprinted from the *Toronto Globe and Mail*.)

Gerlach, Allen. "Who Owns the Falkland Islands? Background to the Conflict." *USA Today* (July 1982): 50-53.

Gil Munilla, Octavio. *Malvinas el Conflictor Anglo-Espanol de 1770*. No. XLI General Serie Ia; Anuario no. 18. Sevilla: Escuela de Estudios Hispano-Americanos de Sevilla, 1948.

Geobel, Julius. *The Struggle for the Falkland Islands: A Study in Legal and Diplomatic History*. Second edition. New Haven: Yale Univ. Press, 1982.

Graham-Yooll, Andrew. *The Forgotten Colony: A History of the English-Speaking Communities in Argentina*. London: Hutchinson, 1981.

Hastings, Max, and Simon Jenkins. *The Battle for the Falklands*. New York: Norton, 1983.

Hernandez, Jose. *Las Islas Malvinas: Lo Que Escribio Hernandez in 1869, Respecto a Este Territorio Argentino y las Noticias Que Acerca de su Viaje a las Islas le Communico*. Edited by Joaquin Gil Guinon. Buenos Aires: Joaquin Gil, 1952.

Hogg, Ian V., ed. *Jane's 1982-83 Military Review:* Second year of issue. London: Jane's, 1982.

Horne, Alistair. "A British Historian's Meditations." *National Review.* (23 July 1982): 886-889.

Housman, Damian. "Lessons of Naval Warfare." *National Review* (23 July 1982): 894-896.

Iglesias Rouco, J. "The First 'North-South' War." *World Press Review* (July 1982): 37-38. (Reprinted from *La Nacion.*)

Kuehnelt-Leddihn, Erik von. "Western Europe Reacts." *National Review* (23 July 1982): 902.

Malvinas, An Unlawful Colonialism (Political and Socioeconomic Regression). Buenos Aires: Republica Argentina, 1982.

MccGwire, Michael, W. Seth Carus and Stephen P. Glick, Peter Jenkins, and Robert Cox. "Battle for the Falklands." In four parts. *The New Republic* (12 May 1982): 9-18.

McLaughlin, John. "Falklands Soul-Searching." *National Review* (25 June 1982): 748.

Meisler, Stanley. "The Anatomy of a 'Betrayal': Why Argentina Sees the U.S. As Villain." *Los Angeles Times* Pt. IV (6 June 1982): 1, 6.

Moneta, Jose Manual. *Nos Devolveran las Malvinas? . . . (Los Actuales Problemas Malvinero(s).* Buenos Aires: Published by the author, 1970.

Moore, John, ed. *Jane's 1982-83 Naval Review:* Second year of issue. London: Jane's, 1982.

Natkiel, Richard. *Atlas of the 20th Century.* Text by Donald Sommerville & John N. Westwood. New York: Facts on File, 1982.

Palacios, Alfred L. *Las Islas Malvinas: Archipelago Argentino.* Buenos Aires: Ciencias Politicas, 1934.

Pereyra, Ezequiel Federico. *Las Islas Malvinas: Soberania Argentina: Antecedentes Gestiones Diplomaticas.* Buenos Aires: Ediciones Culturales Argentinas, 1969.

Pfaff, William. "Will the Falklands War Really Settle Things?" *Los Angeles Times* Pt. IV (6 June 1982): 1, 6.

Phipps, Colin. *What Future for the Falklands?* Fabian Tract 450. London: Fabian Society, 1977.

Plaza, Juan. *Malvinas: Nuestra Proxima Recolonizacion de las Islas.* Buenos Aires: Published by the author, 1970.

Raymon, Henry. "Argentina Miscues." *The New Republic* (9 June 1982): 12-13.

_____. "Errors All Around." *The New Republic* (28 April 1982): 9-10.

Sampson, Anthony. "Of Principles and Power." *Newsweek* (19 April 1982): 47.

"The South Atlantic Crisis: Background, Consequences, Documentation." *Department of State Bulletin* 82 (2067) (October 1982): 78-90.

Tavares, Flavio. "Argentina's Recovery Struggle." *World Press*

Review (November 1982): 25-27. (Reprinted from *O Estado de S. Paolo*.)

Taylor, J. M. "The Falklands and Colonialism." *Atlantic* (August 1982): 22-24.

Taylor, Michael J. H., ed. *Jane's 1982-83 Aviation Review:* Second year of issue. London: Jane's, 1982.

Torre Revello, Jose. *Bibliografia de las Islas Malvinas: Obras, Mapas y Documentos*. No. XCLX in Publicaciones del Instituto de Investgaciones Historicas. Buenos Aires: Univ. de Buenos Aires—Facultad de Filosofia y Letras, 1953.

Wheeldon, John. "A Time to Reassess." *World Press Review* (July 1982): 42. (Reprinted from *The Australian*.)

Index

171

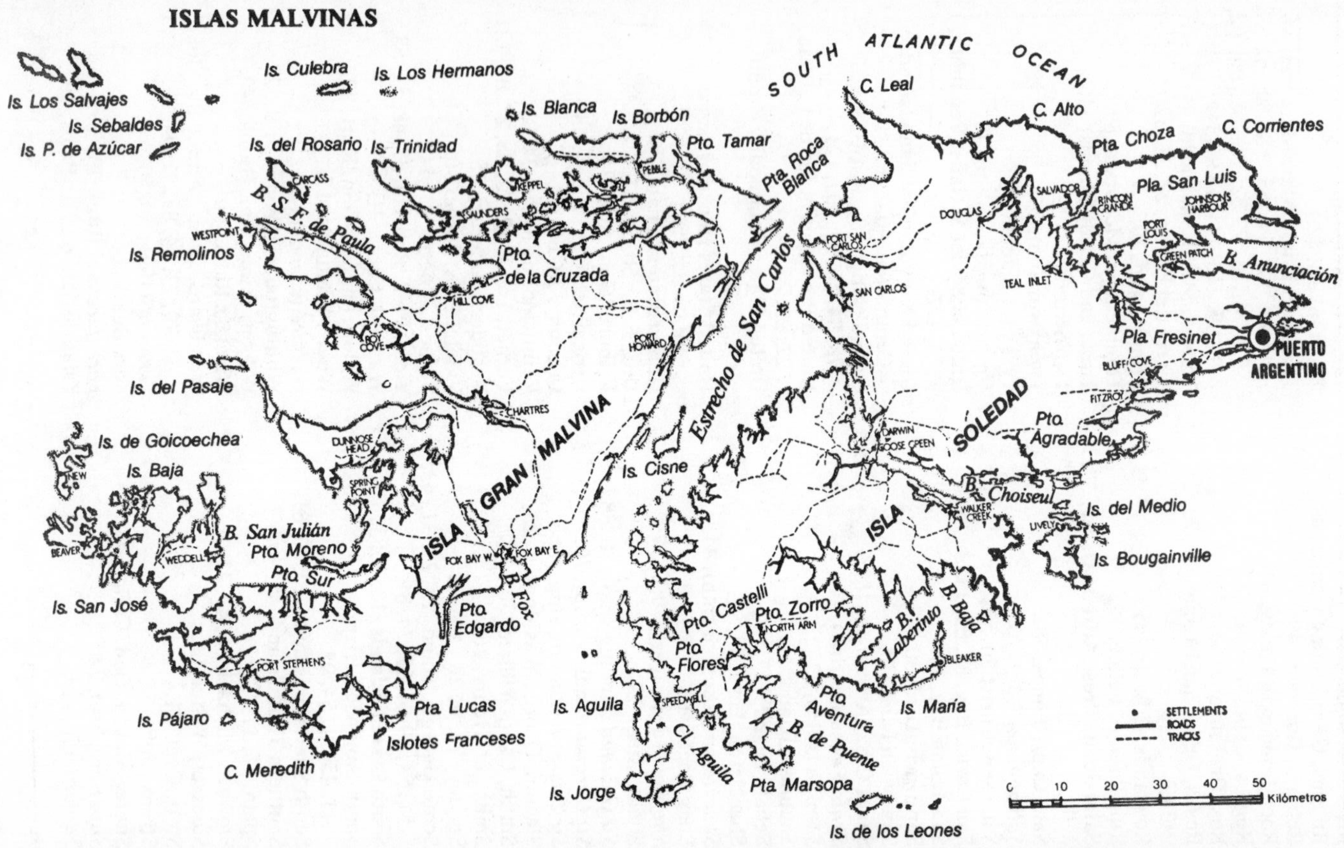
ISLAS MALVINAS
SOUTH ATLANTIC OCEAN
Is. Los Salvajes
Is. Sebaldes
Is. P. de Azúcar
Is. Culebra
Is. Los Hermanos
Is. del Rosario
Is. Trinidad
Is. Blanca
Is. Borbón
Pta. Tamar
Pta. Roca Blanca
C. Leal
C. Alto
Pta. Choza
C. Corrientes
Pla. San Luis
JOHNSON'S HARBOUR
RINCON GRANDE
SALVADOR
DOUGLAS
PORT LOUIS
GREEN PATCH
B. Anunciación
TEAL INLET
PORT SAN CARLOS
SAN CARLOS
CARCASS
KEPPEL
PEBBLE
SAUNDERS
B. S. F. de Paula
WESTPOINT
Is. Remolinos
Pta. de la Cruzada
HILL COVE
ROY COVE
PORT HOWARD
Estrecho de San Carlos
Pla. Fresinet
PUERTO ARGENTINO
BLUFF COVE
FITZROY
Is. del Pasaje
CHARTRES
ISLA GRAN MALVINA
SOLEDAD
Pta. Agradable
DARWIN
GOOSE GREEN
Is. de Goicoechea
DUNNOSE HEAD
SPRING POINT
Is. Cisne
B. Choiseul
WALKER CREEK
ISLA
LIVELY
Is. del Medio
Is. Bougainville
Is. Baja
NEW
BEAVER
WEDDELL
B. San Julián
Pta. Moreno
FOX BAY W.
FOX BAY E.
Pta. Sur
B. Fox
Is. San José
Pta. Edgardo
Pta. Castelli
Pta. Zorro
NORTH ARM
B. Laberinto
B. Baja
Pta. Flores
BLEAKER
PORT STEPHENS
SPEEDWELL
Pta. Aventura
Is. María
Is. Aguila
Pta. Lucas
Is. Pájaro
Islotes Franceses
Cl. Aguila
B. de Puente
C. Meredith
Is. Jorge
Pta. Marsopa
Is. de los Leones
SETTLEMENTS
ROADS
TRACKS
0
10
20
30
40
50
Kilómetros

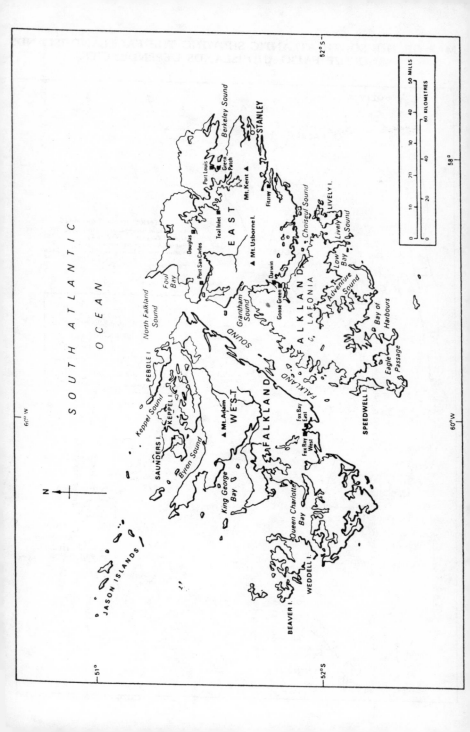

MAP OF THE SOUTH ATLANTIC SHOWING THE FALKLAND ISLANDS AND THE FALKLAND ISLANDS DEPENDENCIES.

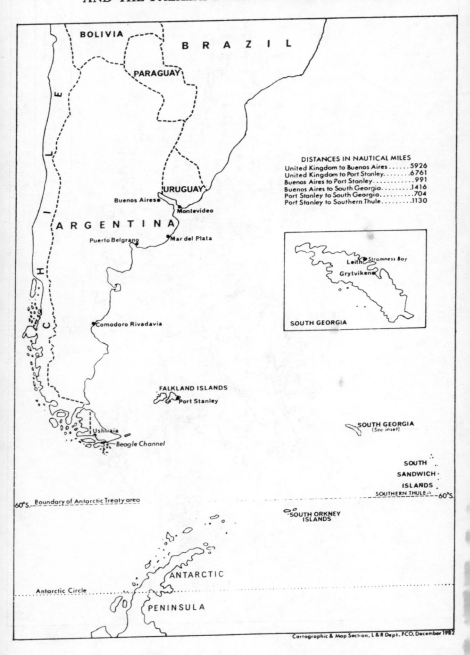

BOLIVIA

B R A Z I L

PARAGUAY

URUGUAY

Buenos Aires

Montevideo

A R G E N T I N A

Puerto Belgrano

Mar del Plata

Comodoro Rivadavia

FALKLAND ISLANDS

Port Stanley

Ushuaia

Beagle Channel

DISTANCES IN NAUTICAL MILES
United Kingdom to Buenos Aires......5926
United Kingdom to Port Stanley........6761
Buenos Aires to Port Stanley............991
Buenos Aires to South Georgia........1416
Port Stanley to South Georgia.........704
Port Stanley to Southern Thule........1130

Leith • Stromness Bay
Grytviken

SOUTH GEORGIA

SOUTH GEORGIA
(See inset)

SOUTH
SANDWICH
ISLANDS
SOUTHERN THULE

60°S.   Boundary of Antarctic Treaty area   60°S.

SOUTH ORKNEY
ISLANDS

ANTARCTIC

Antarctic Circle

PENINSULA

Cartographic & Map Section, L & R Dept, FCO, December 1982

94913

F
3031
.R36
1983

REGINALD, R
TEMPEST IN A TEAPOT.

DATE DUE	

Fernald Library
Colby-Sawyer College
New London, New Hampshire

GAYLORD   PRINTED IN U.S.A.